The Ultimate Route to Market

Global systems integrators, outsourcers and consulting firms are responsible for directly leveraging or influencing most IT investment in large corporations. Original equipment manufacturers (OEMs), software companies and other technology providers aspire to create mutually successful partnerships with the large influencers due to their 'business case' driven approach, their early stage engagement in the sales cycle, their C-Suite relationships with large multi-national enterprises and the often-giant scale of the typical technology spend that their projects and engagements drive. The projects that these companies deliver are specialist and complex, meaning that companies who aspire to work successfully in the sector require skill, knowledge and a sophisticated alliance approach to gain credibility and maintain long term sustainable relationships.

The Ultimate Route to Market provides an insight into the practices, construct and culture of global consulting firms, systems integrators and outsourcers and provides a suggested framework for a successful alliance with them. Here, Ian Shanahan provides organisations with an overview of the global systems integrator, outsourcer and consulting firm sectors, provides insight into their culture and expertly explains alliance best practice methodology.

This is a must read for anyone that aspires to understand the market, how it works and how they become desirable to the large IT services companies, so that they can execute alliance engagements to the sector in a measured, methodical and low risk way.

Ian Shanahan has been in sales, leadership, business development and alliance management for 30 years. His career has included a consistent record of successful channel and alliance execution for a range of technology companies including Sun Microsystems, IBM and Microsoft. During this time, Ian has managed various successful alliances between the world's largest technology providers and leading global consulting organisations and systems integrators.

The Ultimate Route to Market

How Technology Professionals Can Work Successfully with Global Systems Integrators, Outsourcers and Consulting Firms

Ian Shanahan

LONDON AND NEW YORK

First published 2019
by Routledge
2 Park Square, Milton Park, Abingdon, Oxon OX14 4RN

and by Routledge
711 Third Avenue, New York, NY 10017

Routledge is an imprint of the Taylor & Francis Group, an informa business

© 2019 Ian Shanahan

The right of Ian Shanahan to be identified as author of this work has been asserted by him in accordance with sections 77 and 78 of the Copyright, Designs and Patents Act 1988.

All rights reserved. No part of this book may be reprinted or reproduced or utilised in any form or by any electronic, mechanical, or other means, now known or hereafter invented, including photocopying and recording, or in any information storage or retrieval system, without permission in writing from the publishers.

Trademark notice: Product or corporate names may be trademarks or registered trademarks, and are used only for identification and explanation without intent to infringe.

British Library Cataloguing-in-Publication Data
A catalogue record for this book is available from the British Library

Library of Congress Cataloging-in-Publication Data
A catalog record has been requested for this book

ISBN: 978-1-4724-8307-2 (hbk)
ISBN: 978-1-315-61125-9 (ebk)

Typeset in Times New Roman
by Sunrise Setting Ltd, Brixham, UK
Printed and bound by CPI Group (UK) Ltd, Croydon, CR0 4YY

Contents

About the author		vi
Acknowledgements		vii
Preface		viii
	Introduction	1
1	Why do companies invest so much in hiring consultancies, systems integrators and outsourcers?	17
2	Defining the players	25
3	Why partnering is win–win	41
4	Understanding the business model	70
5	Alliance best practice	101
6	Innovating with global systems integrators, outsourcers and consulting firms	122
7	Partnering in the new economy	135
8	The 10 steps to success	153
9	How to put what you have learned into practice	172
	Glossary and definitions	173
	Additional reading	180
	Index	184

About the author

Ian Shanahan has been in sales, leadership, business development and alliance management for 28 years, most of that time spent either working for or partnering with global system integrators, outsourcers or consulting firms. From the proliferation of personal computing (PC) technology, the client server computing revolution, the birth of the internet, the impact of globalisation on technology, the shift to cloud computing and through to the digital age, Ian has been creating and executing strategies for IT vendors who want to differentiate and innovate when going to market with this important market sector.

Ian's career has included a consistent record of successful channel and alliance execution for a range of technology companies including Sun Microsystems, IBM and Microsoft. He has learned the dos and don'ts of how to go to market successfully with the large global influencers from inside and outside of some of the largest names in systems integration, outsourcing and consulting.

Ian currently manages a successful multi-million dollar strategic alliance between one of the world's largest software companies and a leading global consulting organisation. He divides his time between his home in the Cotswolds and his office in London. When not at work, Ian's life revolves around spending time with his wife and two children and pursuing his favourite hobbies – walking his dogs in the countryside, cricket, sailing, sports analytics and coaching rugby.

His motto is 'you get the relationships you deserve'.

Acknowledgements

Many thanks to everyone who has helped me to complete this book either through making a direct contribution to the content, providing great ideas, giving honest feedback or just good old moral support. It is all greatly appreciated.

Special thanks to my peer reviewers and interviewees who gave generously of their time and asked for nothing in return. My dear friend Adrian Ruck is a great source of insight and coaching for any aspirant writer and remains still the world's best unpublished author. Sincere thanks also to Grant Chapman, Paul Emsley-Martin, Alistair Forbes, Kristian Kallaker, Steve Shelsher, Gavin Simpson and Paul Targett for their bottomless reservoir of knowledge about how to make alliances successful – they are all experts in their field that I've got to know and respect through business, but am now honoured to call friends. Thanks guys.

Many thanks to Alex Morris and Petros Bozatzis, my oldest friends at Accenture, exemplary professionals and lynch pins of the dedicated, smart and diligent folk that make up the Alliance Services team. Big up to Georg Seiler, my one time protégé, whose career is now eclipsing my own – exactly the way it should be. And a special mention to Mike Nevin whose priceless intellectual property and recent personal experience of becoming a first-time published author was an invaluable source of background knowledge and inspiration.

From a practical perspective, many thanks to Fiona Morris, who lent her assistance as a legal expert but ended up providing much more advice and input than I could ever have asked for, and Olly, who gave me permission and kind words to set me on the journey. Sincere thanks also to Kristina and Matt at Routledge who have encouraged, indulged and supported me throughout and have shown saint like levels of patience, understanding and empathy with my many broken promises.

There are countless colleagues, managers and friends over the years whose intellect, leadership and knowledge are contained within these pages. Amy, Darren, Gordon, multiple Johns, Mikes and Nicks, Kathy, Matt, Navin, Neil, Peter, Rahul, Scott, Teri, Tim, Tom … even though you may not even realise that this book exists – it couldn't have been written without you.

And thanks of course to my long-suffering wife Fleur who was a constant source of help and support throughout and allowed me to be derelict in my duty as a father many evenings and weekends so that I could write this book. I started this book by saying that you get the relationships that you deserve, but very occasionally, if you are lucky, you get an amazing one that you don't.

Preface

Just like the activities of the companies that feature in this book, the subject matter you will read here is complex and wide-ranging. Therefore, in order to capture the salient points, I have simplified many scenarios. An example of this is the 'typical project' scenario and the roles and personality types of some of the archetypal people involved. It goes without saying that every project, and especially every person and therefore every engagement, is different and one book can't possibly cover every possibility, so please regard the examples used as purely that – examples of a situation, person or set of circumstances. Of course, the book would be worthless if it wasn't written with the basis of experience and a certain amount of knowledge and wisdom, so, whilst generalisations are made for the sake of brevity and clarity, the principles and the spirit of what is intended is valid. You'll get what I mean once you start reading.

Even more importantly, whilst I have referenced many companies within the book, I have done my utmost to keep away from opinion or unsubstantiated content about any company mentioned. This is not a Which? guide to IT services companies and should not be read as such; any references to companies or individuals is to give you a feel for the sector and the players as a whole and is not an endorsement or criticism of any company or individual. I have also changed the name, and in some cases the gender, of the people in the stories that are included at the end of some chapters.

Finally, and of great importance also, I want to make clear that whilst I have pointed out some factors of the culture and business practices of the large global consulting firms, systems integrators and outsourcers that some may see as challenging, such as the expectation of hard work amongst the staff or the relentless pursuit of excellence in order to differentiate from the competition, this is not intended as derogatory. If it is not clear, my over-riding point in the book is that the companies referred to herein, are by and large relentlessly client focused, professional and tightly governed companies staffed by highly skilled, diligent, trustworthy personnel – the point of the book is to explain how other companies need to raise their game to work with them effectively.

So, enjoy the book, take from it what you can, but combine the lessons in the book with your own initiative and judgement of any situation. In short, keep an open mind – this is a guide, not a uniform methodology.

Ian Shanahan, Bath, April 2018

Introduction

An influencer driven sector. How did we get here?

Global systems integrators, outsourcers and consulting firms are responsible for directly leveraging, or influencing, the majority of technology investment in large corporations. Conservative estimates suggest that the large information technology (IT) services companies directly influence between as much as 60–80% of technology spend in Fortune 500 companies. As technology matures and corporations start to source an ever-increasing portfolio of products via the cloud, the ability to engage with the large IT services companies that are procuring, and in many cases retaining, ownership of the hardware and software assets increases the need for technology original equipment manufacturers (OEMs) and other more niche services companies to work with these organisations.

I walked on to the sales floor of a technology company for the first time in 1994, I never saw a 386 PC, but I didn't miss them by much, people were sourcing 486s (average cost of £1500) at that stage and would soon be buying something called a Pentium (586) chip to deliver quicker speeds on the desktop. The majority of large companies and government departments were networked by then, but generally only in the same room or building – most small companies were just embarking on that journey and operated stand-alone PCs, if any at all. Most people had heard of the internet, but hardly anyone used it – either corporately or personally. Even as an employee in a fairly forward thinking company, it would be another two years before I used the internet every day and another five years before I received my first order via email – mainly due to legal rather than technological concerns, which was typical of the sort of suspicion surrounding new-fangled e-commerce.

Back in 1994, technology providers (almost always hardware and software organisations and very rarely as-a-service product providers) were immature, with incompetent supply-chains and incompatible products. Many of today's household names hadn't been formed, or were just small niche start-ups with good ideas and energetic, youthful founders. Even companies that we now regard as mature and established technology brands, such as VmWare, NetApp and Salesforce. com, were still just ideas.

However, life for a sales and marketing person promoting technology products to large enterprises was in some ways much easier then than it is now. Customers had an internal IT staff (ordinarily about 10% of the workforce), they had reasonably straight-forward and unevolved IT systems and, for all but the largest businesses, the organisational structures within the IT department were simple to understand. Primarily, this was thanks to the uncomplicated nature of the IT infrastructure. Decision-making processes were easy – a middle manager in the IT department decided what was required and the procurement department sourced it. Getting hold of the right contact was usually achieved by calling his (rarely her, alas) pre-voicemail desk phone. Then, as systems became more sophisticated and technology-dependent, companies started to see IT as a differentiator. Things were going to change very quickly.

Context and timing was all-important, as ever. The mid-1990s was a time when a painful recession in the early part of the decade was soon being remedied, thanks in no small part to a boom in technology advancement and telecoms. This sort of corporate retrenchment followed by a seismic technology-driven market opportunity is the perfect environment for the growth of consulting services. The major consultancies identified the opportunity to create specialised IT consulting arms to help large corporate clients maximise the opportunity presented by the new economy. As the 1990s progressed, technological advancement (not least the burgeoning World Wide Web), globalisation and a subsequently thriving economy allowed these new technology consultancy players to become essential partners to growing companies looking to be more efficient by concentrating on their core businesses. So, the challenge for the sales and marketing people was that it was no longer as simple as calling up your friendly network admin contact or desktop systems manager – you were now more likely to be dealing with an employee of EDS or Perot Systems who had little or no influence over IT purchases or product selection as they were there with a limited scope to deliver their project only.

As this new model took shape, and in parallel the IT sector evolved and broadened, the picture has become even more complex, with large companies employing multiple outsourcers, consultants and integrators for different departments and projects. Senior IT staff are encouraged to concentrate on strategy and innovation as opposed to the mundane aspects of the supply chain. The latter is now often the domain of the large services delivery company – either as influencer, procurement engine or, increasingly, as owner of the assets which are providing the functionality to the enterprise.

While on the face of things this would seem to complicate the lives of sales and marketing staff for the technology OEMs (or their small complementary services companies), the smart operators see this as an opportunity. Think of it this way: instead of having to create relationships with various complex and daunting corporate clients, you can forge mutually successful relationships with the major influencers and gain highly effective economies of scale as well as guaranteeing successful implementation and adoption of your product by a consistent, high quality delivery partner. What's not to like?

So it makes sense for OEMs and other smaller complementary IT services providers to partner with the large influencers that drive the technology choice. Their 'business case' driven approach to technology usage and consumption, their early stage engagement in the sales cycle, their executive-level relationships with large multinational enterprises and the often giant scale of the typical IT spend that their projects and engagements drive, mean that as a partner to the influencer companies, your proposition can be enhanced, you will have greater reach and have the opportunity to gain genuine economies of scale for less client interaction. Additionally, companies gain credibility and kudos from an association with a large influencer, as well as benefitting from their stand-alone technology products becoming 'business solutions' by the involvement of the services wrap and their industry knowledge.

Not another channel sale

So it's easy, right? Surely it's an old-fashioned channel sale? Wrong! There is risk associated with investing in partnerships with the systems integrators, outsourcers and consultants for exactly the same reason that underlies their appeal. Due to the nature of their work and clients, the projects that this type of partner delivers are specialist and complex, meaning that third-party companies who aspire to work successfully with them require skill, knowledge and a sophisticated alliance approach. This is essential to gain credibility and maintain long-term, sustainable relationships. As a technology solution company you need to get it right first time – often there are no second chances. Typically, technology companies that want to penetrate the large technology influencer market or target a particular player, seek to hire specialist sales, marketing and alliance professionals to lead their campaign – which is a logical approach, but those professionals are in demand and are consequently expensive to acquire. Furthermore, technology OEMs who commit resource in a half-hearted or unstructured way to a partnership with a major global technology influencer tend not to have the patience or deep enough pockets to achieve the breadth and depth of relationships needed to realise a return on their investment in a profitable timeframe. So, it is essential to understand the risks, the most efficient way of working and, equally important, how to qualify the situation before gambling a company's future on the strategy of engagement with a large systems integrator or consulting firm.

I have worked with large IT services companies as a partner, client, supplier and employee since 1994 and I'm still learning. The market evolves and the way that you need to work with these sorts of companies evolves with it. I have seen plenty of salespeople make their yearly target with one successful engagement, but I've seen many more get swallowed up in optimistic sales pursuits and the wrong sort of relationship with an Accenture or IBM and then have nothing to show for it (including no job) two years later. I can't promise that you won't make that mistake, but I can at least help you to navigate the landscape. I will explain to you, the player, how to decide which ones are right for you, how to plan for success and enough pointers to have a chance to be one of the people who succeed. You can live off the scraps of the large transformation projects, they really are that lucrative, but you have to realise that it is a risky strategy – you can spend nine months of very hard work supporting a systems integrator on a complex bid only to find that you backed the wrong horse. Their risk quickly becomes your risk. They, of course, are geared up to roll with the losses, but are you?

Who is the book for?

A lucky break

In the early part of the century I was working for a medium-sized value-added distribution business representing a large well-known technology vendor – let's call them Vendor X. My role was managing a team that were developing a sales channel for Vendor X's products. In a nutshell this entailed identifying, training, recruiting and accrediting channel partners on behalf of Vendor X. Once the channel partners were onboard, we would invest in the relationships and provide marketing, logistical, technical, quoting, contractual and account management support, etc. This meant that the channel partners (our clients, even though we were selling side-by-side with them) were correctly educated, technically capable and commercially supported, which in turn meant they were enabled to originate opportunity, transact the sales and then support Vendor X's products. A standard value-added distributor model, basically.

Vendor X had a portfolio of enterprise class hardware products, so the channel partners in question were primarily medium to large value-added resellers and a few niche resellers who specialised in the vendor's product set. There were also a few independent software vendors (ISVs) whose software solution leveraged the sale of the hardware products in question. Those ISVs sometimes resold the hardware themselves or were happy to work with one of the value-added resellers in order to provide a complete solution to their clients. We had a good reputation with some of the large systems integrators at a company level and I had heard anecdotally that it was a lucrative revenue stream, but we were busy with our traditional reseller channel and also felt that Vendor X was doing a good job at supporting the large systems integrators directly and there was little opportunity for us to add value. In short, it all looked a bit like hard work to develop relationships with systems integrators, so within my department we convinced ourselves that our value to the system integrator channel was questionable and we didn't give them or their consulting firm or outsourcer cousins any focus. Looking back, we also lacked senior contacts and saw the organisations as so large and impenetrable that it looked like a black-hole of effort for our limited resources.

Then one day it all changed. A guy in my team, we will call him Ahmed, took a call from a systems architect at a large systems integrator asking if we could help to source an amount of hardware product to fulfil a substantial client order, because the systems integrator was in danger of missing a deadline. Unfortunately for the systems integrator in question, Vendor X wasn't really geared up to rush through a constrained and complex order. It also looked like a problem that we didn't really want. To our knowledge, the systems integrator wasn't an accredited partner (Vendor X's accreditation process took months and was not guaranteed, and without it we couldn't sell to the system integrator anyway). Furthermore, the product the systems integrator wanted for their project was not particularly common and almost certainly not in stock. A time sensitive order with a large expectant corporate client, where Vendor X themselves were not able to meet the deadline directly, only spelled customer satisfaction nightmare. Nonetheless, we asked the systems integrator to email the bill of materials and said that we would see what we could do.

When the bill of materials arrived, our eyes nearly popped out of our heads, it was massive. It would be our largest deal of the quarter, if not the year, and in terms of our wider market would give us an increase of many points of market share against our rival value-added distributors. The details that make up the rest of the story are unnecessary, so to cut a long(ish) story short, Vendor X waived the systems integrator's obligation for accreditation so that we could transact with them immediately, and the systems integrator sailed through our credit scoring process, which was used to dealing with precarious, technically insolvent value-added resellers. So we bit the bullet and accepted the order. The only cloud on the horizon was the need to meet the very tough delivery expectations. It certainly was a risky move to accept the order in the circumstances. The delivery timescales were optimistic and, as we were dependent on supply from Vendor X (who had already effectively declined the order because of the logistical expectations), we were in danger of missing the deadlines, making the systems integrator look bad in front of their client and therefore alienating them for ever. However, for us it was a calculated risk because we thought we could leverage our superior contacts and greater logistical nous and hit the delivery deadline.

We missed the delivery deadline. Badly. With hindsight it was unrealistic to think that an order that Vendor X couldn't fulfil directly could be fulfilled more swiftly by a distributor dependent on the same vendor manufacturing plant for supply – but there was a happy ending. It's true we missed the deadline, but we were honest and up-front with our new systems integrator client throughout. They wanted the truth and we gave it to them. They wanted daily updates, we gave them daily calls where we updated them on availability of each line item, explaining unflinchingly which were in danger of not making the deadline, offering alternatives and explaining what we were doing to hit their desired timeframes. The daily calls were with our original systems architect contact, the alliance lead for Vendor X within the systems integrator, and the account manager for the system integrator's client. The calls were sometimes difficult, but always productive, positive and professional. What we learned was that our new systems integrator partner was very, very demanding, but when Ahmed, I and the rest of the team were professional, honest and diligent they were entirely reasonable. They were in a brutal business, selling big things to other big companies; they worked tirelessly to give their client the best service, but they were also pragmatic, realistic and grown-up about the situation. We eventually delivered the order. It was later than we all would have liked, but there was no customer satisfaction issue – the client and the systems integrator revised their project plan accordingly. Because the delivery issues were proactively managed, we all left the experience as satisfied partners, impressed by each other's performance and resolving to do more business together. It was indeed our largest revenue deal of the quarter. And not only did we win a new client/partner from the experience, we also put ourselves on the map with Vendor X.

About six weeks later, I visited the office of the systems integrator for the first time. It wasn't what I was used to. My typical value-added reseller client at the time was located on a trading estate on the outskirts of town and the sole receptionist (if there was one) would be multi-tasking reception and incoming calls. But the office of this systems integrator was a different league: located in a glass-fronted office in the centre of London, professional uniformed reception staff, electronic sign-in and interior designed, expensively furnished waiting area. We were met by our original systems architect friend plus a few similar colleagues and were taken to an impressive meeting room with fantastic views of London. There, over tea in china cups (with saucers!), we embarked upon the most lucrative relationship that my team had ever had. By the end of the year, the systems integrator was our largest billing customer. In fact by the end of that financial year, three of our top five clients were members of the family that you would call consultants, systems integrators and outsourcers.

After our initial success, we decided to focus more time on the global IT services companies – clearly they weren't as unapproachable as we first thought and they needed partnerships (in our case primarily as a logistics engine for product fulfilment). Their natural partnerships were the large technology OEMs and household-name software companies, but the reality was that they also required more niche partners to fill in the gaps and help them to differentiate. More importantly, everything they did was big: large volumes, high value, technically advanced high-end product. And, perhaps most pleasingly, they seemed happy for us to make a profit. We were used to dealing with value-added resellers for whom product margin was the be-all and end-all of the transaction. The traditional value-added resellers sold at low, single digit margins, so every percentage point of margin they could extract when buying from us increased their net margin by 20% or 30%. It meant that our relationships with them revolved almost entirely around how much money we could save them by eating into our own profit.

With the systems integrators it was different. That is not to say that they were in any way fools, however. They had great market knowledge, so understood what a fair price looked like. But, because the majority of their profit in any project was in the delivery of their core high margin services, they weren't as interested in wasting time securing every percentage of profit from the hardware. Their most important motivation in the partnership was the level of service they received and how we could provide technical, logistical and commercial support in order to allow them to do their job of delivering the client's project on time and on budget. Their mentality was that we were providing a service and they didn't mind paying for that service with a fair margin in the same way they would pay for the services of a lawyer or architect.

Emboldened by our success, we invested significant time and effort into expanding the systems integrators', consultants' and outsourcers' client base and it became our most important focus sector. But it didn't happen overnight. We had a head start in that other parts of our own organisation were already selling to contacts within these companies and they made introductions for us, so we had an 'in'. This was usually just a name or a mail address, but this crack in the door was usually enough to start an email chain that led us to the right person. Sometimes this was procurement, sometimes it was the alliance team, sometimes it was the person in the firm that looked after the relationship with the particular vendor whose products we were selling. There was no right or wrong answer; it seemed that, for each individual company or project, there was a selection of people who were aligned and valued our support.

With hindsight, there were a few things in our favour. For a start we were acting as a managed fulfilment channel for a global well-established technology OEM who already had a relationship with the large consultants, systems integrators and outsourcers. So I worked the angle of convincing Vendor X's channel management personnel, who looked after the strategic global partnerships, to insert my organisation in the supply chain. If I had been an OEM trying to break into the same companies, I wouldn't have had this door opener. I tasked Ahmed with working the client angle: calling and emailing all of the contacts we had at the consultants, systems integrators and outsourcers acquired from Vendor X (who were effectively playing the role of hybrid supplier/partner), our own company or other 'friends of friends', setting up meetings and asking for opportunities to quote for and participate in projects and opportunities. Looking back, we were throwing darts at a dart board in the dark – we didn't understand the roles, we didn't understand the motivations of the people we were dealing with, we didn't understand the projects or why they were taking so long to close. We had hunger and we were tenacious (though when we became pushy it was always a mistake and it set us back), but we were without structure. To some degree we cracked it in the end, but I estimate it was three years before we had established contacts in most of the large players. Even then, we were really only scratching the surface and there was lots of revenue still going to our competition because we couldn't cover all of the bases. We probably could have done it quicker, more efficiently, at lower cost to our employer and at a greater return if only we had really known what we were doing. There were good days and there were setbacks. Some days we thought we had had a brilliant meeting and had made great headway, and then we didn't hear anything from the consultancy or systems integrator for months afterwards. This disappointment was because we confused these companies, who had a small amount of substantial orders every year, with our usual value-added reseller clients, who had a constant stream of runrate smaller orders, and we were spooked when we weren't quoting every day on an opportunity, convincing ourselves that our pitch hadn't landed. But thankfully, most of the time, just when we had given up on a relationship with a large systems integrator after months of effort, an opportunity came through that made our eyes water.

We also had to change our approach. While selling on price to value-added resellers had obvious disadvantages, there was also a pleasing simplicity to it – you just built personal relationships and the orders came in. But with the large IT influencers the buyers weren't won over just by relationship, they genuinely wanted value: hard work, diligence, innovation and a shared will to win. So the strength of our personalities that had succeeded in securing us close relationships so far really wasn't enough with these guys.

When Ahmed took that initial call, he really didn't have a clue how to manage the situation because he didn't understand the buyer values at all. He didn't know how to maximise the opportunity and he didn't know where it could lead – all he knew was that he had a great big order on his hands and he was smart enough to know that there was huge potential in where that came from if he handled it right. This book is for him – and this book is also for you!

I'm from a technology sales background. I have made a good career selling IT systems, sometimes complex systems, such as large datacentre transformation projects, and sometimes dead easy, low value, high margin components, such as packs of Ethernet cards in the mid-1990s. They've all required a different approach and they've all added to my knowledge.

Well perhaps I exaggerate. Strictly speaking, I've sold very little! Mainly my career has been based on channel selling, so mostly other people have sold things and I have enabled them to do so by putting the right commercial framework in place for them to be able to sell – through product education, right pricing, competitive knowledge and good supply chain support. There's a skill to it, being one removed from the sales cycle and still influencing the sale. Like all sales, it comes off sometimes and doesn't come off most of the time, but the days it does come off makes it all worthwhile.

However, even though my background is mainly channel sales, and this book is written predominantly from that perspective, there are various other people for whom this book is relevant. The common denominator is that you have recognised a need to understand how the world of the global IT influencers works – maybe because you want to sell with them, maybe because you want to sell to them, maybe because you want to work for them, or even maybe because you already work for them and haven't really figured out yet how it all works.

What is your job description? Probably:

Account manager
Business development manager
Channel manager
Sales manager
Partner manager
Alliance manager
Marketing manager
Procurement lead
Systems architect
Technical account manager

Who do you work for? Probably:

An ISV
A start-up

A large, established OEM
A value-added reseller
A value-added distributor
A finance company
A rental company
A company providing IT services
A systems integrator, consultancy or outsourcer

What do you want to achieve? Perhaps:

Create a strategy to work with the large IT services companies
Create a strategy to sell to the large IT services companies
Get more out of your own company's existing relationship with a large IT services company
Understand more about the large IT services companies with whom you work already and how/why they partner
Understand the motivations of those trying to sell to you
Secure a job with a technology OEM who wish to formulate a strategy to work with the large IT services companies
Secure a job with a company that is already focused on working with the large IT services companies
Secure a job with a large IT services company in their alliance function

If you recognise yourself in the above, then this book is aimed at you. If you don't, but still want to understand how the global IT services sector works so that you can keep relevant, broaden your horizons and future-proof your knowledge, then you are most welcome.

I still don't have all of the answers, but I do have experience and I have learned the hard way. To get to the stage where I can write this book about the large IT influencers, what makes them tick and how to engage with them from the perspective of a potential partner, my journey has been enlightening, highly educational and, eventually after much trial and error, incredibly rewarding. But along the way it's been bewildering, frustrating, mentally taxing and at times physically exhausting.

Key learning points: Who is this book for?
1. The companies with whom we are aspiring to work are large, usually globally focused, IT services companies that leverage the sale of substantial levels of technology products and services.
2. The large IT services companies sell big things to big companies and influence the majority of large technology purchases.
3. This book is for you if you are in sales, marketing, business development or alliances and/or have a goal to understand more about how and why alliances work with a large IT services provider.

The routes to reward

Before we go on, let's clear up a few points about the way that you can sell to and with the large IT services companies and some of the implications of those choices.

Sell to (for internal use)

Similar to all large white-collar businesses, consultancies, systems integrators and outsourcers source a lot of IT and related office products for their own use. To be clear: I'm not talking about for use in client projects such as sourcing servers for a client datacentre, I am talking about their own internal IT systems where generally they retain title to the asset. In many ways, this is the easiest way in which to work with large IT services companies because it is effectively just major account selling. They have an internal IT group and a procurement department, and you sell to them in the same way as you would any company with large and complex IT systems. If that is all that you want, this book probably isn't for you. There are better books out there that describe how to plan and execute large account selling on a 'sell to' basis. This book will focus primarily on the 'sell with' model of engagement described in the next section. Of course, if you do forge a good relationship with an IT services company it makes good sense to try and ask them to adopt your own technology for their own use; partly because it's a sale (and that is the name of the game), but, more significantly,because they can act as a reference – it's very compelling to clients when they see their favourite consultancy or systems integrator giving a product the ultimate endorsement by using it themselves. Also, the users (i.e. the staff) of the influencer will become your cheerleaders (hopefully) when on a client's site. Put another way, clients will see your product being used in an aspirational way. There's many a laptop or tablet sale been made because of the advertising provided by a management consultant using his snazzy new technology to demonstrate something to an important client. Conversely, many end-user client deals have been scuppered when the system integrator is asked what they use internally, and the answer is not the proposed solution (aka 'Cobblers' Shoes' syndrome).

Sell with

Hopefully this is why you bought this book – because you realise that the primary value of working with the key IT services companies is that clients are hugely influenced by them. In essence the model is simple: (i) a consulting firm identifies a business improvement opportunity at a client; (ii) the consulting firm is hired to create the process to make the business improvement; (iii) it will always involve the purchase or expansion of technology. There is no unethical agenda at play here. It is true that certain consultancies do have IT practices that then implement and support IT systems, but the real reason that consulting engagements tend to end up being the first step to a large IT sale is that technology moves at such a pace that it is almost always possible to improve a company's business performance by the procurement of a new IT system (assuming of course they are recommended, applied, installed and supported correctly).

Sometimes at the early stage of the sales cycle, i.e. the identification of the business need, the consultancy won't recommend a specific product or brand of IT product, but they will certainly suggest a type of product. For instance, a certain type of tax software for a company to move into an overseas market or a point-of-sale solution to support a retail transformation. If you are already established as a market leader, your product can be recommended at that stage of the process. What is more likely to happen is that, once the management consultancy has recommended the solution, a more technically focused IT business (such as a technology consultancy or systems integrator) will become involved. This is where strong relationships and good product awareness are most essential and your selling and marketing efforts are hopefully rewarded, as this is when the client is usually recommended which products to buy. Sometimes, the consultancy or the systems integrator is even hired to do a formal market appraisal and run a vendor selection process. In all of these cases it is in your interest to be front of mind for the people executing these consulting projects in order to be ahead of the game.

Sell through

This is probably the most 'traditional' channel engagement model wherein a third-party company 'resells' your product to their client. The vast majority of technology OEMs and other product vendors have a channel model that reflects this approach – either by selling to distributors who hold stock and supply the dealers/resellers/retailer channel or by selling directly to the dealers/resellers/retailers. Many large IT services companies like to deal with their technology OEM partners this way and see the resale revenue as a handy war-chest to help with the discounting of the wider project in order to make their services bid more competitive. However, most technology OEMs favour an 'influencer' model for the large IT services companies; this way, they can reward the consultancy or systems integrator for putting their product forward and also ensure that their traditional value-added resellers, who are set up to transact and implement the products, remain motivated. This model has the ability to work well, but increasing rigour in anti-corruption regulation and compliance means that consultancies and systems integrators need to be entirely transparent about all financial rewards from third parties when recommending technology or other products. This, added to an increasing preference by clients to obtain all aspects of a large IT project from as few sources as possible, means that the traditional consultant or systems integrator is increasingly acting as the reseller partner using a 'sell through' model. There is often a strong advantage for the technology OEM or smaller services subcontractor here in that the large IT influencers are usually more financially secure than most value-added resellers and so represent less credit risk in the supply chain. It should be said that large IT services companies are often opposed to this model, as channelling third-party product through their expense and revenue lines can dilute their profit margin and negatively affect share price. This can lead to a pressure on margin models and selectivity about what business they take.

Sell to (for client use)

This is not to be confused with 'sell to (for internal use)' explained above. As cloud computing becomes the norm, rather than the exception, for clients to consume IT, it is much more likely that OEMs and third-party services will be supplied to a large system integrator or outsourcer who will retain title and then provide the benefit of that product (the compute power or software usage, for instance) on a subscription or even outcome-based financial model to the end-user client. This model has previously been known as Managed Service Provision or Application Service Provision and effectively represents an on-demand resource for the client as opposed to the perpetual or all-or-nothing licence traditionally provided. Clearly, this has licence implications for software providers (for instance, if a software licence is bought by the outsourcer who then intends to use it to provide a solution to 100 companies, then clearly the software provider has a right to demand more for that licence). But, the intellectual property (IP) complexities aside, it is a great way for technology OEMs and other companies to reach many clients while the systems integrator carries the costs and risks associated with the delivery. In short, selling to an outsourcer for inclusion in their datacentre and re-usable client solutions is great business. The downside is, of course, that the systems integrator or outsourcer retains title and therefore drives a very hard bargain through their procurement route.

If you have a less-established brand and your product works, then this model is a good thing; the client is, after all, buying an outcome and is often entirely unaware of the brand of software or hardware they are procuring. Accordingly, good quality but less famous brands can forge successful relationships with the outsourcers driving the outcomes.

Sell to as part of a managed procurement arrangement

This is probably the least common scenario, but can be highly financially rewarding. Increasingly, large companies are outsourcing their procurement to third-party specialist companies – basically managed procurement outsourcers. Often, these are the same companies as you may have a relationship with in one of the other areas mentioned above, such as a consulting firm that also executes managed procurement services for clients. Ordinarily, you will deal with a different person in the organisation from the one you work with on other projects – probably a procurement specialist, operating on a client site with a client badge and email address. The interesting angle here is that part of the procurement outsourcer's proposition is undoubtedly their leverage with vendors in the market, meaning that if you are already working with the outsourcer, you will probably have a good 'foot in the door' for their managed procurement contracts. By definition, these

Potential revenue stream	Who retains Title	Pros	Cons
Sell to (for internal use)	IT services company	You deal with the decision maker – there are no other variables	Less leverage, i.e. you are securing a sale to one company only
Sell with	End-user client	Once established, the IT services company can introduce you to unlimited end-user prospects	You are dependent upon the IT services company making the sale – If they lose, you lose
Sell through	End-user client	As above – once established, the IT services company can introduce you to unlimited end-user prospects	As above, plus you will have to sacrifice a margin for the IT services company to retain
Sell to (for client use)	IT services company	Lots of economies of scale; once the product is adopted in the outsourcer's datacentre, many clients can use it	License complexity; little or no contact or influence with the client so deal becomes less about product differentiators
Sell to (as part of a client's managed procurement contract)	End-user client	Straightforward route into a large client and can be an introduction into other procurements contracts managed by the same outsourcer	Outsourcer will have highly trained and aggressive professional procurement personnel who will drive a very hard bargain

Figure 1.1 The routes to reward.

contracts are usually on behalf of large clients, (i.e. substantial consumers of technology and services).

Of course, it makes sense both for the supplier and the large IT services company to work together on as many of the above models as possible as it strengthens their relationship and creates efficiencies and superior commercial models for both parties. So, when embarking on a relationship with one of the large IT services companies, consider which revenue streams listed above are relevant and where you can establish the correct contacts, contractual terms and commercial models to capture all of the available revenue streams. You should also consider which routes will yield those all-important quick wins, which are so crucial to maintaining executive commitment and 'buy-in' across the respective field sales teams on both sides (see Figure I.1).

Key learning points: the routes to reward
1. There are multiple business models. Be clear on your objective from the outset and establish which model makes most sense to pursue for you and your partner.
2. The greatest return will be in working multiple revenue streams with the same partner in order to maximise your effort (i.e. if you are doing 'sell with' and you know your partner likes 'sell to' then make that happen too).
3. For this book, the 'sell to' and 'sell with' models are most relevant and you will derive most value if you are aspiring to these particular business models.

How to navigate around the various routes to market: Stephanie's story

Stephanie is a senior account manager at a company where she manages the 'sell to', 'sell through' and 'sell with' revenue streams from a portfolio of consulting firms, systems integrators and outsourcers. Her story is interesting because, not only has she got a perspective on the different types of sales motions and stakeholders, she is also writing from the perspective of someone who usually deals with the more traditional value-added reseller channel and therefore has some interesting cultural observations about dealing with the global IT influencers. Stephanie is a real person; however, I have anonymised for the sake of privacy.

> I've been working at my current company for 23 years, and from the very first day I was working with one of the large global consulting firms. Our revenue streams with the global IT influencer sector are a cross section of the different types of sales engagement forms including sell to, sell through and sell with.
>
> 'Sell to' is consistent runrate as there is a large amount of project-based work and departmental change to adapt to client needs, which drives technology spend. Also, key internal customers within the large companies often move from business to business – for instance, starting in procurement and then

moving on to a specific project – and as a result they understand what you can do for them.

When I look at the primary drivers for the products and services that I sell to the large consultancies, minimising risk is the key factor. The nature of my business is that we help companies reduce their capex exposure and we find many applications for this within the large global systems integrators because they try to avoid holding assets for every project and engagement that they may be managing. There is also a healthy contractor base, so we find that demand for our products tends to increase and decrease on a daily basis as new people come on board and then leave specific projects.

Regarding the 'sell with' business, it's been interesting to see the big systems integrators and outsourcers buying up names from the traditional reseller channel and integrating them into the way that they go to market and service clients. It's also been important to track the evolution of the alliance function in companies like Accenture and CGEY – they have become vital internal customers and channel partners with highly successful 'sell with' businesses.

In any part of the business, building stakeholders is always a constant. Due to the fluid nature of the workforce, as personnel move from role to role, an internal customer moving on in less than 12 months is common. You find what you thought was a good point of contact and start to build that rapport and then they transfer. Often, they move to another project with which you can also work, but sometimes they move to a different IT services company or to a client. The time is never wasted in building the relationship, of course, but it's fair to say that my LinkedIn page gets a lot of use tracking contacts and keeping in touch. A lot of this personnel fluidity is down to short-term project-based business, but also down to the ambitious nature of the sort of personnel who are attracted, in particular, to the consultancies.

With all this flux in the business and a very flexible workforce and stakeholder base, networking is very important and always pays dividends, whether it's for myself or my team. Even in a sophisticated market like consulting firms, people buy from people and having a good network of allies who will refer business and vouch for you is vital.

As a sales person looking to build rapport and long-term relationships, another change in recent years to which I have had to adapt has been the increase in the digital nature of business. Very often now we are engaging directly with a company's procurement system or, at best, with our customers via email – all of the way through the procurement process. Something as simple as signatures on emails is an example of what I mean – it's not uncommon for there to be no contact telephone numbers at all now.

The other challenge is that the large systems integrators probably make us jump through more hoops than other traditional VAR [value-added reseller] type channel partners, to the point where it sometimes makes you question the viability of a particular deal. This extra admin and governance is driven by typical large companies' operational factors, such as the fact that larger corporations have more levels of sign-off and internal process, and sometimes it is due to the rigorous nature of their business, particularly around data security and health and safety.

I would also say that a bi-product of working with a large system integrator is that there is a lot of very deadline-driven bid work. Sometimes we are asked to put in some quite large and complex bids to support an RFP [request for proposal] that the systems integrator is submitting, but we know that there is rarely an opportunity for us to take it forward – we are just being used as an option B or an option C. It's frustrating and obviously expensive doing business this way, but we acknowledge that the medium-term payback of being a good team player is worth it.

I think that the other point I would close on is one of cultural shift over the years. Some of the ways in which we engage in order to build relationships has had to evolve; for instance, how we approach corporate hospitality or doing business in the pub after hours. The consulting firms in particular do not interact in this way anymore. They run a very tight ethical ship and are very much industry leaders in championing modern day working methods around integrity and neutrality.

Key learning points: Stephanie's story
1. The stakeholder map is constantly shifting – be ready for this.
2. Relationships are all important and you need to figure out how to do this effectively, as 'old school' relationship building techniques are becoming harder.
3. In the short term, the extra work in landing and maintaining relationships with global IT services firms may seem excessive, but the long-term pay-off makes it worthwhile.

1 Why do companies invest so much in hiring consultancies, systems integrators and outsourcers?

How do we define consultants, integrators and outsourcers?

There's a prejudice that says that consultants are expensive, self-serving and tell me something that I already know. So, before we embark on our strategy to work with the top IT services players, it's worth reminding ourselves why they exist. Clearly, their personnel are, in most cases, well remunerated and therefore costly to hire, so why do all of the world's largest companies invest so much in working with them? I've broken the answer down into two groups: consultancies (to include project lead systems integrators) and outsourcers. There is a fair bit of overlap between the two, of course. Essentially, it all comes down to cost, acquiring specialist knowledge and allowing the client company to hand over an activity so that they can focus on their core business. However, the differences and nuances between consultancies and outsourcers are manifold, relevant to you and warrant explanation. Remember, the point of this is that you understand what drives your potential partner's business; in doing so, you can help them to meet those needs by providing your own products, skills or IP.

It is hard to deny that there is a premium and risk associated with the services paid for from consultants, system integrators and outsourcers. So, why do almost all of the largest companies in the world continue to invest heavily in these types of services? Clearly, all projects and client requirements are different, but the reason to seek help from a third-party company almost always comes down to one or more of the reasons discussed in this chapter.

Why do corporations and public sector bodies use a consulting firm or systems integrator?

Staff augmentation

This is the most simple reason for employing an outside company to work within your business. Yes, there is a premium for the cost of their staff, but that premium is easy to justify if it means that, as a company, you don't incur the substantial costs of staff ramp up and ramp down required to fulfil your business's short-term requirements or projects. Leaving aside for now the specialist assistance available from a consultancy, the mere provision of highly qualified, well supported personnel to fill a short-term project skills gap is compelling and essential for businesses who want to remain flexible with their fixed costs. Of course, it is not a given that the consultant's staff will be more expensive than the people in the business – for instance, asking highly paid lawyers to cease earning fees in order to support a project to transform the law firm's operating model would likely be more expensive than hiring consultants to complete the task.

Access to deep experience, IP and resources

The large consulting firms (both management consulting and technical consulting) are usually long established and highly experienced companies with vast reservoirs of industry knowledge. This experience and knowledge sits in the heads of the personnel staffed to deliver projects, but also in tools, methodologies and spreadsheets kept in the consulting firm's libraries and intranet. So, the consulting firms have deep levels of data and knowledge, but they also have pools of personnel that can be brought in swiftly and painlessly to help a failing or changing project. A consulting firm or large systems integrator is also much more likely to have access to best practice methodologies and business models through wider experience of delivering projects across other companies.

A deep focus on a problem

The large IT services companies have a project lead approach. This comes with a project plan, service level agreements (SLAs), client reviews, closely monitored deadlines and so on. In short, an externally managed project receives a focus that most internally delivered projects don't by virtue of the fact that the consulting firm's reputation, client relationship and revenue stream (monthly billing revenues) depends on the consistent and reliable delivery of the project milestones. It should also be said that the work ethic endemic within the large IT service companies is a significant part of the reason that companies hire them: the daily costs for a consultant may be high, but per hour they usually work out as good value given the lengthy days worked during project delivery.

A different perspective is also extremely valuable; often, the staff within a business do not have the time or ability to take a step back and identify the problem with 'a fresh pair of eyes'.

Breaking down political and emotional barriers (aka detached view)

On the face of things, hiring a group of external individuals to execute an important project within, or on behalf of, your company may seem illogical. First, these people are unlikely to have the deep knowledge of your company and business sector; furthermore, they will not fully understand the stakeholder needs in the same way that an internal member of staff does. However, think of it another way: the consultancy is not encumbered by political bias within an organisation and, importantly, it has the ability to cut across levels and functions in an organisation in a way that a salaried member of staff with longer-term career goals may feel inhibited in doing. Put another way: the outside contractor will have the ability to hold a mirror to the business with no deeply held bias or prejudice and will help the leadership to make rational, dispassionate decisions. Let's be honest, there will also be times when it suits the leadership of the client to have an external entity make or recommend a decision that it is tough for them to be seen to make themselves, such as redundancies or board-level compensation. The benefit of a third-party viewpoint can help a great deal in later explanation to customers or shareholders.

Deep technical knowledge

In the case of a management consultancy, deep technical knowledge could mean deep knowledge of an industry sector (gathered and refined over decades of experience in disparate geographical markets), or in the case of systems integrators or technical consultancies in deep product technical knowledge. In the case of the latter, the systems integrator will ordinarily have strong experience and knowledge in its staff that enables it to address a certain implementation or similar technical challenge, but it may also have an extensive portfolio of IP, which could include codes, adaptors or fixes, that can be extremely valuable. Additionally, in the case of the large systems integrators there is also their network of alliances, in the shape of services and products companies with whom they partner and have technical or commercial relationships, that their influence can bring to bear and from which the client can derive significant benefit. In short, you, as an alliance partner, become an important part of the consultant's or systems integrator's sales and delivery proposition.

Key learning points: Why do corporations and public sector bodies use a consulting firm or systems integrator?
1. Hiring and firing staff for short-term projects is very expensive and regulated, so utilising ad-hoc personnel for discrete tasks is usually cost effective.
2. Consultants and integrators have specialist skills and knowledge that a corporation may need for a specific role or project.
3. There are political and practical advantages of dedicating a third party to a specific task or project in order to ensure it gets correct focus.

Why outsource?

Focus on your core business

All companies are resource constrained and during times of expansion or cost-cutting find that key resources and management time are scarce. It makes sense therefore to deploy your most valuable internal resources to revenue generating activities rather than executing or managing mundane or time-consuming back-office tasks. A good example would be an oil company wishing to outsource its human resource (HR) function. It stands to reason that the management of the business wants to focus on the locating, extracting, refining, distributing and marketing of oil, so it is more efficient to pass a function such as HR or payroll management to a specialist business. An example in the mid-market might be a firm of lawyers outsourcing the running of their IT systems to a local technical consultancy with defined SLAs in order that the partners of the law firm can concentrate on the core business of serving clients.

Financial benefits through shared services

It makes obvious business sense that if you can share a function with other companies that are using the same resources, then economies of scale will be created. This is very clear in the outsourcing model where outsourcers will leverage the same resources (staff, facilities, internal systems, IT hardware, etc.) to serve many customers. This is similar to the cloud computing argument, wherein multiple customers can leverage the same infrastructure and therefore bring the cost down for all users. The client also has the distinct advantage of moving fixed assets to variable assets, which brings accounting benefits as well as enabling the client to scale at times of high demand. For example, the high demand might be a spike in business that an outsourced call centre (which has the benefit of serving many hundreds of customers with variable needs) could manage much easier than a company's own call centre (which is likely to have much more modest failover facilities). On this note, it is also common for companies who outsource a function to divest the assets or resources to the outsourcer, thereby improving the balance sheet and generating cash.

Labour arbitrage

Probably the most significant trend in outsourcing in the last 20 years has been the movement to off-shoring, i.e. outsourcing a function or task to a global location where costs (predominantly staff costs) are significantly less than in the home country, therefore allowing 'arbitrage' of the cost of labour. Arbitrage is defined as the simultaneous purchase and sale of equivalent assets or of the same asset in multiple markets in order to exploit a temporary discrepancy in prices. In plain English this means taking a role that costs $15 an hour to employ in the USA or western Europe and sourcing that work at a lower rate in another location (e.g. India or Mexico). This has become possible in recent years due to exponential global improvements in IT and communications links. The IT services companies have invested billions in developing service centres of excellence across the world, and in many cases partner with local universities and educational institutions in order to further develop the local talent and skills. The powerhouse of off-shoring until now has been India; however, recent years have seen significant shifts to the Phillipines, China, Argentina and, in the case of European companies, to near-shore destinations in eastern Europe such as Slovakia and Hungary. Basically, anywhere where the staff costs are significantly less than the country in which the client is based potentially provides an attractive off-shoring opportunity.

Access to high quality and flexible capabilities

This is very similar to the 'Access to deep experience, IP and resources' section discussed earlier. When a company selects an outsourcer, they are usually procuring best practice capability and resources that are highly trained and specialised in the particular function for which they are being hired. Also, there is the added benefit (as previously mentioned) that these resources are flexible in that they can increase or decrease in line with demand. When companies don't have to employ expensive specialist resources to maintain a back-office for non-core functions, there is a double benefit at play. Not only are they most likely paying less for their staff when they outsource, they also minimise recruitment, onboarding and training costs, as well as having superior risk management as they share the burden of delivery with their specialist outsource partner.

Round-the-clock service

Many outsourcers have off-shore capability because they operate in multiple time zones. Therefore, they are still open when you are shut, allowing you to provide a service to your own customers during the hours when you were previously unable to do so. By utilising the services of an outsourcer who can operate around the clock in your chosen markets, you are providing a better level of service to clients and prospects in a world where customers increasingly expect a 24×7 service. They are equally effective when a company has outsourced a deliverable such as creative or legal services because the task can be continued throughout the dormant hours when the business is closed, such that a workload is completed overnight for delivery the next day.

Outsourcing has its detractors. Outsourcers need to work hard to break down both language and cultural barriers as well as potential political pressure to keep jobs 'on-shore'. However, the prevailing market trend is in the expansion of outsourcing. According to Deloitte's 2016 outsourcing survey, the sector is expected to see growth across all functions surveyed, particularly IT, finance and HR.

With customers demanding lower prices and a 24×7 service, combined with pressure from shareholders for greater efficiencies and profits, the outsourcing bandwagon is unlikely to slow any time soon. So my point is that it is incumbent on all technology OEMs to have an approach and strategy to work with this model.

Key learning points: why outsource?
1. At its most simple level, outsourcing allows an organisation to concentrate on its core business by passing the day-to-day 'non-core' admin or back-office tasks to a third party.
2. The rise in off-shore outsourcing is largely down to the advantages of using lower cost, highly skilled resources for functions that can be undertaken remotely.
3. In these days of 24-hour customer service expectation, outsourcing allows organisations to provide round-the-clock access to specialist and skilled personnel who can service their customers while they sleep.

The client-side perspective: Paula's story

Paula has seen the consulting sector from two angles: as a subcontractor and as a client. She has a lot of experience through working for her own consulting firm and also alongside larger consulting organisations 'client-side' (i.e. managing relationships with their delivery partners). Her perspective is interesting and gives a good overall view of what clients and sub-contractors get from a relationship with the large consulting firms and system integrators. She also touches upon some of the friction and challenges of two cultures working together. Once again, Paula is a real person whose name and experience has been anonymised.

> Over many years I have worked with consulting firms in various capacities, ranging from a contractor working 'client side' in the banking sector to overseeing my own independent consulting firm managing entire projects in the public sector.
>
> I recall a role where I oversaw a project to develop a new operational banking proposition with a well-known management consultancy. It involved consolidating operations into one hub that was effectively near-shore. My role was to be CIO [chief information officer] for that project and I was working with the management consultancy as if I was their client (though I was a contractor in my own right). They had a contract that they agreed with the director of the transformation; then I had a team that worked with me on the operations side; then there were other teams working on other parts of the programme. I led the programme and I was also responsible for the procurement. For instance, I would sign-off the management consultant's monthly invoices.
>
> Why was I brought in to effectively do the role of the client? Well, the project was highly political within the public sector. It was merging two regulatory systems and was unusual because it was supported by an act of parliament. The director that I was working for was accountable to parliament for creating this new division, which meant that, in theory, I had an iron-clad mandate. But the issue was that the people responsible for making things happen were the leaders of the two organisations being merged and they had no interest whatsoever in doing it. We were unable, as a programme team overall, to rely on the fact that those guys would work and deliver against the schedule set down. In fact, it was in their interests that the project didn't happen. On that project we had workstreams from three large consulting firms involved in the deal: one firm doing the property consolidation, another consulting firm working on the programme support, and I actually had another company advising on the business integration and governance issues.
>
> When I was working on an oil and gas client, it was challenging in a different way. This was a very physically hostile environment and the client needed an organisation to work with that could understand that. In large oil and gas projects like this, it's not uncommon for the energy companies to be working in partnership, so they are inclined to use third parties to own the project and reduce political issues. I think that, especially in the public sector, cutting

through the red tape is an essential role of the consultant. The disparate departments and geographies stand on their own and they don't necessarily 'buy-in' to the direction of their central executive – they will do their own thing anyway. I found that does happen to an extent in large corporates also, but mainly in these organisations the strategy is followed in the end. There is politics in corporate organisations, of course, but I have found it even worse in the public sector.

When I was involved in vendor selection (be it an OEM or selecting services firms for a client), I was interested in personal relationships. I have to be able to believe in people and engage with them, trust they have the same kind of attitude and be convinced that they are pulling in the same kind of direction that we want to go. In another large banking organisation, where I was delivering a project for a client, some of the large technology OEMs had permanent desks in the building, so, in that case, that was a partnering approach, but in the public sector it was not acceptable to get that close to people.

When I was working with suppliers and partners from the consulting sector, the thing I liked was the intellectual challenge. On the strategic projects, it's really demanding. I also found with them that they offer additional value through their relationships with other companies and from their relationships in other parts of the world. That starts to bring alliances and companies together, so they become a hub. And, of course, you just get a really good quality of personnel.

Cultural fit is always a challenge to be addressed. I had one incident, when I was working for a client managing a project being delivered by a large management consultancy, where I had a revolt from the client's team on the project. They were mainly people who had come up through the ranks or had worked there for 20 years, who were then put into a workshop with a bunch of strangers who had just come out of Oxford or Cambridge. Yes, the consulting team were working until 11pm and turned up at 6am, which garnered some begrudging respect, but the personalities just clashed. We had one night out that was supposed to be a bonding night, but the following day I had to deal with one of the client's team (a long-term servant) who refused to come in that day due to a disagreement the previous night – and that was meant to be a bonding experience! It was a fine example of how there were very different people from very different backgrounds coming together on a project and actually we hadn't thought hard enough about how that was going to work. We just thought that we, as the programme managers, were culturally aligned and so assumed that everyone else was too.

A key characteristic of a good engagement is when the consultancy understands the space well, so you are not having to teach them what the sector is or what you are doing. That way, they put forward relevant people who are engaged and get it and move quickly. The next important thing is stability of resources. Also, the power of their network is not to be under-valued. When I was working 'client-side', the big consulting firms opened my eyes to so many things – particularly around partnerships and strategies for the client – and it showed a value-added angle of those relationships. At least two of the consulting firms I worked with still mail me now. They obviously want to protect the relationship, which goes to show how effective they are at keeping close to clients. There was another example at the same bank, when the management consultancy brought in a large technology OEM. Their experience of working and delivering together meant that we had a degree of technical depth that wasn't even in the scope of the project at the beginning. The technology OEM in this case was also able to dig deeper in and pull other people through. It was a real upside that the consulting firm brought to the engagement through their partnerships.

If I were to give advice to a 'smaller' company looking to partner with one of the consultancies, I think that the issue would be how you can become big enough to address the potential demand. I'm now running my own small consultancy and even when I can persuade that large consulting firm to put us forward, I am challenged by how we add to the credibility of a big organisation, so we find ourselves working mainly on a subcontractor level. Certainly, it helps if you can share the risk as well as the investment these days.

Until quite recently, many of the projects in which I was involved were on a 'time and materials' model, but now we get asked for a 'fixed price' contract every time by the prime contractor. So, I have to look at every deal and figure out how comfortable it will be for my company. Can we all get on? Is the scope such that we can take a reasonable risk on saying this is how we can do it for the organisation? We've responded previously with a proposal based purely on outcome (aka gain-share) and I have to say that nobody has taken us up on it, but sometimes we do a hybrid model wherein we do a piece of work at a lower cost and then take a percentage of the benefits that are seen from the project. For me, the dangerous client is one that has never worked with a consultancy before, because they might be naïve in terms of how things work in the delivery. I very much prefer working with people who have had experience of working with third parties to deliver important projects, and that's what is great about working with one of the large firms as a subcontractor: their clients are used to working that way.

Key learning points: Paula's story
1. Clients do really value the alliances and ecosystems that consulting organisations bring to an engagement.
2. The consulting firms have a specific culture and it isn't always compatible with clients, so you need to work to make sure it is compatible with your company if you want to partner.
3. Very often, even when you think you are talking to a client, he may actually be a consultant working 'client-side', so it is helpful to keep as many relationships as possible because you never know when your consultant friend could suddenly be the key influencer at a client.

2 Defining the players

Before we progress on to the methods used to partner with the large IT services companies, it is worth taking a look at the different sort of companies and terms you will use in the sector. Mostly it's self-explanatory and obvious, but this chapter gives an overview of typical business models, why they engage in partnerships, a typical project and what motivates them to partner. In most cases, the companies listed as examples cut across more than one of the business segments included; for instance, many companies will execute both consulting and outsourcing, often in the same project (see the Venn diagram in Figure 2.1 for a snapshot of the largest players by revenue in the sector).

Systems integrators

According to IT industry analysts, Gartner, a systems integrator (SI) is an 'enterprise that specialises in implementing, planning, coordinating, scheduling, testing, improving and sometimes maintaining a computing operation'. System integrators try to bring order to disparate suppliers.

System integrator as an expression has become synonymous with the IT sector (for which this book is primarily focused), but it is traditionally a generic term and is used a lot in the defence and media industries. As the explanation above suggests, the role of the SI is to pull together disparate systems, ordinarily from multiple vendors, to deliver a specific client business goal. Ostensibly, an SI operates on a project basis and will own all aspects of the projects, managing the entire list of product vendors and sub-contractors as part of their contract with their client.

SIs are generally highly technical organisations. The larger organisations, such as Accenture, HP, IBM, etc., will be generalists in that they will have skills across many technical disciplines, but also have specific personnel and departments to manage speciality areas. Tier 2 SIs may specialise in a specific technology (say, SAP or Oracle implementations), a specific vertical focus or a particular technical area of expertise such as cloud, web or service-oriented architecture (SOA). It should be said that, even when an SI or one of their specific projects appears to be focused on one particular technology only (such as implementation of a SAP system, for instance), there are likely to be many skills and products required outside of that product set. By their very nature (as Gartner states), SIs exist to bring disparate

26 Defining the players

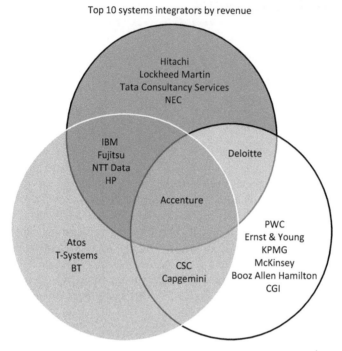

Figure 2.1 Venn diagram of largest global consultancies, systems integrators and outsourcers by revenue.

technologies together seamlessly, so don't rule out a partnership with an SI that specialises in a technology other than your own. A significant component of many large SI engagements will be the integration of existing platforms and technologies, so while IT projects generally represent significant amounts of incremental IT investment, there will also be an element of existing technology integration.

Most large IT projects have design (architecture), build (implementation and integration) and run (support services) elements. A large SI will look to deliver all of the aspects of this project lifecycle. Additionally, most large SIs have a substantial technology consulting element to their business. This aspect of the project lifecycle ordinarily comes before the design phase and is a paid piece of work undertaken by the SI to identify a business need associated with technology, for instance a new enterprise resource planning (ERP) platform or an IT security strategy.

As integrators of third-party technologies, it stands to reason that SIs have an enthusiastic need for relationships and can be very valuable alliance partners for OEMs and smaller services companies. Most of the larger SIs (Accenture, IBM, ATOS, Infosys, for instance; see Figure 2.2) have formal alliance programmes to ensure that they have reliable and consistent links into the major technology OEMs.

Figure 2.2 The top 10 systems integrators by revenue.

Formal accreditation from technology partners is also extremely important to SIs as it will be a key evaluation criteria for any RFP in which they will be involved.

In terms of engagement strategies, SIs are likely to combine a mixture of the models below in any large project:

Influence. The systems integrator will recommend technology, but may not source it themselves and will instead instruct the client to procure.
Resale. As part of the overall cost of a project, the SI will often include product cost as part of their price to the client (in many cases the 'one throat to choke' principle will be the primary motivation in hiring the SI in the first case). The SI will then be compelled to take title and resell the products and services associated with the project as part of the overall project cost. The end-user client will be the ultimate owner of the products.
Retain title. In many cases, the SI retains title to the hardware and software associated with a solution as part of the 'run' arrangement. In this circumstance, the OEMs that wish to work with the SI on that project will be selling to the SI as the end-user of the technology and they will have to decide whether to

tailor the commercial terms as if the SI is the ultimate client or as if the end-user client is the ultimate client. Among other considerations, these matters need to be resolved to address internal compensation issues within the OEM.

Outcome-based model. This is a variation on the above where the SI will retain title of all aspects of the solution, but monetise it with the client based on delivery of certain deliverables, such as a percentage of revenue from a new e-commerce solution or a percentage of billing revenues from a cloud-based solution. This model is a shared risk and gain model with the client, and is largely invisible to the suppliers/sub-contractors unless the SI wishes to ask them to share the risk – more of this later.

Clearly, SIs are a significant influencer in the entire technology selection process for most technology projects, either as technology consultants, architects or the owner of the infrastructure/service, and are arguably the most valuable partner in an IT project lifecycle.

Key learning points: defining the players – systems integrators
1. Systems integrators are highly technical organisations that design, implement and run systems for clients (IT mainly in the context of this book).
2. Systems integrators work ordinarily on a project basis and will often manage multiple stages of the project lifecycle.
3. Systems integrators usually do not produce their own product, like an OEM, so have a need for third-party alliance relationships to create and deliver their solutions.

Outsourcers

Gartner's explanation for outsourcing is:

> The use of external service providers to effectively deliver IT-enabled business process, application service and infrastructure solutions for business outcomes … helps clients to develop the right sourcing strategies and vision, select the right IT service providers, structure the best possible contracts, and govern deals for sustainable win–win relationships with external providers.

There is an important distinction above between business process outsourcing and application or infrastructure services. This section concentrates on the latter two types of outsourcing – business process outsourcing (BPO) will be explained later. In essence, IT outsourcing is the act of contracting with a third-party organisation to deliver an IT focused task in order to reduce cost, increase quality or both. As mentioned previously, there is a strong trend toward outsourcing. Cloud computing, which we will cover later with all its implications, is a form of outsourcing, as is software as a service (SaaS). In the modern world most forward thinking companies are in the process of outsourcing for as many of the services that are not their core business as possible, i.e. they are only looking to retain the services that give them a competitive advantage or that they can use to differentiate themselves in their chosen market. IT functions and projects are prime targets for outsourcing due to their complexity (and therefore high cost and risk to run in-house) and the abundance of skilled technical labour in markets with lower staff costs (aka off-shoring). Common IT tasks and activities to outsource are application services, infrastructure services, maintenance and support. Large corporations often have many outsource partners and will gravitate toward specialists for individual tasks. It's not uncommon for smaller or mid-sized companies to opt for an entire IT outsource.

As a market sector it has fared well during the recession due to its intrinsic business model – reducing outgoings and minimising the risk of fixed costs for a company. Increased globalisation with improved IT infrastructure connections to the developing world, in addition to skilled off-shore resources, have also helped to establish the industry this century (see Figure 2.3).

It goes without saying that outsourcers are very appealing partners with whom to work if you are a supplier of products such as IT hardware or software (or indeed any office related products or services) as they are very high consumers and

Figure 2.3 The top 10 outsourcers by revenue.

therefore purchasers of compute power. If services, and therefore the infrastructure to support them, are sent off-shore, this is not great news (unless you supply products to India). However, many outsourcers are compelled to be entirely based or at least partly based in the country where their clients are located due to data security laws or political reasons, so a large datacentre and/or call centre facility will need to be kitted out.

The business models that are likely to be applicable when an outsource occurs are as follows:

Retain title. In most cases the outsourcer will source the products and services required to service their client's need. In the case of an infrastructure outsource, such as data storage for instance, the outsourcer will source large amounts of hardware, software, potentially other non-IT infrastructure and certain specialist services. In the case of application development, they may use testing, migration or data quality tools. Often the infrastructure or tools are owned by the outsourcer already and they can gain economies of scale from utilising them again and again on new customers (that is, after all, their business) or sometimes they will source new items for each project. If the former, the software company needs to have a clear licence policy to ensure that they are being fairly recompensed for their software being used by multiple end-user clients – this in part comes back to the dilemma of who the software company defines as the end-user, i.e. the outsourcer or the end-user client (see later sections exploring the need for clear compensation models for sales people and a defined channel policy to accommodate this model).

Influence. It is always possible that, as part of an outsource contract, it is only the human resources being outsourced, which could mean that the hardware and software being used remains the property of the end-user client, albeit often located in a third-party datacentre. In this scenario, the outsourcer is likely to have a large degree of influence as to what hardware or software is bought by the client (they will want to know this before they price the contract and will obviously advise the client which products are most suitable); therefore, the outsourcer is a very valuable influencer for any alliance partner.

Resale. As with above, if the client wishes to retain control of the non-human assets that are supporting an outsource contract (almost always hardware and software), then the outsourcer may suggest that the client procure the items from the outsourcer (as they often have superior procurement terms than the end-user client) and see an opportunity to make a profit and create a win–win by acting as a traditional reseller. In this scenario, once again, the outsourcer can be a valuable alliance partner to influence your business.

Outcome-based model. As within the SI sector, occasionally the outsourcer will offer an outcome-based model wherein they charge the end-user client in relation to certain project targets or deliverables (such as cost savings, work orders completed or new business generated in the case of a consumer facing application such as a website). Once again, this model can be invisible to the alliance partner/supplier, but there is an opportunity for an enthusiastic alliance partner to differentiate themselves by creating models to share the risk and reward in line with the outsourcer. We will cover this in more detail later.

> Key learning points: defining the players – outsourcers
> 1. Outsourcing in all forms, particularly IT functions, is a significantly growing market, so it is important to figure out how your organisation can sell to or with the sector.
> 2. Outsourcers are large consumers of computing systems, so appeal as an attractive 'sell to' customer.
> 3. The likelihood that an outsourcer is off-shore will create issues in supplying product to them (in fact it will cannibalise the revenues you are making from your clients), so question hard to identify the on-shore element of the project and figure out where you fit. As ever, don't be afraid to qualify at an early stage.

Consulting firms

Type 'define consulting' into Google and you will receive a number of different answers; however, put as simply as possible, a consultant (in the context of business at least) is an adviser who helps companies improve efficiency. In the context of this book, a consultancy is a company or firm that performs that role for corporate or government clients. There are many different disciplines, such as strategy consulting, change management, market analysis, due diligence etc., but essentially it comes down to the same thing: helping companies make or save money either by the reduction of costs and risk or by increasing their sales revenue. Like outsourcing, it is another largely recession proof business as, when times are good, consultants are hired to increase the top line with new go-to-market initiatives and, when times are more challenging, consultants are hired to help the bottom line by creating efficiencies. Technology consultants address technology related issues whereas management consultants address business related issues – but don't be fooled, the solution is almost always to source new IT products. As mentioned before, just because consulting engagements invariably result in new IT systems being recommended, there is no nefarious agenda here; it is just that in addressing business or technical problems, the rate of evolution of modern IT is such that acquiring and correctly implementing new technology is almost always going to be a profitable activity for a business, either by reducing cost (e.g. more efficient hardware) or improving sales (e.g. implementing a multi-channel strategy for a retail business) – both business problems, both with technology solutions.

You may regard consultancy as the epitome of the new economy, but what we would recognise as the first management consultancies started appearing in the late nineteenth century, shortly after the industrial revolution, formed by pioneering university professors and academics. By the mid-twentieth century, many household names had already been formed, such as McKinsey and Booze Allen Hamilton. The post war years experienced a boom in consulting as the new concept of strategic

32 Defining the players

Figure 2.4 The top 10 consultancies by revenue.

management gained traction and talented newly-skilled MBAs became more plentiful, adding to their effectiveness and appeal. The technology age heralded a new opportunity for the consultancy profession and, as technology boomed in the post-Cold War period, so did the desire for companies to embrace the opportunity created by the new business models that technology brought. By the turn of the twenty-first century, management consultancies and technology consultancies became essential to any alliance strategy due to their early stage involvement in sales cycles, board-level relationships and tendency to be at the heart and, more importantly, the origin of all large technology related projects.

Even though systems integrator architects recommend and implement technology, and even though outsourcers often end up selecting and owning the technology, the consultants (management or technical) are often the most coveted partner of all. Why? Because they are involved so early in the process. It is as simple as that. The consultant knows the client has a problem (or opportunity for improvement) often at the same time that the client learns it, meaning that the consultancy has a chance to start advising the client as to what the solution is (which always revolves around technology, remember) before the involvement of

Defining the players 33

technical architects, integrators or potential hosting partners such as outsourcers. Consultants are very much the 'holy grail' of influencer partners – the more savvy and established OEMs know this and invest heavily in creating alliance strategies and compensation models to work with firms such as McKinsey, Deloitte and Accenture (see Figure 2.4).

The engagement opportunities they represent on behalf of potential alliance partners are not as extensive as other partners in the chain, but their role as influencer should not be under-estimated:

Influence. The consultant influences. Heavily. A management consultancy does not in theory select a particular brand of technology, but they will certainly suggest the type of technology required, so if you are, say, a provider of software for the calculation of tax in obscure countries, then a knowledge of your product will often enter into the consultant's thinking when recommending a solution, i.e. the consultants merely knowing that you exist and what your technology does will help to create demand for your product. Sometimes this means directly for your product or sometimes for a similar (competitive) product, which is why it pays for the management consultant to be aware, and ideally incentivised, to suggest your product. Traditionally, this has been achieved by influencer programmes, wherein a technology OEM will pay the management consultant a fee for recommending their product (pending correct deal registration and authentication process). The opportunity to work with technology consultants is even more obvious – not only are they suggesting to a client that they source a product to improve their business performance, in most cases the client will directly ask the technology consultant what product to buy, either on an informal 'value-added' basis or by actually paying the technology consultancy to make the recommendation. As with management consultancies, technology consultancies can benefit from influencer fee programmes from partners for recommending their product. These fees can be in the region of 5% (for highly commoditised hardware products such as servers or storage) to 30% or even 40% for niche software products. The referral fee model is the traditional method with which to work with consultancies and we will go over the pros and cons of that approach later.

Resale. A management consultancy would very rarely play the role of VAR, but it is conceivable that a technology consultancy may have the appetite to do so as they are highly technically capable and therefore can often see it as a risk free way of earning extra profit and adding value around a project. This is increasingly rare – technology consultants, as all businesses, like to stick to their core business (selling people) and see the resale of product as dilutive to their profit margins and additional credit risk, so they will usually be happier to receive a fee or pass the business to a trusted VAR (once again, often in return for a commercial benefit). It should also be said that the sort of companies that can afford and hire management consultants and technology consultants will generally have established resale framework agreements already in place with one of the larger VARs or direct from the OEM.

We will go into the anatomy of a large IT project later, when you will see the important role played by consultants in the early, and in many ways most influential, stages of the IT procurement process.

Key learning points: defining the players – consulting firms
1. The modern day application of the word 'consulting' in the business world is someone that helps another company improve their business performance.
2. Most consulting engagements result in a new IT system being recommended.
3. Consulting firms make great alliance partners because of their ability to identify opportunity for your product or service and present it in a business rather than technical context that enhances its chance of being adopted.

The other players

Business process outsourcing

Business process outsourcing (commonly referred to as BPO) is a type of outsourcing that involves a company or government department outsourcing an entire process, such as manufacturing or a back-office function (HR, payroll, etc.). As with IT outsourcing, the drivers are: (i) reduced cost, ordinarily achieved by off-shoring the task to achieve labour arbitrage; (ii) a desire for a company to focus on their core business by jettisoning a mundane back-office function; (iii) enabling a new department or function to be created swiftly with minimum management time; and (iv) the ability to scale a department or function as it grows with minimal capital costs.

As with most aspects of the off-shore sector, India is the spiritual home of BPO although the Philippines actually surpassed India in 2010 in terms of BPO revenues. China is rapidly expanding and will no doubt become a dominant force given salary costs and their proven track record of mastering efficient industry processes in the manufacturing sector.

In terms of going to market with the large BPO providers, the news isn't good. The BPO function ordinarily takes place off-shore, so, unless you have a reliable supply chain to India or the Philippines, you are unlikely to benefit directly from any additional revenues. Additional to this is the fact that these off-shore revenues are effectively reducing the in-country headcount of the outsourcer UK customers, so there may be a knock-on effect that will negatively affect the revenues of the OEMs and originators of the products that those enterprise customers used. However, the one angle that can work in favour of technology OEMs is that a BPO can take place on-shore, say a utility company outsourcing their billing process where the data must be processed in-country. In this case there is a remote possibility of your partner (the BPO company) sourcing the IT products to service this new contract – in which case a greenfield sale is possible, though this scenario is not common.

Indian pure plays

Occasionally you will hear the expression 'Indian pure play'. It is slightly misleading, partly because the phrase 'pure play' in reality means any company with a single focus, and partly because it often is not referring to Indian companies. However, what the expression effectively means is an outsourcer (IT or BPO) that exists entirely, or almost entirely, off-shore. The origin of this terminology is related to the fact that the off-shoring opportunity has been particularly well exploited in India, mainly due to: (i) the global communication enablement bought about by the ubiquity of the internet; (ii) a well-timed technology-focused graduate workforce; (iii) the massive need for attractively priced Y2K development skills; and (iv) conducive protectionist government policy, which saw a boom in technology-focused off-shoring on the sub-continent around the turn of the twenty-first century.

In theory, then, these players are undesirable partners in that the services and infrastructure they require is off-shore and it deprives technology OEMs of in-country revenue, but this isn't strictly true. Many of the companies who have built their business on the off-shore model (and originate from India) also have a substantial amount of in-country influence and in many cases utilise personnel sourced off-shore in the country where their clients and contracts physically reside. An example would be Indian resources imported on a short-term basis to work in a datacentre in the USA or western Europe as part of a contract where most of the resources are located off-shore. The on-shore (though outsourced) personnel will often still have a great deal of influence over which products get sourced by the client for contracts that they are supporting, so it is certainly worth establishing and maintaining relationships with the alliance and procurement function of traditional 'pure plays' that may be operating in your geography.

Vertically aligned niche consultancies

As management and technical consultancies are businesses that require deep levels of industry knowledge, in addition to the large consulting businesses that cut across all vertical sectors, many consulting businesses exist just to address a specific vertical sector (e.g. financial services) or even sub-sector (e.g. risk management within financial services). As deep industry knowledge is such a fundamental expectation for consultancies, even the larger consulting businesses will be organised mainly into vertical divisions with highly educated and specialised industry subject matter experts. Outside of the large consultancies, many small- to medium-sized consultancies exist to focus on only one vertical business area.

These businesses establish a strong reputation within their chosen markets and generate loyal networks of contacts that often move from client to client creating new word-of-mouth business for the consulting companies. They trade very heavily on personal approach (speciality and flexibility) versus the bigger consulting brands that offer security and scale. While specialising is a winning business approach for a consulting business, it also leaves these companies open to the risk inherent in their chosen market sector, for instance the recession in banking in 2008 or the halving of the oil price in 2015 that seriously affected the energy sector and therefore the consultancy businesses that relied on that sector.

If you are a business with a strong vertical focus, for instance you create and sell software systems for a particular type of business, then niche consultancies are very much essential to your alliance approach. The niche consultants are talking to your clients all day every day and they are respected as subject matter experts by these clients, so if they can recommend your products, it brings much credibility. If you don't have a niche vertically aligned product, then I would still urge a relationship with the niche consultancies, though it will pay to make sure that your offering is tailored to their chosen market: (i) partner with a complimentary niche ISV in their sector; (ii) create an industry-focused flavour of your technology (maybe a tailored GUI or adaptor with another product that is prevalent in their sector such as SAP); (iii) create and market industry use cases, i.e. a scenario in a certain industry to show how your technology can be used; (iv) promote your industry-relevant credentials heavily and use them as a lever to show that you can make a difference to clients in their vertical sector.

In terms of the routes to market, they are identical to the engagement models for other consulting firms. The most likely business value to you as an alliance partner will be as influencers, though it is not unknown for niche consultancies to play the role of VAR also.

The 'Big Four'

Essentially, this term is a sub-set of the consulting firms section. At one time this group was the 'Big Eight', then the 'Big Six' and then 'Big Five' as they reduced in number due to mergers and acquisitions. Now the 'Big Four' consists of PricewaterhouseCoopers (PwC), Deloitte, Ernst & Young and KPMG. Wikipedia (as they often do) offer as good a summary as anyone:

> The Big Four are the four largest international professional services networks, offering audit, assurance, tax, consulting, advisory, actuarial, corporate finance, and legal services. They handle the vast majority of audits for publicly traded companies as well as many private companies. It is reported that the Big Four audit 99% of the companies in the FTSE 100, and 96% of the companies in the FTSE 250 Index, an index of the leading mid-cap listing companies.

While their background is accounting and finance, all of these companies boast substantial consulting practices that now include alliances formation as a key part of their strategy.

PwC list 29% of their revenues as 'advisory', which will include services such as corporate finance, business valuation, sustainability and crisis management, but will also have a substantial component of strategy, performance improvement and business recovery services, making them a valuable alliance partner to the IT companies that they list on their website as established partners (such as Google, HP, Microsoft, SalesForce.Com, SAP and Workday).

Deloitte states consulting, comprising business services such as enterprise applications, technology integration, strategy and operations, human capital, and short-term outsourcing, now amounts to 33% of their revenues.

Ernst & Young state that 'advisory' makes up 24% of their revenues, consisting of actuarial, IT risk and assurance, risk, and performance improvement. The IT advisory services element is described as:

> helping IT deliver improved business performance ... We help deliver improved business performance by addressing the IT and business agendas together. We work directly with CIOs and others to create a more effective IT organisation. This allows IT to drive process efficiencies throughout the organisation and better support and deliver transformational business change.

Services specifically listed include IT transformation, technology assistance, client-side programme advisory, IT controls services, IT risk transformation, IT assurance, people and organisational change, strategic direction and programme management.

KPMG regard 37% of their revenues as advisory and state that 'KPMGs IT Advisory teams strive to deliver business benefits from a broad range of technologies, helping our clients develop high-performing IT functions and leverage investments in current systems to deliver significant business value'. Regarding investing in their alliance partnerships: 'KPMG has one of the fastest growing Advisory Services businesses and is continuing to invest in growth. Alliances with 3rd parties plays an important role in our continuing growth story.'

Services and vendor hybrids

On 2 October 2002, IBM issued a press release stating: 'IBM and Pricewaterhouse-Coopers today announced IBM's acquisition of PwC consulting, the global management consulting and technology services unit of PricewaterhouseCoopers ... as a result, IBM Business consulting services becomes the world's largest consulting services organisation, with operations in more than 160 countries.'

Since 2000, IBM have made about 140 acquisitions (not far off one a month). They include horizontal software companies (e.g. Cognos, Informics and Algorithmics), vertical software companies (such as Phytem, Explorys (Health Sector) and PSS Systems), many cloud computing companies (such as BlueBox, Cast Iron Systems and ClearLeap) and, most significantly, many IT services companies, including a recent penchant for acquiring creative agencies. It's a good bellwether for ascertaining in which sectors to invest your money if IBM are spending there. IBM are the biggest IT business in the world and a major player in IT services, so none of this is surprising. We will talk more about this later and why it is relevant, but, in short, IBM are a company that has knocked down the barriers between being an IT services business and an IT vendor. They are relevant to companies looking for an IT services partner, but also other IT services partners (such as other systems integrators with whom they now compete) who wish to partner with a company with leading IT products. They dexterously balance these roles using Chinese walls and have an admirable reputation for being an excellent and trustworthy alliance partner.

Six years after the IBM announcement, HP released their own press statement:

> On May 13, 2008, HP and Electronic Data Systems (EDS) announced that they had signed a definitive agreement under which HP would purchase EDS. The agreement was finalised on August 26, 2008 at $13 billion, and it was publicly announced that EDS would be re-branded 'EDS a HP company'.

Once again, this was part of a concerted campaign or acquisition by HP who, since 2000, have acquired nearly 80 software, hardware and services companies to complete their comprehensive portfolio of IT products and services. As with IBM, they satisfy both sides of the alliances equation and have thrived as alliance partners by maintaining strong Chinese wall policies and a reputation for integrity.

Other common sources of influence

This book does not cover this subject well or even at all, but it's worthy of mention. As part of a thorough and comprehensive alliance strategy, there are lots of organisations that will have a key influence over your clients' buying decisions (see Figure 2.5). They are not covered in this book because they are not 'sell with' type organisations – they exist purely as educators or as influencing factors in the market.

According to Gartner: 'Technology buyers spend nearly 50% of their total buying process time engaging with influencers that are independent from their organisation. Technology providers need to expand their investment and attention in influencer relations and marketing to leverage these key resources more effectively.'

Specifically, these companies comprise organisations such as trade bodies, consultants and advisers like Gartner or Forrester, government bodies (such as the CBI in the UK), regulatory bodies and also the influence of peers through social networks like LinkedIn. Covering these influence channels is a specialist area and probably fits more into a marketing and public relations (PR) strategy rather than a 'sell with' alliance strategy, as they are independent bodies and will not show preference or enter into compensation arrangements as a rule, but you should understand which of these types of influencer resources affect your clients' buying process and then work with those influence channels to understand how you can work with them to create a win–win – they may not benefit from your business in a traditional way, but they will have goals and objectives (e.g. gathering up-to-date information) as part of their business model that you can probably play into.

BPOs by revenue	Pure plays by revenue	The Big Four	Other influence sources	Vertically niche	Sector
Automatic Data Processing	TCS	PricewaterhouseCoopers (PwC)	Trade Bodies	Archstone Consulting	Retail, consumer packaged goods (CPG)
Xerox	Infosys	Deloitte	Analyst firms	Giuliana Partners	Public safety
First Data	Wipro	Ernst & Young (EY)	Government Bodies	IMS Health	Health
FIS	HCL	KPMG	Regulatory Bodies	First Manhattan	Financial services
Capita	Indra		Peer groups	Putnam Associates	Pharma and biotech
Accenture	Tech Mahindra		Social networks	AON Consulting	Human capital
Teleperformance	LG CNS			ZS Associates	Sales & marketing
West	Mindtree				
Convergys	Hexaware Tech				
Broadridge	MphasiS				

Figure 2.5 Others to consider.

> Key learning points: defining the players: the niche players
> 1. BPO is a growing sector and will only get larger, but there is little 'sell with' opportunity, only 'sell to', which may be dilutive for markets outside of countries where the off-shore facilities aren't located, such as the USA or western Europe.
> 2. Partnering with vertically aligned niche consultancies can be an excellent way to gain traction in a specific vertical sector, or if you have an offering with a specific industry focus.
> 3. Other market influencers, such as analysts, trade organisations and industry peer groups, have a major influence over your clients' buying decisions, so consider a strategy for benefitting from them.

3 Why partnering is win–win

The anatomy of a large IT project

Now that we know our alliance targets and the routes to market, it makes sense to look at the roles played by each organisation in a typical large IT project lifecycle.

Clearly every project is different – different products, different motivations, different business need, different procurement process, etc. – so, in order to keep it simple, let's distil it down to four very easy steps and consider the role of the large IT influencers at each stage of the process (see Figure 3.1). To be clear, this is a fairly extreme over-simplification of a complex and protracted process, so treat it as figurative rather than literal.

Phase 1: business case

At the heart of every IT project there is a business need. Almost always this will come down to the need to please customers (sell more) or the need to be more efficient (cut costs). It is at this phase of the process that the management consultancy is most often found. Sometimes, the client knows they have a need and actively recruits the management consultancy to tell them how to address the problem or, sometimes, it will take a meeting with a management consultancy to point out that the client has a need. Either way, it comes to the attention of the client's executive that his or her company or department has an opportunity to either improve the way it engages with its customer or the way in which it can reduce its costs by a more effective business process. So, the executive formally engages the management consultancy, who will first do a piece of work to explain to the client that the company can indeed make improvements, and will also explain to the client in high-level business terms what she or he can do to address the situation (by the way, these two things may be different pieces of work or may be within the scope of the initial piece of work).

This is what so appeals to products and services companies that partner with consulting firms: the notion that their product or service may a part of the solution that the management consultant puts forward. In reality, it very rarely happens exactly as the OEM would like it to happen. The management consultancy exists to provide business solutions to a problem and rarely, at this stage of the engagement anyway, goes down to a technology or product level in what it advises to the client. But, what if you did have a particularly unique or innovative product or service that addresses the client's problem? There is every chance that the management consultancy will refer to it or even formally recommend it as part of its solution. It is, after all, their duty to remain market relevant, which means understanding all of the different technological advancements within their sector. As mentioned previously, this is the holy grail of most technology OEMs: being put forward and built into a solution, months or maybe even years before vendor section is formally executed. This is primarily why consultancies – particularly those with a strong specialism (such as a vertical niche player) – are such coveted business partners, because they have an input to technology projects at a far earlier stage than most technology companies formally get invited to be involved.

Phase 2: architecture

Also known as the design phase. As mentioned previously, the solution that is put forward by the management consultancy will, almost without exception, involve the procurement of new technology. Whether the answer is to implement a new billing system for customers, improve fraud detection, engage with shoppers via a new medium such as social media or grow poppy seeds to run cars rather than dig oil out of the ground, the answer will be to implement a new IT system, which will include specialist software and almost certainly a new infrastructure on which to run it. This is the domain of the technology consultancy. To be clear, there is no set convention around who gets to do this work. Sometimes, the management consultancy will have skilled technology personnel who can seamlessly segue into the technical phase of the project (think Accenture or Deloitte) or sometimes the client will choose to go out to the market to select a different partner for this part of the project. It is often undertaken by the company that latterly does the implementation (the systems integrator). Either way, it is very much a different piece of work from Phase 1 and is often contracted as a discreet and separate piece of work altogether – very often to a speciality company. In any event, it is at this stage that things get very interesting for providers of products and services. Sometimes, the company creating the architecture will recommend specific products or services and sometimes they will recommend a more general type of products or services (a lot comes down to how unique the products and services are that are required). Sometimes, they will charge to do the product selection as a discreet piece of work. Whatever the precise scope, now is an excellent time to engage if you wish to supply anything to the project because, once the architect recommends your product or service, you are very likely to end up as part of the solution, hence the fact that technical consultancies (or the large players that have technical architecture functions) are arguably the most desirable alliance partners in the whole project lifecycle.

There is a significant point here around adding value. The technical consultancy has most likely been paid to complete the work considering time (i.e. not on a time and materials basis, but only when they actually complete their part of the project) and, more accurately, the time of the people in the consultancy is the most important cost and outgoing; they will look to leverage the help and assistance from third parties with a vested interest as much as possible. So, providing added value in the shape of resource to help architect aspects of the solution is very appealing to the technical consultancy and will act as a powerful lever to them putting your product forward – as will a finders fee, of course.

Phase 3: implementation

This is the domain of the systems integrator. Often this is the same company as the previous two phases and often it is a specialist company employed for specific product, technical or project management capability. This is normally the most high-cost phase of the overall process and also the lengthiest in terms of timescale. It is also the most critical in terms of product selection. By this stage of the process, the primary software that is central to the solution has normally been selected (think SAP or Oracle, for instance), but there is still an array of decisions to be taken about infrastructure (the hardware of hosting services) and peripheral software (security, migration tools, adaptors, etc.). It is during this phase that the final selection for the products and services will be done and when they will be sourced. If you are not the OEM, but part of the channel employed to provide the product, or maybe the finance company, now is the critical time. As with the architecture phase of the end-to-end project, the systems integrator is almost always paid to complete the implementation (as opposed to time and materials basis), so will look to leverage the skills of the product providers as much as possible, both to provide low cost 'close to the box' services that the OEM or channel partner is better placed to provide or by utilising pre-sales technical assistance in order to minimise time investment of the system integrator's own staff (who can be more productively utilised in other aspects of the delivery). There will also be a fundamental change in the dynamic between the services company (the systems integrator) and the products providers or sub-contractors, in that, prior to this stage, the suppliers will be trying to impose themselves on the process and will be aggressively pursuing the systems integrator, whereas at this stage of the project lifecycle, the systems integrator can't proceed without a great deal of support from the products providers and sub-contractors, so be prepared to ramp up quickly to support the systems integrator because their reputation, client relationship and profit is now on the line and based on strict milestones.

Logistical capability, technical input and commercial creativity is now much in demand by the systems integrator, so make sure that you have prepared for the spike in interest as the project nears go-live. It goes without saying that timelines will differ greatly depending on the scale and complexity of the implementation (e.g. the integration of a large SAP system for a manufacturing company from start to go-live is likely to be years), so ensure that your own project and engagement plan around the project is in line with the needs of the systems integrator.

Phase 4: support

In many cases, your job is done. In the ideal world you have professionally executed a successful alliance relationship with a management consultancy, based on incentives, added value or old-fashioned relationship building. They have built you into their 'answer' to the client's business need and you have successfully navigated the RFP process, legal and commercial hurdles and have your product now ensconced in the recently installed solution. In reality, it is unlikely to have gone this smoothly. Possibly because you are not blessed with the right sort of relationships at the business consulting level, possibly because your product is not sufficiently unique to have been named as the de facto solution to the business problem (no shame here – most of us operate in over-supplied, commoditised markets) or possibly because you lost fair and square during the RFP phase. In any event, there is likely only slim pickings from here on in – the support of the system will be sent off-shore by a specialist outsourcer and the emphasis will be on managing and maintaining the solution as opposed to acquiring new product. But all is not lost. It is not time to move on and forget about this project quite yet. The most obvious revenue stream is the maintenance contract, which will probably require annual renewal. If you are a provider of specialist software or are the OEM of the hardware, it is unlikely that the outsourcer will want to support without backing-off to you for specialist assistance. There will be new and additional users for the solution, which means you will hopefully have a steady stream of licence revenue or upgrades. Assuming you are still on good terms with the client, and your product is doing what it is supposed to, then there is every chance that they will welcome you in to discuss complimentary or new products in your portfolio that can be utilised to support the existing system. However good a job the outsourcer has done to send off-shore as much of the solution support as possible, there will still likely be local datacentres that need to be supported; for instance, those that hold sensitive client data. Probably most crucially of all, the outsourcer will always be looking to run things more efficiently (their time is money, minimising hours to support the solution is profit for them), so should always be open to a discussion about how newer technology can reduce support overhead.

It is possible that all four phases can be executed by the same company, though few companies are geared up to do this. Even if they are, the client may decide that there is a conflict of interest in the same company playing more than one role in the lifecycle, so it's worth considering that all of the IT services companies can be valuable alliance partners in their own right, and are all capable in their own way of leveraging significant spend on third-party products as part of every large project.

Key learning points: the anatomy of an IT project
1. At a high level, think of a project as having four stages: business case, architecture, implementation and support.
2. At each phase there is an opportunity for your product or service to be recommended to play a role, so consider the buyer values at each stage and how you can engage.
3. All four phases may be undertaken by the same company or by different companies, so there may be a need for multiple partnerships in order to ensure you are exerting influence at all relevant parts of the project cycle.

Figure 3.1 The anatomy of an IT project: high level view.

Typical scenario

Let us look at what the above may mean in practice. The same caveat applies here: every project is very different, but, in order to keep it simple, I've picked a fairly basic example (see Figure 3.1). Real life will be more complex, and possibly protracted, so regard the following as an illustrative, albeit fairly realistic, look at how a large IT project may play out.

Phase 1: business case

The client lead for a prominent management consultancy goes to visit a board-level member of a multinational grocery retailer. This may have come about because they have a regular catch-up, maybe because they were reviewing another piece of work, or maybe because they are old business friends and one of them has recently moved roles and thought it would be a good idea to catch-up and see if there is anything on which they can work together. The origin is irrelevant other than to make the point that consultancy is a people business; they sell people, and the knowledge that is their 'product' resides with people, so people are the essence of their business. Ergo, personal connections are all important.

After the pleasantries, the catch-up around their respective personal and professional lives, their mutual friends (possibly even their days working together at 'the firm' – the alumni network is, after all, a very strong sales tool for consulting firms) and overall business scene setting, the meeting moves to its main purpose.

Management consultant (asking a typically open question):	Tell me, what is your main challenge?
Retail executive (after a pause):	You know, I have a concern that when people visit my store they are spending less than they should – perhaps less than the average spend that my competitors are managing to achieve.
Management consultant:	So what is currently the average spend per basket when the customer leaves your store?
Retail executive (whose job it is to know these things):	It's £22.57.
Management consultant (whose job it is to know these things, as well):	OK, that's not too good. It certainly seems quite high for the grocery sector overall, but lower than we'd expect for the supermarket sector, which is in the range of £27.00–£29.00 for a business like yours. How about I do a

	little bit of work for you, to take a look at some of your stores and see if I can come up with the answer?
Retail executive:	Why not. I need to get to the bottom of it. It would be good to know if there is anything that we can viably do.

And so it begins. The management consultant and retail executive agree a scope (remit for the project, i.e. the deliverable) and the management consultant goes back to his office to mobilise his team and start researching why the retailer may have a problem. An initial scope of work is produced, it is sent to the retail executive to sign and a few weeks later the piece of work begins in earnest.

The team from the management consultancy, which consists of personnel at all levels of the organisation addressing aspects of the project suitable for their pay grade and skills, visit stores, interview store managers, interview branch staff, meet with executives at head office to understand existing strategy (e.g. senior personnel involved in brand, marketing, merchandising, pricing, etc.), interview customers, check out social media and so on. They meticulously document their findings against a defined set of criteria and industry best practice. At the end of the process (let's say a number of weeks), the deliverable is produced. In tangible terms this will probably be a PowerPoint deck displaying the findings of the research activity, the conclusions (i.e. why the retailer may be achieving a lower average basket yield than the competition) and suggested ways in which the retailer may wish to address the issue.

The report concludes that the client's business is in good shape, their customer demographic mix is desirable and they are appealing to the right age and ethnic growth sectors; the product selection is good and in line with consumer demand; customer service scores are good and pricing, while not the best in the market, is highly competitive. However, there is one area of the business that is called out: the digital strategy, or, put another way, how is the retailer using its available customer data and modern technology, to which its customers all have access, to ensure that they are targeting the right customers with the right products and at the right times. The competition have done it successfully, and have increased their revenue yield per customer by increasing average spend through effective customer marketing, creating a more efficient shopping experience and creating loyalty. The conclusion, so says the team of management consultants, is to use technology to increase their knowledge of their clients' spending habits, desires and needs and, most importantly, to satisfy these drivers at the optimum time – when the client is walking around the supermarket with a trolley and in buying mode. The management consultancy will also provide some handy projections of what an average basket spend could look like and what that may do to the company's revenue and profit. It will make the money invested in the piece of management consulting work look miniscule and very good value indeed.

So the management consultancy's work is done. They have identified the problem, have recommended how it may be addressed and explained what the result of that can be. If they also have technical consulting aspirations (such as Accenture, IBM, Deloitte) they will now open the dialogue about creating the solution to address the issue. If they are a pure management consultancy, they may just hand the deliverable to the client and wish him luck, with a friendly reminder that they are available to be hired to select the partner for the next phase if required. The client now has the choice to explore the next phase. In this fictional example, let's assume it is a private business (supermarkets usually are) and it can choose to move forward how it wishes; however, in a highly regulated business such as utilities and maybe government, then it may be obliged to enter into a formal process for the next stage before issuing formal purchase orders.

Phase 2: architecture

It is slightly disingenuous to break out this stage of the cycle as it is almost always carried out by the original consultancy firm (as stated previously, many traditional management consultancies now have technical consulting divisions to support their management consulting business) or, more commonly, it is carried out by the company that executes the implementation, the systems integrator. In our scenario, let's say that it is a discreet piece of work carried out by a separate organisation who are hired specifically to design the solution.

Put simply, technical architecture is the act of developing a technical model for an IT solution. One of the results of the architecture design is that the components of the solution (for which all interested third parties will want to be included) are recommended or selected. Put another way, the technical architecture document will act as the 'bill of materials' for the hardware, software and other related architecture that is required to build and implement the solution.

The technical architecture deliverable should consider integration with the existing environment, should detail the required products to make up the solution, should demonstrate a strong knowledge of up-to-date technology and, most importantly, should address the business need laid out by the client (or in this this case the management consultancy). It will be a major contributor to the budget and other business planning associated with the project.

In our fictional scenario above, the technical consultancy look at the business need and decide that what is required is a customer mobility solution, linked to knowledge of the customers buying habits connected via a customer relationship management (CRM) system. The business need relates to modern, contemporary subjects such as mobility, analytics, multi-channel marketing, etc., so it is entirely possible that the team involved will be multi-role, taking in experts from each of these fields as well as specialist personnel to design the user interface for the mobility solution. Additional to that, some knowledge will also be required of existing systems, such as the current loyalty card system, the retailer's existing website, their point-of-sale system and the infrastructure that supports it all. The technicalities of solution are purely illustrative, the important thing to note is that various personnel will be involved in the design and creation of the architecture, so there is very rarely a single person within the technical consultancy whom you need to educate on your offering – many personnel will play a part.

In this fictitious scenario, the retailer is not specifying a certain type of hardware or software for the solution – they are interested in the latest and greatest, so the technical consultancy has a huge amount of influence over what products are selected for the solution. In some cases, there will be few options if a highly specialised proprietary solution is being recommended, though in most cases the technical architect will have many options from which to choose, which is why this such a critical time in the project for aspirant providers of the solution components, such as the technology OEMs or their channel.

In terms of selection of technology vendors, the supply chain or other services, such as finance solutions, the technical consultancies could have one of the following remits:

Minimal influence. Where a client has asked that the technology and associated services are as unbranded or generic as possible, as they wish to retain control of the procurement process and not be tied to any particular technology provider. This gives the client a great deal of negotiating leverage when selecting technology providers for the project.

Significant influence. Where the client does welcome product recommendations, but may not let the product vendors in question be aware of that fact so that they still have power in the negotiation.

Ultimate influence. Where the client asks the technical consultancy to formally select vendors and actually asks them to agree commercial terms with the OEMs so that the technical architecture document acts as the final budgetary price for the project.

Our fictitious example is a combination of the above, where the retailer wants indicative pricing and wants the product commercials to form the recommendations from the technical consultancy, but will still reserve the right to re-negotiate their own terms at the time of implementation.

As a supplier, the above scenario emphasises the need for technical architects to be aware and, ideally, trained on your products. If the company creating the technical architecture is also carrying out the implementation, it stands to reason that they will recommend technology for which they have skills and accreditations. This is even more likely if they aren't guaranteed the systems integration work, as they want to be competing for that business on firm ground, so will be keen to recommend technology or services in which they are expert. This is not as cynical as it may sound; when recommending solutions, all companies want to minimise risk for themselves and their client, so if they know that they have strong skills and credentials around a specific product set, then they are doing the right thing by their client to suggest that product set. Which brings us back to the fact that time invested in training the technical consultancy and investing in their business to build a practice of knowledgeable staff is time and money well spent by any aspirant alliance partner.

There is also a commercial imperative here as well. If the technical consultancy is commercially motivated to recommend a certain technology, because they have the ability to resell it or receive a fee, then that may factor into their thinking.

Although it is unlikely; the tail seldom wags the dog and very few consultancies would compromise the technical integrity of their project to receive a fee that will be a tiny amount compared to the revenue they generate from their core business, so it's not worth risking their reputation. What is more common is that the technical consultancy will be transparent about any fees or resale revenue and use it as a buffer in the project that the client can use for unforecasted costs. If that is the case, then helping the technical consultancy to create this slush fund, that they can use to delight their customer, is a strong lever in getting your products viewed favourably.

Once the technical consultancy has done its job, designed the solution in line with the business needs and budget, created a technical blueprint and ensured that it will integrate with the existing systems and protocols, it is time for the implementation. Bring on the systems integrator.

Phase 3: implementation

So, our client has a business need and he also has a professionally architected solution to address it. What next?

Broadly speaking, they have two options. First, they can go out to tender for the technology platform. Central to the solution will be a software application, so the client may choose to go out to tender for the technology aspect of the solution – primarily the application, but also the infrastructure (or hosting services) and other peripheral software, such as the security or analytics software. Once the client has established the technology to be procured, they then send out a separate tender (aka the RFP) to potential implementers (the systems integrators). There is wisdom in this approach in that most systems integrators have a specific technical specialty (e.g. SAP or Oracle or Microsoft), so the client can ensure that they are focusing their precious time on evaluating precisely the right systems integrators for their chosen solution. It also allows the client to have full control and negotiating power over the vendor relationships.

The other potential approach is that the client goes out to tender for the full solution and gives their chosen system integrator partners carte blanche to recommend whatever technology they want to provide the solution and the results that the tender document dictates. The advantage of this approach for the client is that they don't have to commit the time and effort in supplier management. It also means that the solution is being purchased turnkey (services and products combined), which gives the client less liability associated with technical or logistical issues that may occur during solution delivery or go-live than if they choose to source the products and services from different vendors. There is also an argument that, for most clients, the larger systems integrators will have superior buying terms or commercial leverage over the suppliers which they can pass on to create a win–win, so it can make commercial sense for the client to procure via the systems integrator. For large corporate clients with superior buying terms, this is unlikely to be the case. This comes back to the point, which we have partly covered already (and will come back to in more detail), where the fees or resale margin earned by the large services companies can be used to discount the overall project cost for clients, as most systems integrators tend to use them as a war-chest to make their project cost more competitive and not necessarily as 'extra' profit. With these channel margins being passed on to the client, there is a win for everyone in the chain: the technology OEM, who has earned credibility with his alliance partner, the systems integrator, who will win more work as he uses the product margin (or fee) to subsidise his price, and the client, who pays less.

The bundling of product and services as one price to provide a turnkey solution is more relevant currently as it gives the systems integrator (and their vendor partners) the opportunity to provide software and infrastructure via the cloud on a usage (or even outcome) basis.

There is a third possibility, of course, which is that there is no break in continuity of the partner model between architecture and implementation – the same company does both. This can pay dividends in that the technical consultancy delivering the architecture is more motivated to ensure that it is a credible solution if he is on the hook to make it work. Obviously, no technical consultancy would submit a wilfully unfit solution, but, without the obligation of implementation and management of the solution thereafter, there is a different dynamic at play.

As a company looking to create alliances with a systems integrator, clearly you favour option two. Option one, where the client selects the technology, is absolutely fine of course, as long as you have a good relationship with the client already, as they will come to you and favour you in their product selection, but if you are looking for the IT influencers in the chain to make your market, then you want them to have maximum influence over the selection of technology and related specialist services.

So let's assume the systems integrator is given the responsibility of selecting and providing the products for the solution. They will, of course, choose based on their usual criteria, which will no doubt be a combination of product suitability, value, track record (references) and compatibility. But if they are implementing and building a solution, over a period of months or sometimes years, then they will also take into consideration other facets of the supplier relationship, such as will they add value around implementation? For instance, reasonably priced 'close to the box' services that the systems integrator can bundle and profitably sub-contract. They will also be more inclined to put forward technology for which they have experience and skills themselves, as this lowers risk and maximises profit. As the system integrator staff are all 'on the clock' as well throughout the product sizing and selection, they will look for technology partners that can take cost out of their project by providing good-quality technical pre-sales resource. Clearly, the commercial opportunity comes into play, the systems integrator is in business to make money and so will inevitably be drawn to companies where a win–win is achievable for all. As mentioned above, this is mainly so that they can delight their customer with a lower project price. If economic reward is important, also high on their priority list, they value a partner that has a collaborative attitude to shared risk. Last, but not least, and never to be under-estimated, is personality and culture. If the systems integrator is indeed likely to be spending months or even years working with you, a personal connection, trust and a shared cultural outlook as well as business approach will feature in their decision to work with you or not work with you.

All of these things are good news because, as a potential partner to the systems integrator, you can influence these factors and use them as relationship levers to ensure that you are selected to be part of the system integrator's solution to the client.

Phase 4: support

Unless you are selling specific post-implementation services (third-party maintenance or maybe infrastructure cloud services, for instance), the main opportunity for generating new products or services sales has probably passed.

For our retail client, the project has entered its final phase. Let's assume that during the implementation phase the product was initially tested as a proof of concept, all went well and so the client moved to the development and testing phase and then into change management, taking in important aspects of the solution adoption such as functional training and ensuring that personnel who may be threatened or concerned by the new system are familiarised with it and its benefits to them. We are now in production or go-live; in other words, the system is up and running.

In our example, the solution the client sourced in the end consisted of a primary application, a CRM system, end-user hardware in the shape of tablet technology for the in-store staff, an extensive server and storage infrastructure and myriad additional software products to enhance the customer experience and ensure that they are being effectively targeted with the retailer's most relevant offerings. This complex piece of technology now needs to be supported.

Support means different things, but essentially will come down to three different tasks:

Support. Which will address standard, routine issues that end-users encounter in operating the system.
Maintenance. To resolve any problems that may occur with the functionality of the hardware or software products. This may entail replacement or reconfiguration of source code.
Enhancement. Adding new features, upgrades and fixes to the software and hardware as and when new, enhanced or more efficient products are released.

There is every chance that the client will select one company to manage all three aspects of the support. Ideally (from the client's perspective), they will hold one contract for the entire system and the main support provider (contract holder) will sub-contract different aspects of the support for various hardware and software components of the solution to the OEMs. The support company will provide 'first line support', i.e. log and organise the calls. Much of this will be outsourced, very possibly off-shore for the reasons mentioned earlier: primarily price, but also bountiful supplies of skilled labour and the ability to provide 24×7 cover for users (increasingly relevant in industry sectors such as retail where customers are being served all day and all night).

Of course, many products are now sourced via the cloud. For instance, the server and storage technology required to power the solution could be delivered via a public cloud platform such as Microsoft Azure or Amazon Web Services. In terms of the support, nothing much changes: the company who owns the main support contract will merely take the SLA delivered by the cloud platform company and build that into the SLA committed to the client in the same way as he would have done if it were physical hardware that they were supporting.

During the support phase, if your company's products or services are part of the initial solution, it is common to keep close to the project as there will be ongoing revenues from additional users being added and also from complimentary products that will be required by the client once the users start using the hardware and software in earnest (think extra peripherals for the tablets, enhanced security modules for software or extra storage for unforcasted data levels being driven). There will, of course, be product refresh cycles (though this is likely to be years from original implementation) and also the ongoing revenue stream of an annual support contract. It is distinctly possible that the support company will be contracted to handle requests; it is worth maintaining regular contact with them. If you weren't lucky enough to be part of the original solution, then it's still worth keeping close to the company providing the support, who may see an opportunity to take cost out of their ongoing support to the client if they can integrate your technology seamlessly and at the right price.

In truth, the support role will almost always be provided by the company that led the implementation, as the client will value the extra accountability. A separate tender process for support is also likely (sometimes this is mandatory in the public sector or heavily regulated sectors such as utilities), so be aware that a successful collaborative relationship with the systems integrator does not guarantee that you will have an ally throughout the entire life of the solution – there may be a necessity to create relationships with the specialist support company or outsourcer also.

We've specifically covered the duties and roles undertaken by the third-party services companies as part of the project. In reality, each project will have a project owner (lead, sponsor, project manager or similar role) who will be accountable to a steering committee of stakeholders at the client, such as HR, IT, finance, etc., but this is not a book about managing political webs within end-user clients, we are focusing purely on the large IT services companies and their influence in the process. But, to be clear, at all times there is a client who is paramount in the process and to whom all of the services delivery companies involved in the creation and execution of the solution are accountable.

Sticking with the personnel with whom you will work from the influencers, let's take a look at some of the key roles that you will encounter within your new alliance partner and their potential roles in the project and the influence they can exert on your behalf.

Why partnering is win–win 53

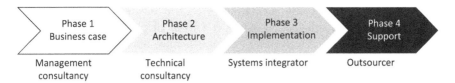

Figure 3.2 Typical scenario: company by type overlay.

Key learning points: typical scenario
1. The business need emanates from a management consulting engagement. This isn't the optimum point to be engaged, but it is helpful if the consultant can consider you at this stage.
2. Consider the technical architecture phase or the implementation phase as the essential time to be engaged in the project. It is when the product gets specced and, normally, specific products are selected.
3. Post-implementation there is also a role to be played: the company providing support will always be looking for chances to reduce cost in supporting a contract and will be open to new ways of working.

Key personnel

Regardless of whether one company wins the entire project from beginning to end or wins individual parts of the solution, there are various personnel who will have potential influence over the third-party products and services that will ultimately make up the solution. As before, the emphasis here is on the personnel related to the services delivery companies that are creating and implementing the solution – not on the client. It is not one size fits all – this rundown of personnel pertains to the imaginary scenario that I created above where each phase was delivered by a different company and the scope limited to that company, but in all deals, different personnel from the IT services companies and the client will have important levels of influence.

As a side note, there are various tools and methodologies that are used in the field of psychology that have been appropriated by the business world to help individuals and companies understand more about the people and personalities with whom they want to work or do business. Most commonly, if you are interviewing for a new job you may be asked to complete a Myers Briggs or similar test, a questionnaire created to identify specific psychological leanings that you have which may affect your outlook, approach and decision-making process. The purpose of instruments like a Myers Briggs test, in this context, is that HR groups (or often other specialist outside contractors employed by the interviewing company) will want to discern your personality type so that they can ascertain whether you are best suited to the company culture or the particular type of role for which you are being interviewed. It stands to reason, therefore, if you're prepared to psychoanalyse your staff, the natural progression is to use the same tools and knowledge to understand your customers and potential customers with the intent of establishing how they make decisions; specifically, the sort of decisions that will affect if or how much they buy from you. There's nothing sinister in this – it's a good way to understand your colleagues, clients and marketplace, with the expected result that you can create happier more fulfilled colleagues and so that you can provide the types of products and services that your clients want to buy.

Management consultant

This role is relevant to the initial business case phase of the project. If the management consultant is employed at a pure play management or business consultancy, this person probably owns the client relationship also. The relevance to third-party companies, such as technology OEMs that wish to be put forward by the management consultant's company, is highly dependent upon the scope of the work and the size of the management consultancy. In our fictional example above, detailing a retail transformation project, the management consultant is highly influential in generating the need for the project (business case) – it can be argued that, without their involvement, there would have been no solution sale at all; however, they played a minimal role in recommending technical aspects of the solution. As a third party with aspirations to be involved in the project, the value of a strong relationship with the management consultant is that you may receive early insight that a project is going to occur (therefore allowing you to steal a march on your competition when it comes to client engagement) or, if you have a specialist product or offering, the management consultant may have based his solution on his knowledge of your offering and the unique business value it brings. Also, it is distinctly possible that the management consultant will play further roles in the project (such as quality assurance, where they monitor and have input around performance at other stages of the project), so they will play an important advisory role to the client. There is also a strong possibility that the client will hire the management consultant once the solution has been up and running for a period of time to feedback on business benefits being driven, so good feedback on your product or service here is clearly a benefit for your ongoing client relationship.

Solution architect and technical architect

In our scenario this role sits within the architecture phase of the project and is executed by the technical consultancy. We should start by acknowledging that there is a subtle difference between a solution architect and technical architect. The difference is subjective and will differ from business to business and project to project, but at a very high level, the solution architect takes a broader view of the solution (i.e. what technology products are required) and the technical architect would take a more technical view of how it works together and the specific brand and spec of the products required. In many projects this will be the same person, though in larger projects, or where a technical consultancy has a wider and more specialist resource pool, these may be different personnel. It goes without saying that both of these roles are incredibly important to you if you want your product or service to be included in the solution. The motivations of these personnel in recommending solution components have been explained already (commercial appeal, technical functionality, compatibility, etc.) and the ways in which you can elevate your product in their thinking will be covered later. For now, let's just agree that this is a very important stakeholder for any third party wishing to be involved in the project. It is also important to acknowledge that this role should be regarded as a collective rather than one person – the architecture function is likely to be a group of individuals, each of which may have a specialist area (say database technology, security, infrastructure or mobility) and all of whom will have influence over product selection.

Alliance manager

This role will most likely exist in a technical consultancy, systems integrator and probably the organisation tasked with supporting the solution (such as outsourcer) also. They are a very rewarding contact to make as, although they aren't necessarily the most influential in deciding which technology is used (this accolade usually goes to the solution/technical architect), the alliance manager exists to help their company liaise with third parties and so is almost always the most approachable person in the process and has the strongest motivation to make you, the alliance partner, look good. The alliance manager is probably goaled in three ways: (i) what extra direct commercial benefit he can drive from the third parties involved in the project, such as fees and resale profit; (ii) helping his company reduce cost by leveraging third-party resource free of charge on a pre-sales basis from alliance partners; and (iii) reduction of risk by vetting and selecting the most appropriate partners based on non-technical criteria, such as their pedigree through legal suitability and relevant history. On this basis, the alliance manager's opinion will be sought by everyone on the various project teams and they will have a large amount of influence over which products and services are included in the eventual bill of materials. Alliance managers are often goaled and appraised on the same terms as salespeople (the most common career background for alliance managers), so, as with all salespeople, it is essential to understand the alliance manager's motivation. For some it will biased toward driving extra revenues for the project, for some it will be biased toward risk mitigation for the project and for some it will be loaded toward the extra services work that can be driven by the involvement of the alliance partners on the project.

Procurement/supplier management/product management

This role overlaps strongly with the alliance manager; however, on larger projects, particularly where the systems integrator or support company (outsourcer) is either retaining title (being the ultimate owner) or reselling the product, then at some stage the procurement group of the systems integrator or outsourcer will be involved. In many cases, procurement has little influence over product selection – they place orders for what they are instructed to order by the alliance manager or solution architecture team. However, for commoditised products or services (e.g. server hardware or cloud infrastructure services), the procurement team (often called supplier management or product management or purchasing, although this is a little old school) can have a strong influence over what products are procured for the project. Also, it goes without saying that, if you are a distributor or reseller selling products that are available from multiple suppliers in a competitive market, this team are of great importance to you as they almost always carry that autonomy to select the fulfilment channel. As with all procurement teams, they will be driven on commercial benefit to their company (cost savings, basically), but they will also be responsible for smooth logistical interface, meaning that, as projects are almost always very tightly time-bound, an efficient supply chain is a strong motivator. Where a systems integrator or outsourcer is looking to take responsibility for the sourcing of the third-party products in the project (as opposed to the client retaining that control), the pedigree and ability of their procurement team will be a key part of their selling story in winning the project at the sales phase.

Project manager

The larger the project, the more influence the project manager is likely to have. In our scenario above there would probably be a project manager for the implementation aspect of the project only. Clearly if some of the aspects of the project were merged (i.e. the same company undertaking more than one phase of the project), the need for a project manager will increase.

According to www.businessdirector.com, a project manager is: 'An employee who plans and organises the resources necessary to complete a project.'

The project manager is unlikely to have a large amount of influence over the selection of technical products or services (once again, the solution/technical architect will guide them), but, as the ultimate owner of the project with a specific emphasis on budget and timeframe, the project manager will have a degree of input about which suppliers do get selected or, just as likely, excluded. Project managers have to be ruthless, but they are always looking to reduce cost and delivery time and will rely heavily on third-party suppliers (often managed by the alliance manager or procurement department) to achieve this, so they can be a very worthwhile stakeholder group to get to know and be brought into your proposition. But remember: they are measured by efficiency and operational excellence, so emphasise this aspect of your selling story.

Client sales lead (aka account manager, client account lead, etc.)

At all stages of the project lifecycle the end-user client has the right to go out to the open market and drive for the best deal. In fact, in most cases it is their company policy or a government mandated rule for this to be the case, in which case there will almost certainly be a salesperson on point at the large services company to manage the sales process and close the deal. During the bidding or sales stage for the various phases for the project, the sales lead will have a great deal of influence over what partnerships are formed as he will very often be driving for a price point that be believes is required to win the work. He will almost always have a point of view of particular products and OEMs as well as good and bad experience of certain partners. Traditional consulting businesses are less likely to have sales leads because they are structured more like firms of solicitors or accountants (more on this later) where the consultant as the fee-earner owns the client relationship, but the more traditional IT companies at the later phases of the project will almost always have a sales lead ultimately responsible for the client relationship. Salespeople by nature are good relationship builders and highly entrepreneurial, so are ordinarily very open to new ideas and collaborations and therefore very significant stakeholders to impress and maintain. They can also be more emotionally driven as a personality type, with great empathy toward other salespeople, and so are likely to be loyal supporters for you and your company if you have added value and make their life easier at any stage of this or any other project. It goes without saying that they will be led by the solution/technical architects and the alliances team and ultimately governed by procurement and legal departments when it comes to the partnerships that they work with (at all levels of the supply chain, from the manufacturers to the implementers).

Legal

Last, but not least, the legal team for the large IT services company will play an important role in determining the basis and terms on which your products and services will be included in the project. While the legal team may not be the obvious route to win new work within their company, building a good working relationship with legal is key to effective and rapid negotiation of contractual arrangements. It goes without saying that their primary motivation will be mitigation of risk for their company and client, but they will also be looking for fair terms around issues such as transfer of IP, data confidentiality and commercial arrangements (fees, costs for services, etc.). As the sector moves toward outcome-based solutions, where the services company accepts far more risk in the project as a factor of how they achieve their fees for a project, the influence of the legal group around the credentials of suppliers and the proposed business models increases significantly.

The above encapsulates the main leadership roles in the creation and execution of a large solution. However, there are additional roles that will play a part, not least the technical and commercial people executing the delivery itself. All of the roles described above will probably have many team members that are working on their behalf, so bear in mind that, while these people will be making decisions around your destiny in the project, there will be teams of key influencers shaping their decision-making process. While all of these personnel are likely to have an involvement with the client at various levels of the large solution cycle, the illustration in Figure 3.3 is a high-level view of when each constituent's involvement is likely to be at their highest.

58 Why partnering is win–win

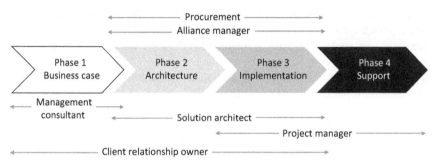

Figure 3.3 Involvement of key stakeholders during project lifecycle.

Key learning points: key personnel
1. As with all major account selling, understand the players and their motivations and shape your selling story accordingly.
2. All of the usual rules of 'decision makers' versus 'influencers' apply to selling with a large IT services company, so use your judgement to ascertain who are the people with the power at each phase of the project.
3. Some people will be, by virtue of their role, more disposed to help (such as alliance managers), so get them on board early and ask them to be your guide through the web of the engagement.

What's in it for the large IT services company?

By now you're getting a feel for why the large IT services companies are such an important part of your alliance strategy and when you should engage with them. So, before we move on to how you go about engaging with them and building lasting symbiotic alliances, it's worth remembering what is in it for them: why do these companies engage with third parties and how do they measure their benefit from the relationship? After all, the large IT influencers have excellent board-level relationships already with their clients, they have skills and IP in abundance and are constantly time constrained. Surely, third parties are a distraction rather than a necessity?

The reality is quite the opposite. The large IT services companies have comprehensive and well-funded alliance strategies, recruit highly paid alliance personnel and always have a prominent section on their public website boasting of their alliance relationships. Clearly, they know that prominent alliances are valuable and, just as importantly, they know that their customers and prospects think they are valuable too. So why do they put such a priority on partnerships with potential alliances, and how do they look to gain a competitive advantage, reduce cost and neutralise risk by utilising these partnerships? Put simply: what's in it for them?

We've explained or alluded to most of the reasons already. Others are obvious, but are worth covering. Regardless, it's helpful to document them in one place to remind yourself – even if you just use it as a check list of how to create a win–win. As you're reading, and before you map out your strategy, it's worth asking yourself: how many of these boxes am I ticking for my potential consulting, systems integrator and outsourcer partners? Is my alliance programme helping to address these needs?

Completing the solution

This is probably the most obvious reason why large IT services companies partner with other technology and services companies. As mentioned previously, by definition, systems integrators are 'an enterprise that specialises in implementing, planning, coordinating, scheduling, testing, improving and sometimes maintaining a computing operation. SIs try to bring order to disparate suppliers'. In other words, they connect together other people's stuff to create a holistic working solution. It stands to reason, then, that third-party product relationships are essential. Most systems integrators and technology consultancies do have their own IP and software components, but these are almost always small, specific pieces of proprietary code to connect systems. Seldom are they stand-alone applications, so, in essence, a system integrator and technology consultancy business model is based on working with other companies. Their relationship with technology providers such as hardware and software OEMs, their ability to work with them and, equally importantly, their customer's faith that they can work with them is therefore fundamental to this credibility. The same concept applies to relationships with other complimentary and sometimes conflicting services companies such as niche players and hosting companies. No services organisation can possibly have all of the skills to cover all of the disparate systems that are in existence, so will constantly want additional sub-contract assistance. Additionally, systems integrators and technology consultancies rarely have business models that allow them to take large risks on the sort of fixed assets required to run a hosting operation, so will look to specialist organisations to provide that infrastructure investment. In conclusion, the IT services companies are just that, services companies, they rely on other technologies to complete the solution.

Additional profit and investment

We've spoken already about the commercial return that a large IT services company attains from a trading relationship with third-party organisations. The routes to commercial market are mapped out in Chapter 1 for working with OEMs and complimentary services companies and include: (i) margin obtained via resale; (ii) fee payments for recommending an alliance partner's products; or (iii) when retaining title, a reduced cost to recognise the large IT services company's channel status (i.e. not the end-user and therefore worthy of a reduced channel buying rate).

When subcontracting work, it is easy to understand that the sub-contracted organisation will often provide a 'trade' or slightly reduced rate to the prime contractor and the prime contractor will add on a margin to cover admin, risk and any profit requirement.

There is also the benefit of 'soft margin', often referred to as MDF (marketing development fund) or by other programme names unique to a particular vendor. This is a notional 'pot' of money accrued by the services company as a percentage of the OEM's revenue resold or influenced. As an example, 2% of the revenue of the vendor's product resold will be accrued in an imaginary bank account and assigned to the IT services company, who can then spend it on activities that will develop business with that partner. Examples would be joint end-user marketing activities such as seminars, mail-shots or hospitality events where the technology OEM and the IT services company joint-market to the clients and prospects. The spectrum of areas that are appropriate for investment are not just restricted to client marketing – the 'soft margin' could be used for demonstration or development product or training courses for the services company's staff. The 'soft margin' is not always a percentage of sales; sometimes it is gifted on an arbitrary basis or donated as a reward for achieving levels of accreditation or hitting training thresholds, for instance. There are also other ways in which an IT services company will look to quantify their relationship with an alliance partner: through the avoidance of cost by logging expenses such as conference attendance or subsidised training, etc. At the end of the period, many large IT services companies will have a clear idea what benefits in kind they received, and the investment by the alliance partner is appreciated by them in helping to manage costs.

Sales competitiveness and differentiation through accreditations

The formal stamp of approval from a vendor is very important to a systems integrator when competing to win business. While skills, experience and all the other details about a large IT services company (in this example, usually a technical consultancy or systems integrator) is considered strongly by all clients when selecting a suitable consultant or implementer, holding the correct accreditations for the technologies central to the project are essential to get to first base in the competitive bidding process.

Almost all IT vendors have formal accreditation programmes and use them to engender loyalty and commitment to selling and supporting their products. Larger vendors, or those with varied product sets, such as IBM, HP or Microsoft, often have different accreditations to govern whether their partner is authorised to perform different support tasks, such as sales, post-sales support and post-sales implementation, or to specify and configure products on a pre-sales basis. The sort of accreditations that a technology OEM bestows on one of their partners is almost always based on the level of trained staff that the partner has. The technology OEM will often tier the accreditation level to reflect this, such as bronze, silver and gold for differing levels of skills. For the larger technology vendors there will be other criteria for one of their partners to join the formal accreditation programme, such as financial security, agreements to report on sales and commitments around management of their IP, etc., but the main purpose of accreditation is that the technology OEM can use it as a way to incentivise the channel partner to invest in more skills for their product. In turn this gives the technology vendor a greater chance of the product being installed successfully, therefore having greater customer satisfaction. It also means that once the partner has a greater financial commitment to the product, they will be more inclined to sell more in order to ensure that those skills are being put to profitable use. Ironically, given the large amounts of skilled resources that global systems integrators have compared to smaller VARs, many vendors will waive the accreditation terms for them and often create a generic systems integrator accreditation (ordinarily equivalent to the highest accreditation) as a means to recognise their partnership and get them in the tent. This is in recognition of the global systems integrator's credibility and also because the vendor really wants the systems integrators and technology consultancies to be incentivised to recommend and implement their products.

How it is achieved is irrelevant. The important thing is that the large IT services companies know that the highest level of accreditation is an important criteria when clients are evaluating potential services partners, so they will do everything that they can to accumulate the most impressive and market relevant accreditations. The converse is true also, of course. For smaller, niche technology consultancies and systems integrators, accreditations from large blue-chip IT companies such as Microsoft, HP or IBM will enhance their standing and credibility and allow them to enjoy the reflective credibility and approval of those brands.

Cost saving through utilising additional resources

This has been touched on before in previous chapters and is a great way for potential partners to endear themselves to the large IT influencers. Large IT services companies make money from selling people. Every member of staff is 'on the clock'. While every employee completes time reports and every hour is accounted for, most large IT projects are sold on a fixed price basis; ergo, every minute of resource that the IT services company can save (avoid) is extra profit. Therefore, they will look to utilise the resources of their vendor partners during the bidding and delivery process of every large deal wherever possible. This is generally a win–win. Most OEMs are pleased to provide pre-sales (free of charge) support to their channel partners on large bids as it gives them the opportunity to have significant input to the architecture, therefore providing opportunity to upsell. It also ensures that the solution being put forward is correct and has been ratified by the people who actually make the product. Finally, and also very importantly, working together into the small hours, against tight deadlines and under pressure really builds long-term relationships and the large IT services company will remember the people and companies that stood side-by-side with them to help them win that important bid – this is, after all, a people business.

The win for the IT services company is even more obvious: the more assistance they can receive from their alliance partner means less cost to them and also less technical and implementation risk. So, it is a given that pre-sales (free of charge) resource is welcome. That's obvious, but also post-sales (chargeable) resource from the vendor partner is welcome. First, because it minimises the investment to be made up-front by the delivery company: why carry the cost of personnel to deliver on every technology when a reasonably priced, plentiful supply of resources exist from the most trusted source imaginable, the actual developers of the product? Second, the resource from the technology partner is often available at a lower price than the delivery company's staff, who are generally highly paid consultant level personnel that are not priced appropriately for certain lower level 'close to the box' type work such as certain engineering tasks (e.g. configuration, or engineering services such as hardware install). Therefore if the technology OEM can provide these resources, it frees up the consultant's personnel for higher return work. Finally, as with providing pre-sales resources from the OEM, it lowers risk to know that the vendor's own personnel are involved in the implementation along with the IT services company.

The technical inside track

Technical consultancies and systems integrators will look to differentiate themselves from their market competition by their technical insight and know-how, and therefore will encourage close relationships with technology companies so that they can have access to early releases of the software and, in some cases, privileged access to the source code through developer programmes and user groups. The advantages to the IT services company is kudos with potential clients, who will be impressed by their potential partner's closeness to the software developer. They will also benefit from their enhanced technical insight into the product and its functionality. Many technical consultancies, systems integrators and outsourcers will be permitted to enrol in their software partners' beta program (the first version of software made available to outside organisations for evaluation or real-world testing) and will use this to convince clients of their exclusive status with the software partner. Another benefit of beta testing is that the technical consultancy or systems integrator can form early opinions as to the potential success of the product so that they can plan resource accordingly on its release. The benefits to the technical consultancy, systems integrator or outsourcer is not only in the prestige of being a trusted beta partner, it also pays dividends during delivery and support of the software if the systems integrator has access to the highest technical levels of software companies. As well as privileged technical access, systems integrators will also value highly specialist technical services and fixes from software companies that allow them to save time, eradicate problems and ultimately ensure lower risk implementation and delivery.

Operational benefits

Operational benefits are particularly relevant for large IT services companies who like to act as resellers on large projects. In essence, the client will want to minimise the number of suppliers and contacts they are managing on their transformation project (as this is costly, brings commercial risk and clogs up credit lines) and the opportunity to work with the technical consultancy, systems integrator and outsourcer to source product to clothe the services is very appealing. Leaving aside the commercial benefits that we covered above, the operational cost savings for the client are that they only have to deal with one supplier, who also happens to be the supplier managing the project. We already know that, when pitching for the work, the large delivery companies will have talked up their close relationship with their alliance partners, so the client will see many advantages to working with a systems integrator, consultancy or outsourcer who is closely plugged into the technology providers and is also dictating the timeframes of the implementation – meaning that they are best placed to arrange the various aspects of the complex delivery of hardware and software. It also means that the technical consultancy, systems integrator or outsourcer is well placed to ensure the correct software is procured at each stage of the delivery (i.e. develop, test, production, etc., all of which will be subject to favourable licencing terms if ordered in the right quantities with correct timings).

However, the greatest motivation for the client to procure as a 'black box' solution is the solution integrity that comes from all products and services associated with the project being sourced from one place. Clients will be sensitive to the risk that sourcing hardware, software and services (core and specialist) opens them up to the possibility that ownership of implementation problems can be difficult to attribute to one party, so the 'one throat to choke' concept can be perceived as a good method for ensuring cohesion in project delivery, although the 'risk and margin stacking' impact will mean that the project is likely to be more expensive. As the IT sector increasingly moves to cloud-based methods of sourcing capability and fewer clients source solutions on-premise or allocated to them, but, rather, hosted within third-party datacentres, the operational benefits of working with OEM partners will diminish for large IT service companies – but, for now, it is still a strong benefit to work with technology partners around project delivery.

Channel networking

Technology companies have well developed and extensive partner programmes. This can be very helpful for their channel because they act as the hub for ecosystems to develop that can complete technical and commercial solutions for large IT services companies. The technology OEMs (and sometimes their distribution partners and agents) organise events, establish online user groups and, if they are switched on enough, actively broker connections between their partners who have complementary product sets (for instance, partnering a financial services-focused technology consultancy with a risk management ISV to create a 'black box' solution). This is a great advantage for the technology vendors who are adding value, engendering loyalty from their partners and hopefully generating incremental sales by helping to create new solution sets among their client base by providing well qualified partnership opportunities. Often, technology companies' relationships cross vertical sectors and geographies, so their services delivery partners can access qualified relationships (with the seal of approval of the technology company) when they need to expand to satisfy certain client needs. In addition to the software companies and hardware OEMs, the role of channel dating agency is played very effectively by accredited distributors and wholesalers, who thrive on creating ecosystems of partners (often across multiple product sets that they sell) who can be matched to create innovative and market relevant client solutions.

New business leverage

Fundamentally, this is at the heart of all successful or aspirant alliances: the belief that together we can double our market penetration and create more business opportunity. This is logical, of course, if there is a solution on which large IT services companies and their partners are jointly invested (i.e. both have their 'product' embedded), then it is in both companies interest to sell that solution. Therefore, both companies are engaged in creating sales leads. If the alliance managers have done their jobs right, then both sales forces will be appropriately trained and incentivised to be pushing the mutually beneficial solution. This is where the alliance starts to pay back its investment, in the creation of incremental opportunity by leveraging each other's sales and marketing resources. Ideally, MDF will ordinarily be used for this type of activity – marketing to sectors for which the OEM and services company have a joint solution. As the sales cycle progresses and moves to costly investment areas such as demonstrations and proof of concepts, sharing costs and lowering the financial outlay for the IT services company is highly appealing to them. This is often an easy win for you, the aspirant alliance partner, as you can usually provide product at very little cost, whereas the perceived cost and opportunity to monetise for the large IT services company is high.

Selling together

This is similar to the above point, but subtly different. While leveraging each other's sales forces and marketing activities for mutual gain is all about the large IT services company gaining alliance benefit from the creation of new sales leads (i.e. the early part of the sales cycle), there is also a great benefit to them when they are embroiled in the more advanced stage of the sales cycle. Once the client has selected technology and is seeking a consulting, systems integrator or outsourcer to deliver, the technology OEM has a lot of power. The client will almost always seek their advice as to which delivery company to select – meaning that the IT services company that has invested in the relationship with the OEM up to that point, and been conscientious in providing value back to the OEM over the course of the alliance (e.g. by investing in training, by taking the OEM into different sales opportunities or maybe just through developing good personal relationships), will be recommended to the client. This happens a lot and if you are a technology provider that has been selected for a project where the services work is at bidding stage, expect a lot of interest from the systems integrator asking for your influence and endorsement. The other significant benefit that the large IT services company gets from selling together is very often that the technology company and they have different stakeholders and client contacts. Technology companies tend to have excellent relationships in IT, whereas a management consulting firm will have relationships with the chief executive officer (CEO) or chief operating officer (COO) and the outsourcing company may have strong relationships with the chief finance officer (CFO) and HR, and so on. All in all, a win–win is achievable because, where ethically appropriate, by partnering with others the IT services company is getting access to a group of stakeholders and influencers with whom they would not ordinarily have a relationship.

Those are a selection of the benefits that a large IT services company derives from establishing and maintaining alliance relationships. In short, they help them to save cost, minimise risk and maximise profit. There is one further reason that large IT services companies and third-party companies start to work together: *because clients tell them to*. When embarking on a large programme, clients need to know that all of their chosen hardware, software and services partners are fully aligned and correctly teamed to deliver the client's objectives. It's as good a reason as any listed above and occurs on pretty much every large project.

Key learning points: what's in it for the large IT services companies?
1. The large IT services companies, in particular the systems integrators, welcome alliances at a very basic level because they need technology partners to complete their solutions as they don't create their own 'product'.
2. It's a genuinely symbiotic concept – as a partner you use the large IT services companies to take your product to market and they rely on your product and patronage to win client work based on implementation of your technology.
3. Leveraging alliance partnerships for commercial gain such as revenues from resale and also avoiding cost by utilising alliance partner resources is a major motivator for the large IT services companies, whose staff are always 'on the clock'.

Why partnering is a win–win: Peter's story

Peter is a senior alliances executive at a world leading systems integrator. He has a great insight into the factors that create a win–win in a successful alliance partnership between technology companies and a large global technology services company. Peter is a real person, but I have anonymised his story for the sale of privacy.

> I've been working in the technology services sector for about 11 years. Companies like mine have partnerships fundamentally because they drive new business and assist us in driving better outcomes for our customers than we would have been able to achieve on our own. My organisation is essentially a delivery company. We find projects that create opportunities for our partners. That's our DNA, so it's important that we work with third parties in order to develop skills that are available to the market and are relevant to what the market wants. Partnering is obviously necessary where the technology (from your partner) is applicable to a big solution that you are putting together; for instance, to address a specific regulation or a specific need.

Sometimes it is a case that there are opportunities where our partners are working on an industry solution, but need help to deliver just because of the scale or the knowledge of the industry.

There are a few ways that a partner can successfully come to the attention of my firm. One of them is through being sponsored by one of our specific business or industry specialists. Another is our research team proactively finding an area or space that we would like to invest in. What would normally happen is that one of those two areas would identify an industry or horizontal technology segment in which we need to invest or spend time. Alternatively, partners may proactively approach us to introduce a solution because they know we have a way of commercialising it into the top 100 or 200 customers globally. Typically, what happens once the technology has come to our attention is that there will either be a technologist or a business lead who will vet that solution. If they think there is merit, they will sponsor it in the business. Thereafter, there is a very sophisticated qualification process that effectively vets the company, makes sure the business proposition is valid, identifies a pipeline for both the product and associated services, and then creates the framework around the governance marketing and go-to-market strategy. Ultimately, the partner gets sponsored and managed by a specific team and that creates the platform. If all goes to plan, the platform is rolled out globally. It's quite a thorough, formal process.

Of course, you have to apply a filter when selecting alliances – relevance, commercial opportunity and ability to collaborate are the three things I look for in a partner initially. Is it relevant to the market? Is it relevant to my business? Could I add value to the proposition? Can we actually influence or specifically improve the solution with our services and/or knowledge? Can I take it to multiple customers, i.e. could it be repeatable? Then, the other important element is the cultural fit. Do we fit in with that organisation? Could we actually work together to build something, and be assured that the relationship would be collaborative and successful rather than just use it a one-off opportunity?

Quite early on, I ask very blunt questions around what's in it for them, what drives them. I then explain what drives my team, my business and what drives our firm. I'm looking to understand both sides of the equation. I hope most of the time they are honest and clear about it, but there have been occasions where we thought we had a common understanding and actually they had a different agenda or what they said they were willing to do, they just couldn't deliver because they were either too insular or not open to a collaboration on terms that we would require from our partners.

The elevator pitch should be: 'This is the business proposition, there is a market that you can address and here is my credibility as a partner' The latter usually comes from credentialing.

When I look back, the characteristics of a successful partner would be innovative, honest, straight forward and commercially and technologically flexible (open standards preferably). Then, you are into the relevance of market trends; for instance, in the current market, cloud is very important. Partner personalities play a role as well. Ours is a people business.

In terms of unsuccessful partnerships, there's the obvious things – none of us like being lied to, none of us like the feeling of being commercially duped or taken for granted. But those obvious things aside, there are other aspects that raise a red flag. For instance, an undefined value proposition, not knowing what they want to get out of the market or not having a defined commercial model that gives the correct support to a partner, by which I mean a commercial advantage to a partner as opposed to the direct model or a model that creates conflict with other partners and can't distinguish or positively discriminate toward the originator of the opportunity (almost always us).

Once the partner is onboard, developing our business together, which often means encouraging them to invest, is a key aspect of what works. Then, as part of that investment, finding out how we discover the next opportunities together. What might happen is that we would create two or three technical experts and two or three proposition experts that would go out and evangelise across the business and to our customers about that specific technology. Simultaneously gaining a sponsor is key within the business – having someone within a practice that will be responsible for a P&L that is related to the services of that technology. If you don't have ownership and specific accountability on both sides, it's impossible to succeed.

Once you've met and found a way forward, you need to maintain it. Initially, you may only need one specific sponsor within one area, but in order to grow it is important that people understand the relevance of level and how they can make that work to their advantage. For example, a CEO of a small company might meet the second or third in command of a certain region of my company. A salesperson going all the way to the top of a global systems integrator would probably not be a wise thing. You need to develop through peer-to-peer conversations in order to scale the business. One of the characteristics of a successful relationship is going a level up and a level up and a level up as the relationship matures. If you have a start-up, and it keeps growing, you need to make sure that you become relevant at the next level up and then the next level up within the business.

Cultural alignment is an interesting subject right now. It was more important a few years ago, when the senior executives in our business clients wanted to see a blue-chip company approaching them and working with them, but the technology world has shifted. I think the size of the partner is less relevant now. As clients progress on their digital journey, the big company approach isn't always the answer anymore, so companies need to be more flexible and more innovative. Big systems integrator firms like mine see that some of the start-ups could be on that wave of disruption, so the big global systems integrators are much more open to innovative new partners than they used to be in the past. Interestingly, there is less onus on the small technology player to adapt to the big firm; often, it is now the other way round.

In terms of the sort of people that work well with us, I would say that in the past you would find the extroverts or the drivers being more relevant, but I don't think it makes a big difference anymore. It's more about diligence, follow up and relevant messaging now, I think – that's more valued than a social animal.

I would say that it takes a potential partner six months as a minimum before you crack it. But then it can snowball quickly, so six months is the minimum to do a proper sales job within an organisation like ours and then take it to the next level. The next level (traction, repeatability, building a practice, sustaining sales pipeline, etc.) could take one or two years.

An interesting feature of the new technology landscape (more start-ups and disruptive niche technologies) is that in the past the 80/20 rule would apply to our business with partners – the 20 would be five or six companies; however, when I look at our partnerships now, it's probably 60/40 and the 40 would be five times more companies than the 20 used to be. Another interesting feature is that multi-million dollar deals are being done by smaller technology companies and niche players, which I never saw five years ago. The most that a previously unknown company used to achieve was a sale up to $1million. Now, you are seeing companies that aren't well-known in the industry achieving $5 million+ deals when their market cap is only $20 million. The sort of deals that we only used to see an Oracle or an SAP close. This is indicative of a big shift in the market, and the credibility that the small, specialist technology providers have. Commercial flexibility is driving this slightly. Many companies are selling the same product – they are just charging it differently, which creates a different model. Some new models (outcome-based or cloud, for instance) are much more interesting and much more aligned to client needs. The financial treatment of some of the consumption models is becoming even more important as well, because some of the ways that clients consume technology and the way that they account for it is becoming more business critical.

I think there is value in smaller, niche technology OEMs and start-ups partnering with big delivery firms, and I don't think small partners should be afraid of the big partners anymore. Most big global IT services companies, if they want to remain relevant, are open to having conversations with new start-ups. I think the value that you can derive in terms of the quality and delivery of the client solution, and also the access that you would achieve by being associated with the big firms, gives you and your potential customers enormous potential. But, as a potential partner, you do need to understand the business of the large global delivery organisations in order to be relevant.

Within the large firm that you want to deal with, the partner (alliance) people are always helpful, and they perform an important function, but you are in danger of not being successful if you don't find a business lead to spend some time with you and coach you on what actually needs to be done. My advice would be to make sure the relevant people are on board and to have a plan as whom you want to speak with next after meeting the partner team. Make sure you do your homework about who you are meeting, what you are trying to achieve from the meeting and what you need to achieve to get to the next level. Make your message tailored and relevant to the person you are actually going to meet. Find out in advance (if you can) their objectives and, of course, how are they measured.

Key learning points: Peter's story
1. Be prepared to be commercially and technically flexible.
2. Get strong sponsorship – a dedicated alliance contact isn't enough. Preferably you need executive support as well as a driver within the practice.
3. Really work hard to understand the core business of your target partner and ensure that is in front of mind in all of your mutual dealings.

4 Understanding the business model

If you are accustomed to working for a new economy business such as an IT or finance company, the culture and business model of the large IT services companies, particularly consultancies, may be unusual to you. It's often unique and in many cases more like an accountancy or law practice than a sales-led technology company. It's important to understand this model – the sort of people you are dealing with, how they are goaled, how they are rewarded and how you can gain close lasting relationships by understanding and addressing their business.

Culture

Below I have tried to explain the culture of large IT influencers. This will affect the type of personnel they hire, their skills, their limitations and the sort of behaviours that their culture and recruitment policy drives. Clearly, how you as a potential alliance respond to that culture is vitally important for how you succeed in the relationship.

To those who are unaccustomed to dealing with them, the most bewildering group is the consultancies, so this section does relate more to the companies at the consulting end of the delivery cycle. However, as we have seen in the Venn diagram in Figure 2.1, many of the large consultancy businesses are also the large systems integrator businesses and also outsourcing businesses, so for now let's treat them the same. Obviously, every company is different in their culture and behaviours, so it is dangerous and misleading to suggest that the following applies to absolutely all players in the large IT services sector, but, like most generalisations, it is rooted in fact and experience.

I have based my knowledge of culture on three things: (i) my experience; (ii) the experience of friends and collaborators; and (iii) the values that companies publish as central to their approach. It's easy to be cynical about these stated values, but in reality they are often the cornerstone of the company culture and do dictate the conduct and behaviour of the personnel.

One last thing: a lot of the following is what every business does every day, but without the fancy language. My local butcher will cheerfully tell you that he works 12 hours a day (he has a strong work ethic), that he has exceptional butchery skills (he is a subject matter expert), that he treats his staff well (he behaves with respect and integrity), that he doesn't discriminate in recruitment (unwittingly he practices exemplary diversity attitudes), that he builds up close and long lasting relationships with his customers (client-is-king approach) and that he contributes to his local community (has a commitment to social responsibility). So, perhaps the following is common sense and doesn't need spelling out, but trust me on this, there is something about the religious zeal with which management consultants, systems integrators and outsourcers evaluate their people against the culture and core values which means that you have to be prepared to understand how non-negotiable they are when you embark on a strategy to deal with your potential IT influencer alliance partners.

Hard work

I love this joke, I've heard it a few times, but I got this version from the Independent Consulting Bootcamp website:

> A lawyer, a doctor and a management consultant were discussing the relative merits of having a wife or a mistress.
>
> The lawyer says: 'For sure a mistress is better. If you have a wife and want to divorce, there are a number of complex legal problems to resolve and it will probably be very expensive.'
>
> The doctor says: 'It's better to have a wife because the sense of security and wellbeing lowers your stress and your blood pressure and is good for your health.'
>
> The management consultant says: 'You're both wrong. It's best to have both so that when your wife thinks you're with your mistress, and your mistress thinks you're with your wife, you can go to the office and get some work done.'

We all live in a world where we are 'always on' (we have smartphones, tablets, wi-fi and all other blandishments of the modern work environment to thank for that), but more than any sector I have ever experienced, there is an expectation within the large IT services companies, particularly, it seems, the consultancies, that hard work and commitment to the task is paramount. No-one has risen to a position of significance within one of the large IT services companies without great personal sacrifice and more than one story about a project or sales pursuit that consumed them night and day for months or even years.

If you read any memoir of people involved in the consulting sector, there is one common denominator in people's accounts of their time at a consulting firm, and that is an expectation of very hard work – not just long hours, but application too. When I asked a friend at a consulting firm if he had a 'dress down day', he replied 'yes, Saturday'. In previous jobs I used to be able to differentiate myself with hard work, but when I first started for a large IT services company, I realised that was no longer the way to career enhancement. Working into the night, weekends or even during family holidays is a given – that in itself is not enough, the standard of your work also has to be of the highest quality to stand out.

The umbrella explanation is that hard work is cultural in the large consulting firms (note that I've mentioned before that they have much in common with firms of lawyers and accountants, where long hours are also a cultural norm), but the explanation probably comes down to three things:

1. Consulting firms, systems integrators and outsourcers exist in a very deadline-driven environment. This includes the process of winning work through competitive bid process (surely the most strictly deadline-driven aspect of sales and business development) and then delivering work, both of which have very rigid time commitments on which the delivery company's reputation and ability to win and retain work is based. Where immoveable deadlines are involved, there will always be pressure to work until the job is done.
2. A competitive career environment (we will go into this in more detail in the next chapter) means that it is difficult to say 'no', and progression, or even job retention, is often contingent on high levels of personal commitment to the firm.
3. A competitive market means that large IT services companies are constantly striving to deliver more work within tighter budgets, with the attendant consequences. This goes for the process of winning work by competitive bid as well. Many RFPs are works of art when they are submitted; they include many hundreds of thousands of words and well thought out answers to the 'exam questions', but also a great deal of extra information to differentiate the bidders and win the project. This extra collateral that makes up the bids, such as credentials, testimonials, case studies, company information and so on, is tailored to the theme of the bid and entails a great deal of research and application in short timeframes to pull together. Bearing in mind the personnel are not chargeable at this time, it is often collated and presented by bid teams out of hours or with minimally resourced teams.

There is another side to the equation in most cases. Staff within the large IT services companies are rewarded well and are professionally supported by top quality back-office operations, which allows the personnel to be highly productive and focus on their 'day job'. In my experience, from within and from working with the large consulting firms, there is a healthy recognition by the leadership that sacrifices are being made, and a great deal of institutional and personal support is provided to the workforce to ensure their health and happiness despite a fairly 'full on' working environment. Often, there is a comprehensive private health care, pension and maternity/paternity package, generous holiday allowance (with strong encouragement to take it) and a no quibble, highly supportive approach when employees need to take time off for personal, family or health reasons. There is, therefore, a strong two-way expectation in the corporate culture.

Diversity

The workplace is far more meritocratic in the twenty-first century than it ever has been. Generation X and the millennials will experience considerably more social mobility than our parent's generation. This is reflected very keenly in the large IT services companies – they need the best people and there is no place for any form of discrimination. Fortunately, most of us in the developed world live in a country where discrimination in the workplace is illegal, so there is an obligation for corporations to be inclusive, but the large IT services companies take this to new level. I don't believe the cynics on this one: they will tell you that the conscientious commitment by these global consulting firms and systems integrators to be inclusive is in order to hit quotas and win awards that they can use as a marketing tool to win more public sector and corporate clients (with whom a diverse workforce plays well). But it's just not true. The large IT services companies' success is dependent upon attracting the most capable and skilled personnel – their business is people, that is their product. Simple as. Therefore, their workforce is made up of the best people available to them, and, guess what, it is a fair cross section of society if you take into account the strict educational and skills requirements of the role. It should also be said that the vast majority of intelligent people are enlightened and not bigoted in the slightest, so, regardless of institutional policy and company brand, the staff of the large IT services companies would not tolerate working for a company that was not entirely egalitarian in their employment policies. Technology has been a great social leveller as well. Many of the skills that the large IT services companies require in order to be market competitive cannot be sourced from the USA or western Europe, and countries like India and China are producing vast quantities of highly skilled and technically capable graduates that are required by the global delivery companies. It's not just racial diversity that is relevant here. IT services, like most 'technical' careers, has traditionally been male dominated, so the large influencers are committed to programmes increasing the numbers of women and supporting LGBTQ employees in technical roles by funding public initiatives and programmes within schools, universities and the wider workplace.

This isn't an after-thought or a gesture, this is a serious commitment. It's not driven by a demand to please clients, it is a reflection of a far more significant societal change, and the large IT services companies are leading the way.

Knowledge capital

Most management consultancies and systems integrators are very asset light. It's different for outsourcers; they own and maintain datacentres and call centres and other infrastructure by their very nature – after all, they are providing those assets so that their clients don't have to. But for consultancies and systems integrators, their assets and their value is within only one thing – people. This is why consultancies and other IT services firms are so difficult to put a valuation on when they are assessed for takeover or merger, because their value is essentially what is inside the heads of their staff, who could, in theory, walk away at any time, particularly if a listed company finds itself the subject of a takeover that greatly increases the share price and therefore the wealth of the staff. So, knowledge and IP is everything to the likes of Deloitte, Errnst & Young and PwC. This is of course why they are hired and also why they are great value to partners, because they bring subject matter expertise to business problems in the shape of deep sector knowledge which (as we have learned previously) is then addressed by the sale and implementation of transformational technology solutions. The academic bar to entry for consulting firms is very high and usually entails not just very good grades from a top university, but also evidence of exceptional performance in some other walk of life (think captain of the football team or lead in the university dramatic society). The large firms hire people with a proven track record of academic achievement and attract 'experienced hires' with deep subject matter expertise. This may sound obvious, but it's worth remembering that, when you are selling people, to a large degree you are selling knowledge. The quid pro quo to you, the partner, is logical: the IT services company opens business opportunity by identifying business need and then relies on partners to provide the products to complete the solution. As a partner, there is an expectation that you can bring to the relationship or project an equally deep knowledge of your products and the technology segment in which you are operating. If you are looking to culturally align with the IT influencers, deep knowledge and expertise is respected as much as your high quality product.

Integrity and reputation

As with knowledge capital, reputation and trustworthiness is difficult to quantify, but it is absolutely essential to the global IT services company's ability to continue to win work successfully. There are two very good reasons why reputation as a safe pair of hands is essential to this sector: first, because they have so much access to client data (and in turn their customer's data) and, second, because the large projects with which they are involved are often so central to the successful running of a company's operations going forward, any delay or failure could cost the client everything.

Unsurprisingly, all of the professional consultancies, integrators and outsourcers have very rigid polices to cover all aspects of their strict integrity policies – competitive information, security policies, treatment of client and company data, receipt and payment of fees and hospitality, etc. With all businesses that employ people, it is never a perfect process, humans are fallible and, either by accident or for avoidable reasons, will make errors, sometimes which end up on the front of the newspapers if they affect a government department or household brand (such as a high street bank). Any search of the internet will find lots of examples of where global consultancies, systems integrators or outsourcers have had their brand affected by high-profile failure, but it is rare and this is largely down to the rigour and robust processes that these companies have in place to select and recruit the right people and then manage their conduct. This is extremely relevant to you as a partner – strict non-disclosure agreement (NDA) terms and other policies must be observed. Where the reputation of the IT services company is on the line, they cannot tolerate any risk from their partnerships (for whom they share a reputation for the duration of the engagement) and so will greatly favour partners that have stated and demonstrably implemented policies and procedures around all matters related to integrity and personnel conduct. Mostly, the expectations will be mapped out in the alliance or teaming agreement when you embark on the partnering journey, but it is not to be under-estimated because, for your new partner, everything is at stake.

Corporate social responsibility

Go to the website of any large IT services company and it won't take you many clicks to find how much they value and invest in activities related to social responsibility. This takes the form of investing in their local geography supporting charities and government initiatives through to helping the young or disadvantaged in that country find work, but will also extend to large global initiatives supporting significant charitable activity in developing countries, particularly where they have outsourced operations.

Large IT services companies and social responsibility are a natural fit. First, they have a lot of knowledge and skills inherent in the business that charitable causes require. Second, they have a model wherein not all of the resources (personnel mainly, but could refer to infrastructure such as servers or storage space) are utilised at any given time (the concept of a 'bench', which we will cover later) – they have a global outlook and are geared up to help developing nations due to their geographically distributed workforce. As mentioned before, when talking about issues of integrity generally, there is a cynical viewpoint here that detractors will like to espouse: that good deeds are a PR ruse, that they elevate the donator's reputation, credibility and image, particularly to government clients, or that it is merely a tactic to help colleague engagement, as the staff are generally emotionally intelligent folk who want to feel that their day-jobs aren't only about wealth creation so the feeling of being part of an enterprise that is doing something great helps moral and staff retention. My personal experience is that it is generally done for altruistic reasons. When the leaders of these large organisations meet, it is often the corporate social responsibility topic that dominates the conversation and the thing for which the leadership is most proud.

It's important to be cognisant of this when working with large IT services companies. What are your company's initiatives and how could they relate to that of your potential alliance partner? is this yet another opportunity for kinship?

Colleague respect

It's a people business, so the motivation and wellbeing of the individuals within are of paramount importance. There is also a practical imperative at play here: lawsuits for inappropriate behaviour, discrimination or HR matters such as allegations of constructive dismissal, will cost money, sap management time and, most importantly, effect reputation, so the large IT services companies, like all large enterprises, attach great importance to a culture where colleagues are professional and respectful at all times. Clearly this is impossible to enforce on 100% of the personnel 100% of the time (as with the wider integrity points, all organisations that employ people are populated by fallible people), but, as a cultural trait, any form of inappropriate comment that may be construed as racist, sexist, homophobic, etc., is strictly forbidden and policed. Also, as a rule, blame culture, shouting, belittling and all other facets of what was maybe synonymous with the professional services sector for our parent's generation (watch *Mad Men*) is not tolerated and would breach strict HR rules and processes. Do not underestimate this when looking to partner, and certainly when you are on a partner's premises. They will not be accustomed to certain management styles and certainly not used to off-colour humour in the workplace. It will cause significant embarrassment for you, effect your credibility as a partner or, worse still, result in the termination of the alliance. If you're unsure (though really this is about common sense and decency), check your partner's policies and their implementation and policing of those policies.

All of the above is good news for the clients. They get to work with an incredibly dedicated and committed workforce who adhere (and for that matter are strictly governed) to strict ethical standards. The whole operation at the large IT services company is geared up to deliver client value by recruiting the most educated and knowledgeable people and then managing them to ensure that clients, colleagues, partners and society maximise that benefit. Like the butcher in my example at the start of this chapter, this is second nature for most businesses, but within the large IT services sector it is recruited, stated, taught, governed and reviewed in a rigorous way to ensure that the values of the organisation and the culture is what dictates the tone and business model of the company. As a potential alliance partner, this is only a problem if you are unable to respect the approach and adapt to the model, at least for the times you are working with them. On the plus side, by understanding and acting in line with these cultural traits, you can forge closer and longer lasting relationships with the people within your new alliance partner and become entrenched as one of the family.

A final word on culture: decks

I can't go through this whole book without referring to the role of PowerPoint in the life of a management consultant. Or to use the correct terminology: decks. There's an excellent section on the managementconsulted.com website, that I strongly recommend reading, called 'The Management Consulting Lingo Dictionary'. It's a slightly tongue-in-cheek, but highly informative, glossary of terms you will hear when working with and for management consultants. It describes decks as: 'Your PowerPoint slides (anything more than three slides), and sometimes referring to the master deck for the team.'

Coming from a fairly traditional IT sales background, I wasn't familiar with the word 'deck' and it took me a few times of hearing to realise that what was actually being referred to was a PowerPoint presentation. It is difficult to over-estimate the role that decks play in a management consultant's life. Decks are by far the most frequently used format for conveying information, both internally and to clients. This sounds obvious – that is what PowerPoint was invented for, after all. The difference in a management consultancy though, as opposed to most other businesses, is that the deck is used as a stand-alone document – it is the primary source of the content. If, like me, your background is sales, you will have been taught that the PowerPoint presentation is a prompt to the speaker's presentation, and we have all been given advice like 'keep the content on the slide brief as it will distract the audience', or 'if a slide is too detailed or informative your point will be lost', or 'use pictures not words as it complements the words that you are saying', that sort of thing. In short, the salesperson's approach to PowerPoint is that it is there to act as a backdrop only, because the presenter is the real focus. In consulting, this is not the case. Very often, a deck is actually the deliverable to the client, so when the consultancy is presenting the strategy document at the end of the project, it will be on PowerPoint, or when the consultancy is reporting market data or research as a deliverable it will usually be displayed on PowerPoint. The deck is used in the same way that other businesses use Word documents: to deliver factual content. So, why does this matter to you? Well, for a couple of reasons: (i) if your consulting partner asks for a deck to be sent to them, don't be afraid to load it up with data, content and facts, they are used to this style of slide and this is what they expect; (ii) because it is the tool of their trade, people in consulting are really good on PowerPoint and create beautiful, informative and content rich slides, so be warned when you stand up to give your presentation or when you send in your company overview PowerPoint, they will be checking out the quality of your PowerPoint skills.

> Key learning points: culture
> 1. The staff in the sort of companies with whom we are dealing here have very strong work ethics and there is an expectation that you will stand with them shoulder-to-shoulder, so be prepared for long hours and challenging deadlines.
> 2. Knowledge is their business, so make sure that you are prepared to have a point of view and that you can add value to their business by increasing their knowledge capital.
> 3. Integrity and propriety is a non-negotiable, so ensure that your standard of conduct and behaviour is exemplary or risk undoing all of your good work.

Career model

Unless you have previously worked in a professional services company, much of the way that a large IT influencer operates and motivates its personnel will not be familiar to you, as it is removed from the working of a typically sales-led operation (e.g. a technology OEM or software company). We've talked earlier about the difference in cultural perspective, it's also worth looking at the way that people are goaled and their career paths. By understanding this aspect, it will be considerably easier to understand the motivations of people with whom you are working and also to understand where they may fit in the organisation and how that may affect the influence they may have over your activities together. To be clear, this is a slightly different topic from what was covered in Chapter 1 when we talked about roles, this is to do with career levels, the progress through which is a very important motivator for the sort of dynamic, career oriented personnel that the large IT influencers attract.

The following pertains more to consultancies, but, as we have seen in the Venn diagram in Figure 2.1, we know that there is a strong crossover between these companies, large system intergrators and outsourcing firms, so expect a high degree of similarity from a career model perspective also.

Career levels and performance management

As ever, the exact detail varies significantly from company to company, especially when related to the job titles, but the following is a good guide to the career levels typical in a large IT services company, in particular a consulting firm or global systems integrator. To reiterate the point made above: to understand this will help you to ascertain the seniority of your stakeholder and therefore their level of influence and other factors such as approval level. It's also handy to talk the language, as empathy around career paths and how you can help them to achieve career goals is a great way to build strong relationships. In most cases there is no commission or incentive scheme for 'sales' performance – the reward is career progression (and eventually equity and status related to that), so the carrot of career progression is important to a stakeholder's career progress.

Level 1: analyst, business analyst, associate, associate consultant. The point at which most graduates enter the organisation. In theory the lowest level in the organisation and the lowest chargeability cost to clients. Typical tasks may include data collection, interviews, surveys, market reports and analytical modeling. Typical tenure 1–3 years.

Level 2: senior analyst, senior associate, senior associate consultant. Very similar to level 1, but with greater responsibility, i.e. larger examples of the same tasks, more complex models. Typical tenure 1–3 years.

Level 3: consultant. A common level of entry for experienced hires. Consultants will generally own a specific aspect (workstream) or a larger project or engagement. There will be much more client engagement responsibility and the consultant will probably also be responsible for upward liaison with the firm's management. The consultant will often have a specific area of expertise, such as industry sector knowledge, or a specific technical competency. Typical tenure 2–4 years.

Level 4: manager, case team leader, engagement manager, project leader. As the name would suggest, managers have usually excelled within their roles as consultants, which means they have mastered a high degree of knowledge in their chosen specialty and are now tasked with leadership responsibility. For instance, this is the typical grade for a project manager, who will be responsible for the leadership of a team of analysts and consultants. They will also have significant client-facing responsibility. This will typically be the level at which an expectation of new business generation is expected. There are also likely to be people-developer duties outside of the manager's specific project, such as community leadership, career counselling or mentorship. Typical tenure 2–4 years.

Level 5: senior manager, principle. This is in many ways the toughest role in the firm in that it is incredibly competitive, there is an expectation of very hard work and commitment, but making the next step up to partner is a much tougher process and ultimately proves elusive for many. This level will lead significant client engagements or relationships, will manage sizable sales pursuits and will hold significant people-developer or community leadership responsibility. Typical tenure 3–5 years.

Level 6: partner, vice president, senior executive. In a privately held business, partners are the owners of the firm. In public companies, they are likely to have a substantial stock holding (and are unlikely to be called 'partner', which has legal connotations that aren't relevant to a PLC). The entry process is very rigorous and, certainly in private businesses, will be subject to a vote among the other partners. Like all leaders of a large business (think in terms of a board of directors), the partners will hold important client relationships, set the strategy for their departments or, in some cases, the whole firm, and be responsible for important strategic initiatives and investment decisions.

I can't emphasise enough that the above is a guide, not a hard and fast rule across all firms. In particular, watch out for the fact that the same job titles can be used by different companies at very different levels, for instance at Oliver Wyman, the title 'Director' is the equivalent of level 6 in my guide above and is effectively the highest role in the firm, whereas in Accenture, 'Associate Director' pertains to level 4 in my guide. Within Booz Allen a 'Senior Associate' may be a level 4, whereas in BCG it pertains to level 2. It is also true that there are grades, pay scales and milestones within each career level for which employees strive in order to ensure that their careers are moving forward on an annual basis.

You may hear the phrase 'pyramid' or 'staffing pyramid'; this refers to when IT services companies (and the large projects that they execute) attempt to maintain a pyramid staffing cost model with an appropriate balance of personnel at each level and with (usually) diminishing numbers at each level all the way to the top of the firm or project (see Figure 4.1).

In terms of career progression, another shorthand expression that you may hear is 'up or out'. This is a term associated with robust career management in highly competitive sectors such as professional services firms, where the expectation and career support/feedback model is that you will progress within particular timescales (as indicated above). In the absence of this progression, it may be more attractive to look for opportunities elsewhere. Although this can seem hard nosed, an honest and constructive feedback culture means that people are clear on where

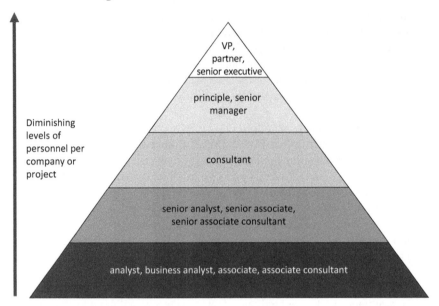

Figure 4.1 Career levels pyramid.

they stand and where their strengths and development areas lie. In my own experience, I believe that the career levels system is more commonly used as a carrot than a stick with equity based rewards and high degrees of professional respect for those that make it to the top.

In terms of annual appraisal, a popular form of HR process in the sector remains a 'normal distribution' or 'bell curve' performance management model, although this is being increasingly abandoned in favour of a more personalised rewards model. If you have worked for a large IT company you will be familiar with the bell curve model. Writing in *Forbes* Magazine in 2014, Josh Bershin, founder and principle at Bershin by Deloitte, describes the bell curve far better than I can in an article entitled 'The Myth Of The Bell Curve':

> The Bell Curve represents what statisticians call a 'normal distribution.' A normal distribution is a sample with an arithmetic average and an equal distribution above and below average … this curve results in what we call 'rank and yank.' We force the company to distribute raises and performance ratings by this curve.

As mentioned, the bell curve is a model that is going out of fashion and was recently discontinued by Microsoft, KPMG and Accenture, but it is still very popular among many of the large IT services companies. Its critics say it encourages blame culture, creates an unhealthy level of competition, inhibits collaboration and affects personal relationships. But it certainly drives personnel to care about their performance and objectives, and encourages a need to differentiate by hard work and exceptional performance. As an alliance partner this can count in your favour as it encourages entrepreneurial spirit and innovation and means that the people with whom you will be working will be more inclined to adopt your interesting new product or innovation.

> Key learning points: career levels
> 1. In most large IT services companies, the career levels will be transparent and easy to understand, which helps to ascertain the seniority of a particular contact or stakeholder within a project.
> 2. Commission plans in a typical IT company are rare, especially within consultancies, so career progress and the opportunity for increased equity as result of rising to higher levels within the company are the motivator.
> 3. Often, the staff with whom you will be working will be in a competitive performance management environment and this can be used to your advantage as you can help them to create differentiation ahead of peers by selling/delivering to a higher standard using your offering.

Billing revenue

Perhaps the most obvious distinction between the roles listed in the previous section is that the companies with whom you are looking to partner can charge different hourly/day rates for each level. One of the things that new employees to a large IT services company find surprising is that every hour is accounted for. If you are not chargeable to a client, then you will have a different charge code to cover your time – probably paid for by someone's business development or corporate overhead budget. Either way, you are 'on the clock'; everyone in the company is. Even the back-office personnel within a large consulting firm or systems integrator are charging their time to a code, which in their case may or may not be a code related to a client account (therefore a client is not being billed) but to a central code created to fund their activities and time.

Hopefully the explanation of this model, where every hour is accounted for, is illustrating the point as to why value-added services, in the form of architectural assistance or other technical services, on a free-of-charge basis from an alliance partner are so appreciated. The arrangement releases a member of staff from the project or department either to become billable to a client, and therefore revenue earning, or to allow the project team to save costs on a member of staff that otherwise would need to be funded to do that work, e.g. via a charge code allocated to business development (a pot of money for colleagues to access when working on non-client-chargeable sales pursuits). Hence, any relevant resource and manpower to help an IT services company deliver on a sales pursuit or client project is money saved and will greatly enhance the value and regard of an alliance partnership.

There is another very important point here. If everyone is 'on the clock' and chargeable at all times, it means that the personnel have very little time for frivolous or irrelevant meetings to hear sales pitches or talk about speculative business opportunities. If you are reading this as a salesperson for a traditional hardware or software company, then you are encouraged to go to meetings and generate business. It is your job to build personal relationships, evangelise your products and generally brainstorm opportunity with clients and partners in meeting rooms with coffee and white boards and marker pens. You know that, in sales, 'face time' builds relationships and enhances your chance of building a profitable long-term relationship. There is a place for that within the large IT services companies, but the staff are very selective about what alliance partner meetings they will attend because every hour not chargeable to a client is costing their company money and also will impact their chargeability rate. In turn, that will impact their rating vs their colleagues (remember the bell curve). Think of it like this: if every time you attended an hour meeting to discuss a long-shot business idea it cost your company £400 of your product, you would be much more discerning about the meetings you attended. That is not to say that you won't ever get time with the chargeable personnel within an IT services company, but it probably does mean that they need to have a good reason to see you, i.e. a specific client need or a particular requirement within a current project that has warranted the meeting.

There is a way around this. Some people within the large IT influencers are employed to meet with and qualify potential new ideas and partnerships; they're called alliance managers. Your aim should be to get them bought in to your offering or solution as early as possible so that they will network and open doors on your behalf, or represent you within client teams. This will mean that you are not constantly imposing upon chargeable activities and finding that you cannot get sufficient traction.

Key learning points: revenue streams
1. Everyone with whom you are working is 'on the clock', so ensure that every meeting has a point and a value or else you may find that it is difficult to get the next meeting.
2. Use the resources that are not expected to be chargeable to a client (such as sales or alliance management personnel) because they will be more amenable to investing the time to work with you.
3. Get into the mindset that every meeting you attend carries a cost for your partner and could impact the chargeability metrics, so don't be frivolous with people's time as they probably don't share your desire to build relationships for the sake of it.

Deal shapes and shared risk

The technology landscape and the way the large companies consume technology is changing. There is a strong trend toward consuming computing functionality through managed services and the cloud. Clients expect to source capability, a user experience or an outcome, not necessarily products that they are obliged to own and run. This is strongly reflected in the way that the large IT project delivery companies are being asked to operate and how they are shaping their business to reflect this trend. If you want to provide your new alliance partner with innovative and relevant solutions that reflect the way that they work with their clients, you need to understand the fundamental 'product' that they are selling and how you as a partner fit into that offering. To add more colour and context, I refer back to the 'Routes To Reward' section in the Introduction to indicate the way that you may engage commercially in each scenario. I also refer back to the retail client scenario described in Chapter 3 to show how these different 'deal shapes' may have applied to that client's need.

Time and materials

This is one of the two 'old school' models to which project delivery may be subject. In this model, the client will source their own product (potentially through the cloud, but also in order to retain title and host 'on-premise') and then source the related services from a services company. This is a very attractive model for the typical large IT services company because it involves very little inherent commercial risk. Essentially, this entails the consultancy or the systems integrator (not outsource contracts) providing a day rate for the services of its staff to the client (tiered as per career level) and then consuming the services and paying fees on an ongoing basis as and when they use them, including any relevant 'materials' (which could, of course, mean product, but also expenses such as flights and hotels). While this could seem overly fair to the delivery company, it is sometimes seen as the best and most transparent cost construct for all parties where there is a degree of uncertainty, either on the part of the services company doing the project delivery or the client about what the project entails. In other words, the project scope or its evolution is unclear. This flexibility can work in the client's favour as well because the client can cease the project or engagement at any stage, or either party can amend the scope of the project as they go along to reflect changing circumstances or findings.

In our fictitious client scenario involving the supermarket chain in Chapter 3, it is plausible that this model could have been used during the initial business case phase of the project. This was when the client was exploring whether there was an opportunity for business improvement, but wanted to monitor progress as the project began in case the findings at certain checkpoints were not conclusive enough to justify completing the exercise (although in fairness the client would probably still have gone for a fixed price contract with a break clause if this was the case).

This business model is largely invisible to you as a partner. It would prevail in a fairly typical IT project where the products and services are sourced separately and the client takes overall project responsibility. Your direct involvement will probably be where the consultancy or systems integrator has recommended your product and left the client to engage with you directly, so it is a straight influencer model. It's not ideal because the very nature of the model suggests a certain level of disconnection between the delivery company and the client deliverable, so the consultancy or systems integrator is likely to have questionable influence.

Fixed price contract

Of the traditional deal shapes, this is by far the most common. It is where the client and their delivery partner agree a fixed price for ultimate completion of a specific deliverable, i.e. a fixed scope. Rather like paying a builder to build an extension on your home, rather than run the risk of paying him by the day with no pre-agreed end price (i.e. time and materials), in this scenario the contract will not refer to how many days or 'materials', such as expenses, but will only refer to an agreed completion for the project (or phase). The large IT services company must then take all of the risk of delivering a profitable project by being as efficient as possible with their costs to deliver the solution as promised. As well as downside risk, there is, of course, upside opportunity if the company delivering the project can manage the costs of the project effectively (see the 'Hard Work' section in this chapter), or indeed leverage the value-added services of partner companies to subsidise the cost of the delivery team.

There is obvious reward for cleverly priced contracts, but substantial risk too, especially with many companies competing for work in competitive bid situations where the tendency to offer lower and lower pricing is a temptation. From a client perspective, fixed price may seem a safe and effective way to contract, but it is a relatively inflexible model in that the scope needs to be battened down and set out in full before the contract is signed. This may often be difficult to do, particularly if the contract is signed at an early stage (e.g. prior to technical specifications being settled).

In our fictitious client scenario, this is the most likely method for the first three phases of the project, where the client pays the consultancy or systems integrator to deliver the business case, technical architecture and integration, respectively.

Once again, this pricing model is most likely to be a more traditional IT solution sourcing model, where the client is acquiring IT services and product from different sources. However, it is possible that the overall project will include product costs as well, in which case the delivery partner is even more heavily incentivised to not only acquire the lowest priced product, but also to look for interesting and innovative products to lower the cost of delivering the solution for sign-off at time of completion.

As an alliance partner, you have three obvious ways to be appealing to the prime contractor: (i) providing value-added services to bring down the cost of delivery; (ii) providing low priced product when the large IT services company has contracted to provide a fixed cost to include product and services; (iii) building in a resale margin for the prime contractor when they have contracted to deliver the services, but are tasked with sourcing the hardware as a value-added service.

Business process outsource

We've covered this model in Chapters 1 and 2. In essence, a client takes a function or task that they are currently managing 'in-house' and pays a specialist outsourcing company to execute that function or task on their behalf. This may be a large undertaking, such as the HR department for a blue-chip corporation, or it may be a much more modest task, such as support of a specific application. In its most basic form, the commercial model is very straight forward, the client and the outsourcer agree a fixed fee for the period of the outsource activity, usually 3-5 years. As we have discussed previously, this is often bad news for the client's current suppliers as the infrastructure required to support that task in-house (or the personnel executing the task) will move to another company, who probably already have an infrastructure in place. Your main hope as an aspirant alliance partner to the outsourcer (or as a supplier to the client) is that the outsourcer may wish to procure products or services to support the outsource and you benefit from the recommendation, although for reasons stated above, most notably geography, you are probably clutching at straws and there is minimal alliance opportunity.

Gain-share

Things now to start to get interesting. This deal shape is becoming increasingly common as the large consultancies and systems integrators start to blur the lines between their traditional business models and the domain of outsourcers. In the context of the large IT services companies, a gain-share model is a model wherein the consultant, system integrator or outsourcer (and in most instances they are performing all three roles) are rewarded for the financial contribution they make to the client.

A good example is a procurement department outsource arrangement. The outsourcer will be building their business case to the client based on their ability to save the client costs, partly through the client not having to employ a procurement department (or a greatly reduced department) and partly because the outsourcer will argue that their greater expertise (specialist people, processes and market knowledge) will mean that the client sources product on the client's behalf at a lower cost, ergo their spend is less. This scenario is a perfect example of where a gain-share model could be a win–win. The client proposes that the outsourcer should take part of his fee based on the savings that the client achieves from the reduced personnel costs and any savings the client makes. This is a perfectly reasonable request, of course, especially when an outsourcer believes in his business case and has strong precedent to support it. A very basic example is shown in Figure 4.2.

Figure 4.2 assumes that the outsourcer managed to save the client 5% on their spend through their specialist expertise. The outsourcer also saved the client significant staff costs, partly through efficiencies and partly because they off-shored the personnel costs. If the outsourcer charged £600k for the 10 personnel, it probably cost them in the region of £400k. So, in this scenario, there are significant benefits all round; the outsourcer makes £200k and the client saves £5.4m.

But let's consider another scenario. How about if the client had said: 'Rather than us pay you $600k to outsource our procurement department, what about if we pay you 20% of savings on our spend instead?' The table would now look like Figure 4.3. The outsourcer benefits by an extra £1.4m even though they took the cost of funding the client's personnel costs. You could argue that this isn't

86 Understanding the business model

	Current costs for client	Client costs after outsource	Profit for outsourcer
Client procurement department (10 personnel)	£1m	£600k	£200k
Client spend through procurement department	£100m	£95m	
Total current client costs	£101m	£95.6m	
Client saving after outsource		£5.4m	

Figure 4.2 Basic gain share example.

	Current costs for client	Client costs after outsource	Profit for outsourcer
Client procurement department (10 personnel)	£1m		−£400k
Client spend through procurement department	£100m	£95m	
Gain-share fee to outsourcer		£2m	£2m
Total	£101m	£97m	£1.6m
Client saving after outsource		£4m	

Figure 4.3 Basic gain and rick share example.

a win–win and that the client is actually £1.4m worse off than in the previous scenario, but they aren't taking any risk on an outsource contract that may not work out, so most companies would see the £1.4m hit as fair – particularly as it was money they didn't have in the first place and they are still £4m better off than before the outsource.

What does all of this mean for you, the partner? In this scenario, very little. It is probably just bad news because the outsourcer is unlikely to require any products or services to run the outsource (all they are doing is creating efficiencies and moving some personnel off-shore). It is conceivable that, if the client previously bought products that you supply, but did not buy them through you, then you could help the outsourcer by supplying them with reduced price product, or alternative products of equal quality, to help them meet their procurement savings goals – so that would be a win, but it is a long-shot.

Understanding the business model 87

   This is the important bit: this business model can really start to benefit you as an alliance partner of an outsourcer (or consultancy or systems integrator) when they are running a technology system or solution on behalf of a client and agreeing to take a percentage of savings from the running of that system. You then have a great opportunity to help the outsourcer run the system more efficiently using your product or service because they will be very open to any solution that assists them in doing so. The particularly interesting angle here is in you starting to share the risk. Say the solution above was not about saving costs through procurement, but about saving costs through processing cheques quicker for a bank or issuing bills quicker for a utilities company. What is to stop you, as the supplier, enjoying the spoils and 'giving' your product or service free of charge to the outsourcer in return for an element of the gain-share. There may be extra revenue in it for you (a risk you may be very happy to take if perhaps you have a software product that has already been developed and the cost sunk), but, just as importantly, you are creating a lasting and trusting relationship with the outsourcer who is benefitting greatly from the shared risk and lower exposure. Clearly, you need to do your due diligence around the contract and the commercials, but, if you execute this deal shape correctly, then you could enjoy uncapped reward, increased stickiness with your alliance partner and a great deal of respect and kudos.

Outcome-based (aka shared risk–reward pricing model)

Now we are moving to how the future of business will increasingly work, so this bit is important to get your head around. There's a popular cliché that states: when someone buys a drill, they don't want a drill, they want holes. It's a metaphor for IT systems. In our example of a retailer sourcing a new system to create incremental sales, this is an excellent illustration. Of course they don't want a new IT system per se, they want the extra money through their tills from selling more items per shopping trolley. Inevitably, they will have doubts. Was the initial analysis work (business case) accurate? Will the system fail technically and leave them with substantial costs to repair and maintain it? Will it work functionally, i.e. will it actually result in extras sales in sufficient quantity to justify the investment? So, there is risk and it's this risk that will very often stop the project going ahead.

   Rather like the gain-share example, what if the client said: 'We don't intend to accept the risk of acquiring the system, so if you believe in the opportunity and business case, why don't we install it for no cost and you share a percentage of the incremental sales?' This is subtly different from the gain-share model described above, which was about the large IT services company sharing the cost savings. This is about your services partner actually owning a business solution and using the retailer (in our example) as the route to market. Traditional high street retail is a good example of where this model works well (sale or return), but this business model is more commonly starting to be seen in the e-commerce space, where a large IT services company will build a web presence on behalf of a company (could be a retailer, but could just as easily be a utilities, bank or oil company transacting with their corporate clients) and then agrees to share in the revenue through that new channel.

This business model requires tight and relatively complex contracting and a great deal of trust between the client and their partner, but as a business model for future growth it is perfect. The client gets access to a new revenue stream at no risk and the large IT services company gets to leverage the client's customer base and revenue stream. No longer are they selling people and restricted by the finite amount of resources that they can recruit and sustain, they can now gain revenues from retail sales of baked beans, or a share of a utility company's income from providing power to homes, or a share of sales from pizzas because they own a pizza delivery company's online ordering system.

This model is becoming increasingly popular, and the large IT services companies are gearing up to do business this way. As with the straight gain-share model, this opens up interesting new opportunities and dynamic ways of doing business for alliance partners who can share in the risk and reward by implementing exactly the same model. They don't actually bill the company who delivered the transformation for the use of the product or service, they just licence and contract their product or service to the delivery company to run the client's specific solution for a return of the client's incremental sales revenue. As with the large IT service company, the benefit to the technology OEM is the opportunity for unlimited sales by leveraging the end-user client's customer reach. It also provides recurring revenues, which is liked by the stock market, makes the technology OEM (or similar alliance partner) more appealing to investors, increases the depth of the relationship with their alliance partner and presents new logos and success stories to attract new business.

The examples I have provided in the gain-share and outcome-based sections are fairly extreme cases of the delivery partner taking all the risk. In reality, a large project such as the retailer scenario may well have elements of the various different models. For example, the client may have asked for the initial business case work to be undertaken on a time and materials basis because it allowed them to evaluate progress frequently and gave them the flexibility to continue with the piece of work only if a potential business need was shaping up. There is then every chance that the retailer and large IT services company could have agreed a fixed price to implement the system, but at minimal cost with no profit for the services company and maybe with no charge to the client for the actual physical system. This way, at least the services delivery partner doesn't take the full hit for the risk of implementation and can 'back-off' the product (hardware and software) to his alliance partners. But then the run element could have been done on an outcome basis, where the client pays no ongoing charge for the running and execution of the system, but the services company takes all of the cost and risk in return for a share of the extra retail sales on an outcome-based model.

These last two examples represent the most significant trend in the way that alliance partners are choosing to work with large IT services companies. No longer is it merely about the technology OEM providing the product and the large IT services company providing the services, with the client owning the system and

Understanding the business model 89

Deal Shape	Who typically retains title (order of likelihood)	Typical route to reward For OEM (order of likelihood)
Time and materials	Client	Influence Resale
Fixed price	Client IT services company	Resale Sell to
Gain share	Client Large IT services company	Sell to Resale
Outcome based	Large IT services company OEM	Sell to Outcome based
Outsource	Large IT services company Client	Sell to Resale

Figure 4.4 Deal shape summary.

taking the cost and the risk. Clients are getting savvy to the opportunity of protecting their cash investments and using their services delivery partners (and, in turn, their partners) to really share the risk. While it's a scary model in some ways for the product and services providers, it is also a way of tapping into forward revenue streams and gaining true leverage for the privilege of having high-profile and successful clients. Wouldn't you like a little bit of money every time someone paid a utility bill on time or ordered a takeaway pizza online?

A summary of the variety of deal shapes is set out in Figure 4.4.

Key learning points: deal shapes and shared risk
1. The way that large consultancies, systems integrators and outsourcers transact with their clients is evolving. This creates fantastic opportunities for alliance partners who want to share the risk and reward.
2. By understanding the terms under which our IT services company alliance partner is transacting with their client, you can find innovative and compelling ways to shape your proposition or licence your agreement with them.
3. As 'outcome-based' deal shapes become more common, start looking at your core offerings and risk profile and ascertain if they are still fit for purpose for partnering within this business model.

Going 'client-side'

This is a straight-forward concept to understand, but worth spelling out. Most of the discussion to this point has concerned a consultancy or systems integrator working with an alliance partner in order to create a complete solution for a client. In doing so, the consultancy or systems integrator identifies and then recommends products and services that deliver the correct functional and commercial solution for the client. Put another way, the right product at the right price. If you wish to be the company whose products or services are put forward, obviously it is essential to have an offering that fits the scope, but it is also helpful to have the correct commercial construct as well (both for the client and for your partner, the large IT services company). In essence, the vast majority of the time, the product evaluation and recommendation is a value-added service, i.e. not chargeable, and bundled as part of the wider project. In fact, it is precisely the sort of specialist knowledge that the client is looking for when they hire a consultancy or systems integrator. But there is another engagement type that may prevail, where the client is actually paying someone (almost always the consultancy) to make a formal vendor selection. This was touched upon in Chapter 2 when we looked at the project lifecycle. In our imaginary retail client scenario, it is likely to be during or at the end of the architecture phase. The usual process would be that the client identifies what sort of technology products they require, then they go out to the market to select the technology platform to deliver it; for instance, a CRM or ERP system or a mobility platform. Once they know the answer, they select a partner for the implementation phase, which is a wise approach as it allows them to select the correct product and then go and find the very best systems integrator to implement it. The company tasked to execute the vendor selection project could be a specific consultancy hired for that specific task, or could be be the original management consultancy who put together the business case, or could be the technical consultancy that drew up the technical architecture. It could also be the systems integrator who has been selected to implement the system, if they are of a size where they have multiple vendor relationships that include all of the relevant potential players for this project and therefore can be entirely trusted to be impartial. Once the consultancy has been hired, they are often referred to as 'client-side' and the way that they engage with partners will be much more formal and restricted.

The basic process will be that the consultancy engaged to do the vendor selection will look closely at the business processes required, prioritise them and document them into a scope. They will then draw up an evaluation document within which to evaluate the products in the vendor selection process against that scope. It is possible at this stage that a client may wish to meet the likely candidates in person and ask them to demonstrate their software. However, if the consultancy has that knowledge already, this is not required. Once the consultancy is aware of what is required, has seen evidence (a working demo and credentials) and is convinced that it fits the bill, they have two choices: (i) make the decision there and then and then enter into negotiations with the software company concerned; or (ii) ask the short-listed software vendors to complete a pricing exercise (most likely an RFP) where they match their own software against the functional scope of the project and provide pricing. Even if the client knows which software they wish to use (or at least strongly favours), they may still go through the RFP process in order to drive the best price from the selected software company, who will be more aggressive with their pricing if they think they are in a competitive situation. Thereafter, there will be a formal tender review process scoring the responses against various criteria related to functionality, price and ability to deliver, which will be very individual to the project and will be mapped out in the tender document.

The significant point here is that this entire vendor selection process is executed in a very official and formal way and there is minimal opportunity to influence choice of your product outside of the formal process. As described previously, the large IT services companies will ordinarily encourage partnering and welcome as many value-added services as possible in order to augment their skills, save costs and even generate extra profit for the project via fees or resale. But when it is a formal, paid vendor selection process, expect a different approach. Protocols will be in place and, as a potential partner, you will be subject to the similar sorts of rules that relate to formal RFPs. So, 'selling' to the company making the vendor selection is banned in order that they can be entirely neutral in their vendor selection work. Don't be surprised if phone calls are not returned and invitations to events or seminars are declined, to avoid undue influence in the process. You will not be let in on a personal level at all.

Of course, human nature plays a part in any process. While the consultancy will, no doubt, run a very clean process in the vendor selection (for 'clean' read 'strictly by the rules and not subject to any undue influence'), they will still be subliminally influenced by previous dealings with certain vendors. After all, it is their job to give the client best advice. If the consultants executing the vendor selection have recently been trained on the technology and were impressed, received some high quality relevant marketing in relation to it or, better still, have direct experience of working successfully with a certain vendor, it is inevitable and sensible that they bring that into their scoring, which is of course always subjective.

In short, when a consultancy is 'client-side', many of the usual routes of influence are probably closed, but this is when the hard work that you put in to build relationships in the months and years previously will give you an edge.

Key learning points: going client-side
1. When you enter into a vendor assessment process, ascertain early if this is a formal process where the consultancy is 'client-side' or a less formal engagement that the consultancy is providing. This information will help you understand what product to put forward as part of a solution bill of materials that they 'control'.
2. There is a different and more formal protocol which needs to be observed for dealing with your large IT services company alliance partner when they are 'client-side'.
3. There is a still a place for you, and your hard work to this point in socialising your product or services with the consultancy will increase your chances of being involved in the formal vendor assessment process.

The protocol of fee programmes

The background

For years the accepted business model for compensating consulting firms and systems integrators for successfully recommending a partner's product would be to pay a commission or fee to the influencer. This practice is now largely discredited and in certain situations illegal, even if the benefit is passed down to the client or they are entirely aware of it. So how do OEMs and software companies trying to incentivise channel or alliance partners navigate this potential moral and legal maze?

Let's go back to the beginning. The business model of large IT services companies is that they are high gross margin businesses and their financial results are geared up to this model. In the case of publicly quoted companies in the sector, their share price is often predicated on comparatively low revenue and high gross margin, which is an equation that stock market investors like. Therefore, from a high-level financial perspective, the large IT services companies are not keen on reselling product because (depending on the resale model) it can dilute their gross margin, not to mention the pressure it puts on cash flow and the increased credit exposure to a client. Additionally, there is the added disincentive of investing in the skills to sell, support and deliver on technology products, with all the potential customer satisfaction issues that brings. So, the traditional method of compensating consulting firms or systems integrators for recommending a technology OEM's products was to provide a fee. As covered in the 'Routes To Reward' section, this brings benefit and risk.

At a very basic level, the benefit for the company that recommended the technology is that they receive a fee that can be taken to the bottom line. This sounds like a conflict of interest; after all, there is an expectation that companies playing the role of consultant are being entirely impartial in their advice and are being paid as such. However, the reality is that the IT services sector is so price competitive that the fee is usually taken to merely prop up the deal economics. Put another way, the client is the beneficiary as the services delivery company uses the extra profit derived from the fee to further cut price the delivery element of the project for the client. This produces a win–win for the client and the IT services company supported by the technology vendor's fee programme.

The downside of fee programmes for the IT influencer company is being open to accusations of impropriety, i.e. they favoured one product over another in order to receive a fee. Even when that money is put to good use to keep the project costs down for the client, it is still a very precarious ethical situation to be in. In the case of government owned clients, it is prohibited pretty much worldwide, as it is in highly regulated government influenced sectors such as utilities and telecoms. So, at best, receiving commission fees is ethically complex, and at worst strictly forbidden. As a form of doing business, its days are numbered and already unacceptable by many of the consultancies and systems integrators.

This has lead to the increased appeal of resale as a model for large IT services companies, to derive margin enhancement from selling solutions that involve a significant product element. Notwithstanding the potential for the margin dilutive aspects of reselling mentioned above (there are financial treatments that can avoid this, but let's park that for now), reselling product has significant advantages: (i) it allows the technical consultancies and systems integrators to be close to the product supply for a project, which brings logistical benefits; (ii) it brings profit to the project even if it is at a lower margin than they are accustomed; (iii) it means that the technology partner in the relationship remains engaged and provides lots

Understanding the business model 93

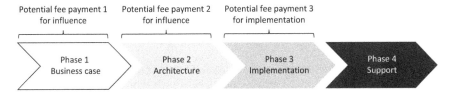

Figure 4.5 Sample fee payment model.

of value-added services; (iv) it provides recurring revenues in support contracts in coming years; (v) it strengthens the bond between the company doing the delivery and their client and negates the need for the client to work with a VAR that may be looking to encroach upon the large IT services company's revenue streams.

What you need to know as an alliance partner

Fee programmes are a very powerful lever and, in situations where it is possible to implement them in compliance with the relevant legal and client requirements, they are an excellent way to incentivise IT influencers to build your product into their solution. It also allows you as a technology OEM to keep your VAR channel sweet because they take the traditional reseller margin and the influencer takes the fee, allowing you to maintain satisfaction within your channel. This, of course, means paying twice, but if the deal is incremental, this could be a small price to pay.

A typical way of incentivising using a fee programme is by paying for different levels of participation or contribution at different stages of the project cycle. The usual mechanism for this is for the IT influencer to 'log' involvement in a project and explain how/when they recommended a certain technology in order that the OEM or product supplier can ensure that the correct party is being recompensed – as opposed to the wrong partner claiming retrospectively when another partner was actually responsible for the original recommendation.

Creating a single fee payment for influencing the business can sometimes be fraught with conflict, so it often makes sense to recompense for different stages of the cycle in a modular way (see Figure 4.5). Of course, all stage fee payments could be accrued by the same company, but there is often a need to recognise the disparate organisations at each stage of the project lifecycle.

Key learning points: the protocol of fee programmes
1. Fee programmes to incentivise are a very effective way for a technology OEM to motivate the IT influencers to recommend their product, and also keeps an existing reseller channel intact because the two partners can co-exist.
2. However, most consultancies and systems integrators will have policies around how and whether they can accept fees, so be sure to understand those constraints before making firm offers.
3. Look to tier incentive programmes to weight for the behaviours you want to drive in your partner, such as origination or deal closure as opposed to delivery only.

Co-opetition and ethical walls

You may have heard of co-opetition. If not, there's a good explanation on ft.com:

> Simultaneous competition and co-operation between a company and external players such as rivals, government agencies, suppliers, distributors, and partners ... It develops win–win scenarios in which a business strives to gain more, not necessarily by taking market share or profit from a contender, but by creating a bigger market in complementary areas.

In the modern technology landscape, certain companies that are providing IT related services also have software or hardware businesses. Some would argue that it is the perfect model for clients and shareholders, others would say that a influencer like a services company should be about providing the best products and shouldn't be open to the criticism that they have unfairly favoured their own product offerings. Conversely, traditional software and hardware OEMs have implementation and even consulting departments that conflict with the core business of the large IT services companies.

So, how do the successful companies manage this potential conflict and ensure long-term, successful trust-based partnerships? If you are reading this as a technology OEM, you'll want to know how you can augment your product sales with services revenue without annoying your large services based alliance partner. If you're reading this from within a large IT services company, you'll want to know how (if at all) you can work with a technology OEM that offers services as a proposition.

A great example of a company that finds itself in this position is IBM. They are the ultimate in channel hybrid: part hardware company, part software company and part service company. They even have their own finance arm. To put it bluntly, they compete with everyone. But they also have a reputation for being an excellent channel partner and have a hardware and software business with other services delivery partners that they count in the hundreds of millions of dollars despite being a formidable opponent of the same companies when competing in mutual clients and prospects. How do they pull this off? Part of the reason is that they are very adept at delineating between the different parts of their business and creating ethical walls (known in the past as Chinese walls); another reason is that they have strict governance and processes; but maybe the most important reason is that they are culturally hard-wired for co-opetition.

If you're a technology OEM and want to sell services, it's probably for one of two reasons: (i) you want to ensure that you have a hands-on involvement in seeing that your product is delivered correctly; (ii) you want to generate revenue and profit. Both of these reasons are fine and there is a place for them, but if you do want to enter the services market and remain friends with your channel, be mindful of the following rules:

1. Ensure that your delivery services alliance partner is aware of your strategy from the outset of the relationship and work with them to agree how you will approach potential conflict in a real-life scenario.

Understanding the business model 95

2. Don't mislead your alliance partners by encouraging them to invest in training resources that will later clash with the skills that you want to sell along with your product sale. Ideally, look to train them in complimenting services.
3. Agree a teaming agreement on each sale so that you are clear who should be the delivery partner and how it is appropriate to divide the services revenue associated with a sale or implementation. It goes without saying that a 'fit for purpose' teaming agreement must include NDA and IP terms. We will cover this in detail in Chapter 5.
4. Create a reduced 'channel price' for your services so that your delivery services channel can make a profit when 'selling' or subcontracting your services at your rate card price.
5. Learn from IBM and create ethical walls. If there is a potential that different parts of your company conflict with your partner, ensure that the correct protocols and governance exists internally to guarantee that only those with no conflict of interest work with your alliance partner. If you are potentially looking to sell services associated with your product deal, and you have agreed with your services-focused channel partner that this will not be collaborative, and will indeed be in competition, then ensure that the personnel working with that partner, such as technical architects or sales staff, are not also working with your services arm.
6. Amend your salespeople's compensation plans to reflect your strategy. Incentivise them for business with your channel and de-incentivise them for conduct that may impact your longer-term channel strategy.

But despite all of the above, even more importantly:

7. Understand the law very carefully and take advice as required. For good reasons, competitor collusion is illegal and you should fully understand the implications of entering into any agreement, formal or otherwise, wherein you agree with any partner about who should do what in a client engagement. You don't want to upset your channel that you rely on to influence the sale of your goods, but, more importantly, you do not want to disrespect your client or break the law.

If you are on the other side of the fence and you are working for a IT services company and you have products that conflict with your technology OEM alliance partners, such as niche software products, the same rules of best practice apply.

Key learning points: co-opetition and ethical walls
1. Co-opetition is the act of offering competing products with the companies with whom you are also partnering. It takes skill and sensitivity to get right.
2. Create a model where there is adequate skin in the game for your alliance partner and ensure that the services you provide are complimentary and not core to their value.
3. Be transparent, but get very good legal advice before entering into any engagements, either tactical or strategic, that may suggest collusion.

Alliance excellence in the new economy: Georg's story

Georg is a director for an award winning global consulting and design business. He is responsible for guiding the sales and delivery of programmes, which include 'Tools for Digital Transformation', 'People Engagement' and 'Next Generation Learning'. Prior to this, Georg worked in IT and business transformation and alliance services at one of the large IT influence companies, shaping and delivering client programmes, working with an ecosystem of partners. His story is interesting for anyone looking to understand the relative cultures (say between a large established consulting firm vs a fast-paced, multi-disciplinary digital firm) and what these growing IT consulting firms value in a partnership. I've deliberately left in the bit about Georg's journey as well because it is helpful if you want to acclimatise to the mindset.

> I have worked in consulting for 10 years with a focus on business development, alliance partnerships, large-scale change, learning and people engagement programmes. What I love about my work is the collaboration, versatility and creativity required to deliver new ideas at scale. Technology is fundamentally shifting what is possible and I am fascinated both by the business opportunities this presents and our human connection within this landscape. A common thread throughout my career has been a desire to find new and exciting ways to leverage technology developments and connect seemingly disparate areas to create something that brings value to people. This is at the heart of what attracts me to business development through ecosystems and partnerships.
>
> When I started my consulting career I was focused on strategy, digital and technology solutions. Prior to that I had studied English and German law, with a masters in comparative jurisprudence and worked as part of the CEO's office for an innovative music-based start-up. This experience instilled in me a desire to work at the entrepreneurial side of business, finding and growing new opportunities. Having seen how strategic alliance management works, both from the perspective of a global organisation with many hundreds of thousands of employees covering over 400 alliance partnerships, and from the perspective of a smaller, fast growing digital agency environment, I can reflect on both the shared practices and some potential points of differentiation between the two seemingly disparate worlds.
>
> I believe that, regardless of size, companies need to think in terms of ecosystems and partnerships to achieve their full potential. Who and how you partner with has wide-reaching implications, and there are many factors to consider. It is true that navigating a larger company can be difficult. There can be a huge amount of stakeholder management, process and due diligence required to form a new alliance. When dealing with well-known brands, it can often be a 'high stakes' environment to flesh out new growth areas. The potential for returns is significant, but the 'cost' can be equally so. This cautiousness can sometimes impede the speed and scale of new partnerships.

Understanding the business model 97

My personal reflection is that regardless of size, good alliances management can be distilled into four principles: (i) entrepreneurial mindset; (ii) clear value proposition; (iii) trusted relationships; (iv) operational excellence.

I define the entrepreneurial mindset as having the business acumen to recognise an opportunity and set up a strategic partnership model around it. The parties must be able to spot a market gap, identify complementary offerings, evaluate the potential rewards and be able to influence their respective organisations to shape a joint solution. This is true for both larger and smaller companies. However, I have observed that within a smaller company, things can move quicker, which provides advantages.

When I made the move to a smaller organisation, I found the alliance opportunities to be fast-paced and varied. You have creative freedom in the sense that you can quickly put together solutions that test a hypothesis or an idea for an innovative solution to a client challenge, then build a business area around this. In my role, this may involve taking a 'bleeding edge' technology, or something that is popular in a B2C environment, such as interactive VR [virtual reality], then work with clients to put an enterprise level solution in place. This solution will adapt the experience into a B2B environment within the parameters of the client's IT estate, KPIs, brand and other requirements to create the most-advanced-yet-acceptable (MAYA) solution that delivers a great experience and meets the core objectives. Therefore, something that started as an arcade style interactive VR idea can quickly become a large-scale learning experience to deliver sales and customer service role play scenarios to train a global workforce.

From an alliances perspective, this involves connecting with leading providers from different backgrounds, such as the B2C world, then working together to adapt the solution into an enterprise environment that retains the innovative experience, but is compliant with client IT, security and process requirements. Once the solution is proven and there is wider demand, we can quickly scale up a practice to market, sell and implement this new offering.

Working in a smaller, agile company allows you to operate in this entrepreneurial way. At a larger company, there would inherently be more rigid processes involved to partner and scale up a new solution. In my view, there is an opportunity for larger companies to recognise and embrace this fast-paced way of partnering to innovate and disrupt markets by using the full weight of their resources. You don't have to be small to be nimble.

The second principle of having a clear value proposition is also essential. No matter how exciting or innovative an alliance partnership seems on paper, without a clear and attractive value proposition for all sides, it is unlikely to succeed. There needs to be value for all of the parties involved, especially for the end-user. Also, the value for all sides needs to be well articulated and easy to understand in order to achieve the 'buy-in' required from everyone. This, for me, is the litmus test for the strategic partnership.

What constitutes value for the parties may be weighted differently based on each company's situation, but, in my experience, there are a number of common drivers, which apply to both large-scale and smaller high-growth companies. These include things like new client relationships at the right levels, driving innovation and shaping new markets, delivering quality at scale and reducing delivery risk, creating intellectual property, positive brand association, access to a sales and marketing engine, neutralising or blocking potential competitors.

It is all about matching interests to create something that is valuable for all sides. For example, a large consulting company could be an attractive partner for a high-growth technology player for the potential impact they can have on their company valuation. A large consultancy could potentially shift the needle on all of the above drivers, but what is in it for the consultancy? They might be much more interested in the overall direction of the market and securing their stake within it. Also, it could be about showing innovation and relevance with their client base much more than simply growing revenue.

A smaller high growth company may have the advantage of greater flexibility of deal shapes to construct something that works for all parties without the same constraints that a larger company might face. This isn't always the case, but typically a larger company will have quite rigid parameters from which to negotiate with in terms of what is and isn't acceptable to them. It often requires vision and tenacity from key people within the larger organisation to push through a ground-breaking partnership deal. In comparison, a smaller company can be creative about what the optimal deal shape looks like and move forward quickly. This may bring more risk for the smaller company, but their speed to market could also increase the potential rewards.

Regardless of the deal shape, an important aspect of the value proposition principle is that everyone understands it and can articulate the value for the different parties. Otherwise, a sales team won't be motivated, a client won't understand why this makes sense for them and key stakeholders will not buy into the alliance or measure the right KPIs to evaluate the effectiveness.

The third principle is about trust. All good business and personal relationships are built on trust. The importance of trust in forming and developing alliance relationships is paramount. It takes a lot of trust to open the doors of your company and share ideas, knowledge and strategic plans with a partner. Many companies today also need to establish internal 'firewalls' for situations where another part of the business is a competitor, so called 'co-opetition'.

From what I have seen, trusted relationships both at a personal and organisational level are just as important regardless of the company size. Trustworthiness is the currency that wins you a seat at the table. One observation between larger and smaller companies is that with a larger company, where the alliance is already established over many years, the trust is automatically built in. Therefore, when you come to deal with a new person from the partner company, the parameters are already in place.

When working with a smaller company or forging new ground, trust needs to be built up and earned. All aspects of the 'trust equation' are constantly in motion. Even though NDAs, teaming agreements and memorandums of understanding clearly lay out the principles of engagement, there is still a high degree of trust required. This is one of the aspects I really enjoy about new business partnerships, getting to know the values of the organisation and finding a common ground from which to shape new ideas.

It is also interesting to consider the role of personal relationships in the context of trust. It would be easy to presume that personal connections matter more at smaller businesses, but actually they are just as important in the context of large companies. I have witnessed numerous examples of individuals within a large company acting as a catalyst for an alliance relationship based on their trustworthiness and credibility, which they have built up within their own organisation and with the clients they serve.

Trust is therefore a universal principle to good business and is a critical aspect of an alliance partnership, regardless of the size and nature of companies involved.

The fourth area is operational excellence. This is essential. You need to know if the alliance is performing well, delivering value and providing a good return on the joint investment. This comes down to operational excellence and it applies to all areas of the alliance in practice. Operational excellence includes formation and monitoring of partnership agreements, measuring of sales and marketing KPIs (e.g. new leads/news coverage), regular executive reviews and touch points, training and enablement of teams, regular monitoring of key performance metrics and ensuring the right culture, tools and processes are in place.

The alliances I have seen succeed, both within large and smaller company environments, are not necessarily the ones that seemingly had the greatest potential at the outset, but rather it has been the ones where the operational side is managed very well. There is inherently a high degree of planning and administrative work involved with launching and growing a new partnership arrangement or offering. It is this hidden graft, much like the production of a great event, that makes the difference and gives the impression of effortless success.

Some key aspects of this include setting up the right commercial and legal frameworks at the outset in collaboration with the leadership teams of all sides. This gets the partnership up and running. Then it is about crafting the go-to-market approach and processes with all the supporting elements, such as sales and marketing collateral, training and incentivising of different teams. This must all be underpinned by ongoing leadership involvement and a strong KPI reporting function. These elements, though seemingly easy to put in place, are essential for a slick end-to-end partnership experience.

While every company has their own approach, I typically see larger companies making resources available to dedicate to these elements, which is positive, but may risk process over engineering if not reviewed regularly (e.g. in the leads management space). Smaller companies tend to move faster, but can get stretched when business picks up, often due to their own success, and they can lose the discipline quickly. In my opinion, it is about getting 'the basics' right, even though getting it right is far from basic.

When looking at alliance management through the lens of these four principles, it is clear that larger and smaller companies actually have a lot in common. I think smaller companies can learn a lot from the process discipline that larger companies have in place, while larger companies should recognise and reward flexibility, creativity and agility in their alliance professionals.

One way I have seen innovative larger companies adopt this approach successfully is through an incubation or innovation programme that tests, nurtures and iterates partnership offerings in the market with trusted clients. This generates the right entrepreneurial environment, giving access to large company scale, while creating a safe environment for developing ideas that still protects the core brand and business.

Ultimately, it comes down to a commitment for establishing mutual value through well executed ideas built on a foundation of trusted relationships. This is particularly important as we enter an unprecedented age of partnerships and ecosystems enabled through digital working.

Key learning points: Georg's story
1. The large IT services companies provide interesting and exciting careers and attract ambitious personnel.
2. Innovation, creativity and imagination are really important in the new digital integrators when selecting partnerships.
3. The 'trust' word is as essential to partnering successfully with a modern fast moving consultancies as it is to the established players.

5 Alliance best practice

It's important that we re-cap on the important aspects of alliance play at this point. Some of the principles in this chapter are alliances 101 and apply to all channel relationships, but where possible I've tried to tweak the messaging to reflect the way that the large IT services companies are goaled and motivated. One thing that they have in common is that they are complex in their business models, so a greater degree of organisation and a systematic approach to establishing goals, creating a plan and then delivering on that plan in a methodical, structured and consistent way is required.

Objections

Before we go into why establishing formal alliances is a good idea, let's not ignore the fact that there are good reasons why that approach comes with risk. While you may believe in the logic that says 1+1=3 and that a well structured and executed alliance strategy is a productive and cost-efficient business model, there will be people in your organisation that mistrust this approach, especially the idea of engaging with large complex global organisations. They are right to be wary, and in many places in this book I also recommend caution when it comes to the very strategy this book is promoting. It's risky and can be an expensive mistake to make. So, let's examine the three most common objections that you will receive from your colleagues and leadership, and look at ways in which you can address those concerns so that they can also see that, if planned and executed correctly, it can be the right way for your company to be introduced to and close large sales opportunities. Once again, these points apply to a wider channel strategy, but I have made the responses relevant to how you would address these objections specifically related to a proposed alliances model with the large consulting firms, outsourcers or systems integrators.

Objection 1: 'Why would I hire an alliances person? They can be very expensive and don't actually close deals directly with my clients.'
Overcoming this objection: The answer is very simple and is related to economies of scale. If you hire an effective alliance lead and they create relationships with motivated business partners such as large consulting firms or delivery

organisations, then you will create a sales force of many thousand advocates. The same applies to any well delivered channel model: a few good-quality channel or alliances personnel can manage relationships with many face-to-face sales organisations, who have their own effective professional sales forces, and you will gain penetration into their customers.

It's a simple time-honoured model and we see it everywhere across all industries. After all, retail is merely a channel model; CocaCola sell via a supermarket or a restaurant. It's a model that takes skill and subtlety. If you are 'once removed' from the actual customer/buyer, then you need to motivate the people who are dealing with them (in the context of this book, the personnel listed in Chapter 2) to push your agenda forward. So, well planned and generous programmes that allow your business partner (your route to market) to be successful are vitally important as well as making your company's products the easiest and best supported. More of this later. This is, in essence, what this whole chapter is about.

Objection 2: 'When our own skilled and focused employees – our sales representatives or technical account managers – are dealing directly with a customer and are in charge of a sales cycle, then we have greater control and a better chance of closing the sale.'

Overcoming this objection: It's true that, when it is your own personnel owning the sales cycle, you will probably have more knowledgeable people promoting the product, but this misses the point of why you are considering engaging with a channel: you want to leverage their network and contacts. While your organisation will be very adept at impressing the technologists and other department-head personnel, the consultant or systems integrator is probably dealing with the C-Suite. So, while they may not have the depth of product knowledge that your own sales and technical representatives have, they are offering you a greater chance of success because they are dealing with a level of the organisation that makes the important buying decisions and controls the large budgets.

It is also worth pointing out that 'knowledge' comes in many forms. While your own client-facing personnel will know your product, and often the immediate narrow market sector in which your products fit, better than the people who are 'selling' for you within a large influencer, it is still very likely that the large influencer personnel know the client, or the wider vertical market, or, more importantly, the business benefit better and so can position your product in the most effective and relevant way. It's a cliché, but the saying 'the man who knows *why* earns more than the man who knows *how*' is very true.

Objection 3: 'If I work with a third party such as a consulting firm, I will need to give away some of my margin either as resale or as a finder's fee, so I'm actually worse off.'

Overcoming this objection: First, I would take a look at the response to the two objections above. It's true that you may end up giving away some of the margin on each opportunity, but you can placate the sales guys giving you this objection by telling them that their chance of closure will be greater: 80% of something is better than 0% of nothing. If it is your CFO making the point, you can respond that it will be more-profitable business because the channel model has less fixed cost to maintain than a full-time sales force, and also that the better access to key decision makers will mean that revenue is likely to hit your books sooner as deals will get closed faster. But probably the best response to this objection is in the size of deals. Large IT influencers like global systems integrators and outsourcers sell big things to big companies, so your margin may be reduced, but the sizes of deals on which you are working will be far bigger.

Objection 4: 'Large systems integrators are very complex and therefore it takes longer to navigate to the correct people in the organisation, thus extending the sales cycle.'

Overcoming this objection: This is a fair point, but there is also risk in working directly with an end-user client and ignoring the systems integrator or outsourcer who is delivering the project. You may discover later in the sales cycle that they are required to sign-off on all technology (or related) decisions, or even that they need to take ownership or support each platform used. This could mean that your technology needed to be vetted, approved and, in some cases, acquired by the implementation or consulting partner, so there could potentially have been many hours wasted by not partnering with them. Additionally, the time argument is offset by the fact that the large systems integrator or consulting firm is likely to have the senior relationships that could minimise many pointless extraneous meetings socialising your product or solution with lower level stakeholders.

Key learning points: objections
1. Investment in a well executed alliance policy, far from being costly, will save money by extending reach and creating economies of scale.
2. Working with clients alongside and through alliance partners will not dilute your influence, but will increase your sales contacts and messages within the same client and give you a greater chance of success.
3. While incentivising a large IT influencer like a systems integrator will affect your margin, the increased average deal value and greater conversion percentage of your pipeline will justify that investment.

Establishing goals

It's a platitude to say that an alliance relationship needs to be a win–win and makes obvious sense, but what about when a congruent goal isn't obvious. If you are working with a large IT services company, such as consulting firm, in a traditional way (i.e. you are providing a product or niche service, they are providing services such as systems integration or project management), the win is easy to define: when the client places the order, both parties effectively make a sale and we go and celebrate.

But what about when you have sold the client the software many months or even years previously and the delivery services company is now competing for their share of the deal? Or what about if you have sold the large IT services company your product in the past and now they are taking it to market? You must be vigilant to show empathy, respect the fact that your goals are not aligned 100% and sacrifice time and effort for the longer-term good of the alliance. Likewise, it may be you that has the burning need, an end of quarter or a specific sales accelerator you want to hit and you want your influencer channel partner to help encourage the client to place the order; or, even better, maybe your channel partner will buy up-front to allow you to recognise revenue in a resale situation (unlikely, but you can make it worth their while with greater margin to cover the risk). In this scenario, you are relying on them to see the bigger picture and be good team players.

This level of empathy and shared goals takes time to establish, and re-enforces the point of this section: agree all of your goals and objectives from the relationship up-front. Document them, put timeframes on them and, where necessary, be specific and detailed about what precisely merits success. What follows is a list of what you should consider putting in an alliance plan with a large IT services company (see also Figure 5.1). It is not exhaustive and, conversely, may be too long a list (your expectations may be far more modest), but the following is probably a fair template for the typical types of metrics that both sides of the alliance relationships would regard as important in order to gauge the success of the alliance.

For the large IT services company:

Services revenue. This is their business and therefore their most basic of goals for the relationship. How will your relationship with them help them sell and deliver more and higher quality work by partnering with you? This may be what work is executed on your technology platform, or by using your financial products, or by providing add-on services to your services proposition.

	XYZ Software Co FY'00	Large IT services company FY'00
Revenue generated	$2m software	$10m services
Resale profit / fee revenue generated		$400k
Marketing development fund generated		$100k
Incremental lead generation	5	5
Accredited personnel		5 x technical architects
		5 x implementation personnel
		3 x sales personnel
Published joint credentials		2
Other goal	Regarded as strategic partner	Establish position as number 1 partner globally

Figure 5.1 Establishing goals: example overview.

Resale margin or fees. In the traditional VAR community, this is the number one goal. When working with large IT services companies, it will also be important for the reasons mentioned earlier, i.e. it allows them to drive more profit from the project that they can use to feed back to the client in discounts in order to be more competitive. It is in your interest to record this, as it is a powerful contributor to the story at the end of the year when reviewing the value of the alliance.

Marketing development fund (aka 'soft dollar'). Marketing funds are valuable to large IT services companies. While they benefit the alliance partner, as it compels the partner to spend time and money in investing in their alliance to generate more mutual business, it will also add profit to their bottom line because they offset marketing costs that otherwise would have impacted their profit.

Cost avoidance. This is a sub-set of the above. While marketing investment saves your services channel partners money from their bottom line, so does other cost avoidance, such as loans of demo hardware, subsidised product training or conference entrance fees, etc. Once again, though it may seem peripheral to the relationship overall, it is worth logging and recording and using in the final review at the end of the year because a pound saved by your partner is a pound earned.

For the technology OEM/alliance partner:

Product revenue. Assuming you are reading this as a technology OEM, the main interest that you have in the successful execution of the alliance is in the sales of your core product. As mentioned above, this could be services also.

Accredited personnel. Presumably you want to grow the skills for your product in the marketplace. It helps a better quality of delivery, and therefore greater customer satisfaction with your product, but also creates a bank of hungry, skilled resources that will require feeding for years to come. Consequently, you may choose to target, and record as one of your KPIs, the level of training commitment made by the services channel partner to support the sale and delivery of your product set.

For both parties:

Qualified leads. In essence, the whole idea of the alliance is that you can leverage one another's sales and marketing activity. Your alliance partner wants to be brought leads by your sales force as a sign of commitment and to repay the time and investment in them skilling up to sell and deliver the product. In turn, you, the alliance partner, will expect to be brought into new projects. It's not a truly profitable relationship if all the large IT services company is doing is delivering the business that you have created. So, it's an important metric for both parties and, if it is a positive story to tell, very little is more powerful in ensuring the annual review goes successfully and that key stakeholders, on whom you rely to invest in the alliance going forward, will be satisfied.

Joint wins, credentials (aka logos on the alliance deck). The thing that you both have in common is the pursuit of new business wins, not just for the obvious business benefits, but also because it adds a new client logo to the sales deck. It's a healthy joint goal, where possible, to be included in any comprehensive alliance plan.

Like all objectives, make them SMART (specific, measurable, achievable, relevant and time-bound) and regularly review with all interested parties and stakeholders (quarterly is traditional).

Key learning points: establishing goals
1. Like every aspect of an alliance relationship, goal setting and regular reviews of progress are essential to the long-term health of the alliance.
2. Don't make the list of goals and objectives too long. Concentrate on three or four for each party and, of course, make them SMART.
3. The rubber really hits the road when you are bringing opportunities to each other. Ultimately, this will be how the relationship is judged: what incremental business did we win because of our partnership?

Stakeholder management

Who are the key personnel involved in a typical project or sales pursuit? How do they differ from a traditional IT software or hardware company? Who holds the ultimate decision-making power? Who selects the products to be used? Who manages the commercials? Who runs the areas of the business for which you and your company's products are most relevant? You will never full understand the answer to these questions unless you have regular structured engagement at all levels of a large IT services company partner because most are complex, and a robust, methodical approach to stakeholder management is required to navigate their 'matrix organisation' model.

There's a good definition of this on businessdictionary.com: 'An organisational structure that facilitates the horizontal flow of skills and information. It is used mainly in the management of large projects or product development processes, drawing employees from different functional disciplines for assignment to a team without removing them from their respective positions.'

To the outsider this is a complex model, especially if you are not accustomed to it, but it is increasingly popular in all businesses. It requires patience, a methodical approach and ideally some good navigation advice, but it is logical and does create aggregation points where your key decisions and stakeholders are easy to pinpoint once you understand the structure. To explain the roles within a project would be going over the same ground that was covered in the 'Key Personnel' section of Chapter 3, also there is a more detailed view of governance (i.e. regular controlled contact with your key stakeholders) later in this chapter, but, as a high-level overview, your main stakeholders will probably fit into five important groups (see also Figure 5.2):

Stakeholder group	Typical role
Account-based	Sales executives, account managers, client leads (consultancy model), technical account managers
Project-based	Project manager, technical/solution architect
Executive	Managing director, relationship executive sponsor, alliance leads
Functional	Technical speciality lead, respective legal contacts, training lead
Vertical sector alignment	Vertical sector lead, vertical sector business development, vertical sector technical lead

Figure 5.2 Stakeholder categories.

Account-based. Large IT services company employees that are specifically aligned to a client with which you are also involved or wish to be involved.
Project-based. As above, but personnel connected with a particular project with which you are also involved or wish to be involved.
Executive (leadership). Senior management who may also be the executive sponsors for the alliance and are empowered to make important investment decisions around the alliance.
Functional. Key personnel who are aligned around particular product areas (e.g. the head of IT security) at your partner who would face off to the lead of your security products or specialist business areas, such as your partner's legal representative.
Vertical sector alignment. As most large IT services companies operate a vertical sector alignment model (industry knowledge depth is important in their proposition), it is important to align your own specialist sector heads if your organisation has a comparable role.

If sales and alliances is your goal in life, then it goes without saying that spending as much time in front of your customer as possible is desirable. This is a people business, after all, so use your team. The above represents many touch points that may exist within a serious alliance alignment, so, if you can achieve regular contact, it will increase your profile, develop the network of supporters within the client and also ensure that there are amenable relationships when the big opportunity or occasional problem comes along.

A key aspect of managing these relationships is an ongoing structured governance strategy (i.e. ensuring that these important stakeholders are constantly updated and appraised on the progress of the plan). It is a given that the alliance

108 Alliance best practice

Stakeholder group	Typical role
Account-based	Business update (mutual business in client) Account intelligence Progress on existing sales cycles New offerings to take to client
Project-based	Project specific milestones
Executive	Business update (key alliance metrics) Key deals Key mutual business development opportunities Roadblocks/issues to overcome
Functional	Business update (mutual business together) Product update Capability update (training and accreditation) Innovation
Vertical sector alignment	Business update (mutual business in sector) Sector intelligence Progress on existing sales cycles in sector New industry-specific offerings to take to client

Figure 5.3 Proposed review meeting content.

leads from the large IT services companies and their aligned partner(s) will be in regular contact and should develop a close working relationship, but, in addition to that, the governance model should include regular updates for the stakeholder groups listed above. In the case of executive engagement, this is typically quarterly, in the case of technical and functional stakeholders, this would be monthly. Mostly, sales and business development functions, such as vertical sector stakeholders and key account teams, should meet monthly and projects in delivery should meet as and when the project plan dictates.

The agenda will change based on the maturity of the relationship and the type of product that the alliance is based around, but will include the types of topics listed in Figure 5.3.

> Key learning points: stakeholder management
> 1. Identify your stakeholders (across both sides of the alliance) early and ensure that your strategy and approach is in line with the wider requirements of both organisations.
> 2. Implement a structured governance and reporting model to constantly monitor success and value to both organisations.
> 3. Your large IT services company alliance partner will probably operate a matrix organisation model, so take time to map out your relevant horizontal and vertical stakeholders.

Going to market

As discussed previously, arguably the most significant motivator in forging partnerships is to gain synergies from marketing joint solutions to your respective clients and prospects. This rarely happens without any encouragement or a concerted approach, so there are five obvious steps that you can take to help the process. Ultimately, this comes down to motivating sellers, so it's how successfully you achieve that which will dictate the success of the joint go-to-market sales activities.

Ensure that compensation for your own sellers reflects the importance of the partnership

Within your own business, the salespeople may well acknowledge the long-term benefit of working with a large influencer like an Accenture or a Deloitte, as they will be intoxicated by the client base that they can introduce to your salesperson, of course. They will also appreciate the credibility that comes from being associated with a larger brand; it's so much easier to making that initial contact when you can say you are calling as part of an arrangement with Fujitsu or IBM than saying you are calling from a lesser-known start-up.

But, in the thick of a deal, things are not quite as easy because clients will have their favoured delivery partner or will often just not value the partnership that you are bringing. In those circumstances, it is quite normal for you as the technology OEM or the smaller services player to forsake the partnership in order to take that client objection off the table, The other inhibitor for the salesperson is that, if the large influencer wants to act as the reseller of the product, you will be obliged to provide them with a discounted (trade) price. This can be quite substantial, say 30% or 40% for some software products, which is a large revenue hit for the salesman to take. One minute he's selling a £100,000 deal to a client and the next minute he's selling the same deal to the systems integrator, who's delivering the project for £60,000, and seeing £40,000 of his margin going to someone else. For someone who has a sales target linked closely to their earnings or retaining their job, this is a bitter pill.

The answer, of course, is to move the compensation model in your favour. Salespeople are conditioned to respond to incentives and if you are determined that your company strategy is an alliance with a particular consulting firm, systems integrator or outsourcer (or several of them), then you just need to tweak the sales compensation model to reflect that. At a simple level this means ensuring that the salespeople don't suffer any revenue degradation when the channel margin is applied. So, if the influencer is given a discount of 40% from list, then just compensate the salesperson at list price, not at the discounted price. The same applies to fees: don't take that from the deal value that the salesperson sees. If this is a truly strategic relationship in which you are committed to invest, you can also take the next step of providing accelerators, say a 20% or 30% uplift on sales revenue transacted through (or with) the alliance partnership that you are looking to nurture. This inevitably drives salespeople's behaviour. Be mindful of this sometimes driving the wrong sort of behaviour, because salespeople may be incentivised to over-complicate sales cycles to benefit from this uplift.

If you're reading this from within a large IT services company, and looking for tips to help your alliance thrive, the same rules apply. Either financially incentivise your personnel for service revenue that is delivered on a certain OEMs platform, or, if you (as is more likely) don't have a traditional commission model for your personnel, then build a volume of deals or sales revenue with a certain technology OEM into a sales executive's, client lead's or even technical architect's performance objectives.

Account mapping

The ultimate way to focus the mind on the opportunity between two potential partners is to start talking specifically about mutual and potential clients. It's likely that your original contact with the large IT services company was based on a sales lead or opportunity within a particular client, so there is already a connection with one particular client. It makes sense to explore the common ground with all of the others. There is no better way to do this than with a tool so beloved by consultancies: Venn diagrams (see Figure 5.4). These are three examples of different approaches:

Venn diagram 1. I have looked at established clients. This is helpful when identifying common ground, but possibly serves very little purpose because, in most cases, the technology OEM will already be successfully selling into that client and already have a delivery partner. So, unless they are looking to move their chosen delivery partner, or want to move into new areas of the account, this may not be a win–win. However, it will be interesting for the large IT services company who is looking to collect easy revenues for supporting the OEM's product or managing upgrades.

Venn diagram 2. I have shown potential target clients, i.e. where each party has aspirations to do business or maybe where they have a fledgling business that they want to develop. This is a valuable view of potential business together, though, if both parties just list companies where they have no relationships or traction currently, this can be a fairly academic 'wish list'. It's useful if there is a genuine belief that the relationship has a unique market relevant proposition and where identifying 'white space' clients is required.

Venn diagram 3. I have created the view that is most interesting for the technology OEM or niche service provider, as opposed to the established IT services player. This is where the large IT services company has successful relationships and where the alliance partner aspires to do business. This can be the most powerful for both parties as it is where the large IT services company has client relationships and credibility and where the technology OEM aspires to do business. So, it is a winning combination of using the brand of the big global consultancy or outsourcer and their relationships, combined with the incremental sales opportunity of the technology OEM's product to create a new sales opportunity.

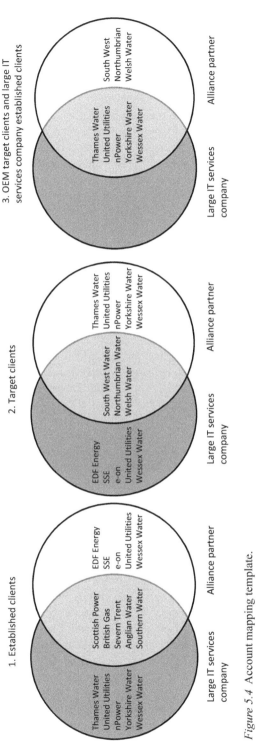

Figure 5.4 Account mapping template.

Bring a deal

As much as it is in everyone's interest for an alliance to be an egalitarian win–win, sometimes it requires a spark of selfless sacrifice to get things moving. A great example could be you benevolently bringing a new piece of business to your prospective alliance partner, i.e. introducing them to a client with whom you have an advanced sales cycle from which they can benefit.

Mostly. this is unnecessary. In my experience, a large percentage of alliances between a technology OEM and large IT services company are born because the OEM is in talks with a corporate client and the client instructs them to go and work with a specific large IT services company. There are several reasons why the client may do this. It could be that the delivery partner in question is owning a project, and the client wants them to qualify and effectively take the risk on the choice to use the OEM's technology. It could be that the client has a strict supplier management policy and only wants to work with approved suppliers and therefore wants to transact with the OEM or smaller partner via the contract with the delivery partner. Or it could be that the client feels that the technology OEM lacks the ability to execute, and wants them to partner with the large IT services company in order for them to gain the credibility to deliver. Whatever the reason, the alliance is often started because the OEM and the large IT services company are thrown together by the client.

This is excellent news for the technology OEM if they are looking to build a long-term alliance strategy with the large IT services company in question. From this initial introduction, relationships are made between key sales and delivery personnel on either side of the potential alliance. If the sales cycle progresses into a project, then skills are acquired by the delivery partner, resulting in (as described earlier) that partner being keen to monetise those skills by doing more business in the future with the OEM. Arguably most important, a credential is created. Large IT services companies like selling what they have sold before, partly because they have in-house experience so can manage the delivery in a cleaner way, partly because they can monetise their skills and partly because a previous delivery experience with a technology OEM means lower risk for them and in turn their client, meaning a safer engagement and a higher likelihood of a time-consuming sales pursuit being successful.

All in all, an established book of business is desirable. So, if it doesn't come naturally, you may have to make it happen by taking an existing warm deal on your sales forecast to the large IT services company to work with you. If they can be convinced by the product, their ability to deliver and monetise, plus the chance to develop their client relationships with a route into a new part of their business, will encourage them to jump at the chance and take the lead enthusiastically. This is not without pain for you if you're the technology OEM, as you may end up having to take a hit on margin if your partner wants to resell. Also, by bringing another variable into the sales cycle, another client objection may be created; so, a leap of faith and an appetite for investment is required, but only once both parties have that initial sales under their belts can the relationship flourish.

Awareness/training and collateral

If the respective sales and client-facing personnel are pivotal in promoting the joint solution, then not only do they need to be incentivised, they also need to be educated and supported. This can be summarised into three areas of activities and content.

1. Fully understand and document the win–win. We can go into the formalities of this later when talking about teaming agreements, but at a basic level this includes the alliance owners (may be full-time alliance people or related functional people or interested sales executives) meeting and agreeing a typical deal shape and who contributes what. Once this is established, it should hopefully be clear what is in it for each party (typical revenues for each party based on an average deal size) and, crucially, what is in it for the client. There may be other third parties that also benefit and in large complex companies there will also be different departments as well (say IT infrastructure and management consulting), so make sure they are in the mix. Document this output, it will become a vital document in the months and years ahead when articulating the background to the alliance at reviews and when meeting new stakeholders.
2. Once you know the advantages of the relationship, then create collateral and materials to be able to articulate it. A brochure should be a given, but also create a YouTube video, TCO tool, sales deck, white papers, microsite, working demo, etc. – whatever works for you. The important thing is to create materials to make it real.
3. Promote it. This comes in two flavours – internal and external. We will go into an internal comms strategy in detail in the next section, but suffice to say: a vital part of the process is ensuring that, once you have established the solution or collaboration and have documented it, there is minimal chance of success unless the people who are out there talking to the clients understand it and are able to 'sell it', or at least identify an opportunity for others to sell it later. In terms of external promotion, if the relationship is valuable to you, then use your current marketing plan to sell it hard. Include your alliance partner's name on your website and specifically reference a joint solution if you have one, create a press release, jointly demo at your chosen trade shows, and so on. This isn't a book about marketing, and that is a specialist area that changes constantly given the emergence of new social channels, but if you have invested the time and effort to get this far, then it is worth making the alliance a significant part of your story.

Show preference

This is a tough one. If you are an established brand with an established sales channel, then this is really tough. But here goes.

What will really make your name with a large IT services company is when you get off the fence and show preference for them . By which I mean, tell a customer that they are your preferred partner. Sometimes this is easy: (i) when the client is only talking to one delivery services company and there is no conflict; (ii) when the services partner that you want to back is more accredited, so it is ethically OK to back them above the competition; or (iii) if the services partner in question created the opportunity in the first place and assuming in all cases that you are not 'dominant' in your market in competition/anti-trust law terms. In all of these scenarios, it is ethical to show preference. You need to be secure on your legal footing, but there is no ethical dilemma in backing a particular player under those circumstances and you should be able to defend your position and retain your reputation for fairness in your channel strategy.

When it gets trickier is when there is a genuine channel conflict, i.e. when the client has selected your product or service and is now undertaking a competitive process to find a suitable delivery partner. You have a choice here: remain entirely neutral or pick one partner and make a friend for life. It's a risky strategy, but if you have set your heart and bet your alliance strategy on cracking a particular consultancy or systems integrator as your most important partner going forward, then this is as good a way as any to show your commitment.

This is usually articulated to the client as: 'We [the OEM] do a lot of work with this particular partner [the large delivery company]. While there are other partners that you might choose, we have not worked with them before, so we can't specifically recommend them, but we have worked with partner X, which means we have a successful precedent of working them.' In other words, you can use another partner with us, but there is a higher degree of risk.

Comms strategies and promoting your company within the large IT services company

As mentioned many times already, most of the large IT services companies are large complex, global organisations. So, how do their vendor partners ensure that they keep their profile high within the departments that are relevant to them? In the digital age, how can concepts such as enterprise social networking be utilised to give a partner organisation maximum exposure to relevant business groups and communities within a large IT services company? The truth is that even when you have established contact, integrated into a project or two and maybe even started doing business with a global influencer, you are still in an ongoing battle to establish yourself as the partner of choice. Even if you do have the best product in the world and have undertaken a successful track record of delivery with a particular alliance partner, there are so many projects going on at any one time within large systems integrators that most people will have no idea that this is the case and you will have no profile with them at all. Internally publicising your product and the success stories takes hard work, a combination of the old-fashioned approach of 'walking the halls' and using the various internal

Alliance best practice 115

comms mechanisms that exist within your partner company to promote your offering.

Remember, the large IT services companies employ (in some case) tens or hundreds of thousands of geographically dispersed personnel on thousands of clients sites, so they need very effective internal comms strategies to inform the various departments, project teams and communities of the company's news. It is these comms mechanisms that you need to understand and master if you want to get to the desktop of your potential stakeholders (see Figure 5.5). While we have spoken already about the key people in a deal or project delivery team, it should also be noted that almost everyone in the large IT services company is engaged in either talking to a client or working on behalf of a client on a daily basis, so can be a key influencer or channel for what you have to offer.

The whole issue of a successful marcomms plan merits a whole book in itself, but in four simple paragraphs, this is enough to get started:

1. **Establish your plan**. Within your alliance partner, to whom do you want to promote your message? What message do you want to promote? What is your objective? That is, what does a successful comms campaign into the large IT services company look like? Understand how that company promotes to their staff currently, and do what you can to find out why other companies like yours are being successful in getting their message across.
2. **Create collateral**. Think to yourself: if I wanted to understand my offering and be able to go and sell it, what would I need? Then create that collateral (see Awareness/training and Collateral section above). Then work out in what departments and communities your target audience work and find out what comms mechanisms they use to communicate with their personnel.
3. **Deliver the plan**. You know who you need to promote to, and you have the collateral so go ahead and do it. You need to get the correct network on board. If you have an alliance manager, they can help you with this, if not then

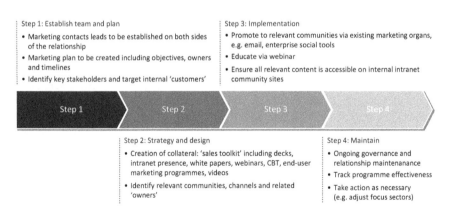

Figure 5.5 High level internal comms plan.

you will be reliant on your sponsor to introduce you to the relevant internal comms personnel that can help you to post your content on to the intranet or staff portal and push out the messaging via the comms engines – email, newsletters, enterprise social tools, putting up posters in the tea room, giving away cup cakes in the canteen, leaving postcards on seats – whatever works for your audience.
4. **Monitor and maintain**. Do everything you can to record progress and regularly feedback to your alliance contacts and/or sponsor. Let them know what is working and ask them for their help in doing more of it; after all, it benefits their business.

Then repeat. This is a journey that never ends. Staff attrition, the likelihood of messages not being read and the constant need to re-inforce sales messages means that this is the archetypal 'painting of the Forth Road Bridge' – once you finish, you go right back to the beginning and start again.

Key learning points: going to market
1. I cannot repeat enough times: the success of the joint sales motion, specifically how much truly incremental revenue that you mutually generate, will be the deciding factor in how you continue to get funding for your joint alliance strategy.
2. Ascertain a set of joint targets and clients and use your respective client relationships to leverage new sales for the partnership.
3. When you have been successful, shout about it, both internally and to the outside world.

Governance and tracking

Now that you have identified and established the correct contacts, it is of paramount importance to correctly track the health of the alliance and to use this governance to ensure consistent, ongoing 'buy-in' from all stakeholders.

The regular contact between stakeholders is the cornerstone of the relationship: it keeps visibility high, engenders trust, builds relationships and allows you to deal with issues and challenges before they become problems.

Each relationship will require a different level of connection, based on frequency and the method of meeting. It goes without saying that meeting face-to-face is always best, but considering busy diaries and transport costs, the pragmatic approach is often to arrange conference calls on, say, a monthly basis with face-to-face meetings achieved quarterly.

The matter of stakeholder management has been covered previously, so does not need repeating here, but it stands to reason that some relationships need frequent and brief touch points, whereas senior-level executive sponsorship (say, CEO to CEO) will be in the quarterly/half-yearly timeframe.

Each stakeholder meeting will have a different emphasis and set of priorities, but you will want to consider as a minimum the following important points to ensure that the relationship is progressing:

Metrics. How is the relationship performing to the targets set by each party? As discussed previously, each partner will have different needs and goals from the alliance. This will always come down to business revenue generated, but also issues such as client satisfaction could apply.

Delivery. Where we are working together, are things going OK? Do we have a happy mutual client? Are the projects delivering what we need? Are there any risks? In truth, this will usually be addressed by project management as part of the project, as opposed to the alliance discussions, but a heads-up to the overall quality of the work you are doing together is important.

Business development. What can we do to generate more business together? This may entail new products that your partner needs to be made aware of. It may entail a new project that your partner has recently won in which their partner would like to be involved.

Roadblocks. This is often the most important agenda item of all. What is inhibiting the business? If there are senior people in the room, it can be the most important item too, as the chance to have people available who are able to make a difference, and approve that piece of funding or lend their weight behind a meeting that isn't happening, can be invaluable.

Forecast. What is the sales forecast? What business can we look forward to together in the coming weeks and months? In particular, what can the people do as a team to make the deals happen?

Skills/accreditations. Monitoring the skills and accreditations held is an ongoing task. Are the skills relevant? Are they up-to-date and, most importantly, when compared to the pipeline projection, is there enough cover for the new business?

Milestones. Are things moving at the pace that everyone needs in order to hit the annual plan? If not, what should we do? It will usually entail extra focus or investment, but it's better to establish that now than at the end of the year when goals have been missed and relationships are on the line.

Next steps. So what happens next? We have identified the problems and the opportunities. Let's ensure that someone is owning all of the actions to make sure that the plan is moved forward and commitments met before next time we meet.

Regular governance is the cornerstone of the relationship. If neglected it can mean that the relationship loses the momentum you have created and all of the good work up to this point is wasted. Whereas regular governance, backed up by clear, accurate statistics where colleagues/partners can understand their role and how they can help, will ensure business plan success. Of course, governance will not be executed successfully without authority and this is where executive sponsorship becomes essential; escalation to ensure that a business plan is being delivered by all relevant parties is often necessary.

118 *Alliance best practice*

> Key learning points: governance and tracking
> 1. Be disciplined about your governance and do all that you can to accommodate all key stakeholders, but do not wait to have the full list there. Maintaining momentum with regular meetings is more important than a full meeting room.
> 2. Strive to make the governance model peer-to-peer so that the correct tone is set for the alliance.
> 3. Use the regular connections to cover the main metrics of the relationship, but also use the seniority of the people in the room to remove roadblocks in the relationship and get things done.

The alliance partner's perspective: Gavin's story

Gavin has worked for many years in various market-leading technology companies at a senior alliance level, owning relationships with the major systems integrators, consulting firms and outsourcers. Here, he explains his experience and how he sees working within this sector from the perspective of the alliance partner.

> When it comes to partnering with the large global IT services companies, the analogy I use is that of an aircraft carrier. The aircraft carrier is the most potent fighting force on the planet, but not the most manoeuvrable. So, if you're trying to get an aircraft carrier to sail up a small estuary to dock in a little local harbour, it isn't going to happen. If you're trying to get one to do a U-turn on a sixpence, it isn't going to happen either, but if you get it pointed in the right direction, that thing is going to blow everything out the way and I think that happens when you get someone like IBM, Accenture, Capgemini etc. focused and standardised on your technology. We had that when I was at a previous software company; one of the large integrators standardised a whole delivery function on the technology and we pretty much won every deal together. In the end, we were acquired by a much larger player, which spoiled things somewhat, but it was great while it lasted. In that case, we did such a good job at making ourselves relevant and culturally aligning, it turned into a bona fide practice within the partner.
>
> But it's not just about scale of projects. It's also about reach within the end-user client. My large systems integrator partners can get to C-level executives in a way that I, as part of a medium-sized technology vendor, will struggle to. We'll get bounced down to IT or procurement. The large systems integrators are outwardly agnostic, so you can drive a completely different discussion in the client if you can harness their approach. Delivery capability is probably the third benefit: taking a great product and standardising, globalising, setting up offerings that we can deliver at scale and in a consistent fashion. Your product can then truly become a solution.
>
> In my time, though, I've worked at other technology vendors where it wasn't as cut and dried. At one, we had a huge debate, about whether the timing

was right for a partnership with the large global systems integrators, down to two fundamental issues. The first was technical: we didn't have data centres in Europe, so a number of vertical markets were completely off limits and certain countries too. Such is the perceived importance of having customer data in the region. The second issue was a commercial consideration: the absence of a clear revenue opportunity for the partner, because the SI is often more interested in the service upside than the ability to resell the technology itself. To address both issues simultaneously, we built a platform approach to show how our solution plugs into the wider ecosystem of applications which the SIs are investing in (e.g. the salesforce ecosystem). This helped move the discussion with those SIs to a much more strategic basis, focusing on client business value from an end-to-end solution stack rather than features of an individual product.

What really mattered in this instance was our ability to tailor our solution pitch to the SI community and their own delivery priorities. Technology vendors clearly each have their standard pitch, but this is simply not enough to turn up with at a large SI. You have to turn it into something relevant; you have to change the language. For example, don't talk about deals and transactions in quarter, talk about how the solution assists with client value and the transformational agenda. You also have to be crystal-clear on where the services revenue opportunity comes from, as tech resale is usually not enough in its own right.

I like to think I have grown to understand the drivers and motivations of client teams within the large SIs well. One of the most successful programmes I was involved with was when working for a large cloud services provider. We closed a significant opportunity in a net-new client that was sourced, nurtured and closed by the SI, involving the vendor sales team literally to close out commercial terms at the end of the process. It was a huge incremental win for us at an important client for the SI. It came about because a middle manager on the SI client team saw an opportunity during an awareness session we delivered to position our technology to accelerate the digital transformation changing the way the client was working. This took over a year to close, but led to the creation of a repeatable offering and a pseudo practice which we could then leverage to drive further opportunities. The value of this first reference win cannot be overstated, as few client leads want to be the first one to take the plunge with a new technology!

When I think of the process to getting a deal like this done, I think the vendor alliance manager has a key role to play in bridging what is often a culture gap between the technology vendor and the SI. SI practitioners tend to be different animals from vendor sales guys, with the former focused on long-term relationship and value creation and the latter typically goaled on in-quarter revenue, which can lead to short-term thinking or even a 'hit and run' mentality. The alliance manager tends to focus more on the big picture, the long-term relationship with the SI, and is typically goaled on driving a sustainable stream of revenue versus a 'one-hit wonder' deal. We're looking to build something rather than just sell something. The proof-point is when you're able to move to a new company with a new solution set and call on the same contacts at the SI again because of what you were able to build together in the past. That makes me feel good about what I do. It's not always easy, of course, so the key is really to maintain close proximity with the sales teams on both sides ensuring expectations are clear from the outset and that progress toward the deal (through the ups and downs) is governed appropriately without anyone lapsing into 'short-termist' behaviour, which could derail the long-term alliance momentum.

Despite the big deal we closed at this particular vendor, I wouldn't say we ever really 'cracked it' with that SI. The fit between our solution and the various SI practices was never quite strong enough to enable repeatability at scale.

If I think about that long-term alliance momentum, I think about a two-year process split into three phases. The first phase is awareness creation, driving sessions with people you know (or get to know) and conveying where your solution plays, how it links with the SI's existing offerings and, hopefully, hooking an architect (ideally someone relatively senior) who sees potential value for their client. This gives you a chance to road-test the value proposition in the field.

The second phase, which is probably 6–12 months in, is all about enabling the alliance to function smoothly and scale; for example, getting a formal alliance agreement in place, enabling resale and formalising service delivery capabilities and the support infrastructure needed. Getting the right executive support within the SI is key here; someone from the practice, not just the alliances function. Then the third phase is about cranking the handle and turning those initial wins into repeatable offerings that begin to drive demand as a function of their success. This could take the form of a formal commercial relationship, like a 'joint initiative' or 'joint venture', or, at the very least, a set of offerings that both parties get behind with joint collateral and go-to-market commitments.

Of course, there are no guarantees that the process will go to plan, and it is fair to say the larger SIs are definitely the hardest to crack. However, the rewards are significant, given the power and strike force of the 'aircraft carrier' mentioned earlier, coupled with the value for the alliance manager in terms of career progression and market reputation.

I would make an additional comment on how the market is also evolving in terms of the opportunities for smaller, agile vendors (notably in the cloud sector) to make an impact with the larger SIs, who perhaps previously would have been tough to reach, preferring instead the trusted blue-chip players.

Nowadays, with clients under pressure to innovate, and cloud technology disrupting even established markets like ERP, it's totally possible for a hot new player to aspire to meet with senior executives at the major SIs – providing they are clear on the proposition and how it fits, in line with the process discussed earlier. Being 'hot' can get you the first meeting, but the second and subsequent meetings come from being structured and aligned.

To sum up, if I were the GM of a hot new start-up with a great product, and one of my team came to me and said they were going to 'break into' Accenture or Capgemini, the advice I'd give would be very clear: we're not breaking in anywhere until we've mapped how our solution fits within their practices and thought through how they can drive revenue as well as us. This is not the feedback which sales people like to hear, but it is unfortunately what they need to heed if they want to drive anything meaningful and sustainable with the partner and get that particular aircraft carrier fuelled and armed and sailing in the right direction.

Key learning points: Gavin's story
1. Research and understand the priorities and focus areas of the partners you want to work with and how your solution fits in. Think about how the solution owners in the partner can drive client value and also advance their own standing by working with your solution.
2. The path to a functioning alliance typically takes two years. Focus early efforts on trying to identify an early-adopter sponsor who is senior enough to make stuff happen (but not too senior as to be tough to maintain focus with). Invest resources to land that first joint win, even a small one, as nothing sells better than a reference.
3. Today's technology trends have opened up opportunities for smaller vendors to gain traction with the largest partners, but the fundamental process steps of linking the product to the partner's ecosystem and offerings must still be followed.

6 Innovating with global systems integrators, outsourcers and consulting firms

Why does it happen?

Why is mutual innovation and asset development relevant to the alliance, and how does creating repeatable solutions result in long-term, loyal, profitable relationships?

First, let's set the rules here. Businessdictionary.com has a good definition of innovation in a business context:

> The process of translating an idea or invention into a good or service that creates value or for which customers will pay. To be called an innovation, an idea must be replicable at an economical cost and must satisfy a specific need.

I like this definition because it doesn't stipulate that the idea must be new. More importantly, the emphasis is on the invention being useful and marketable, and it also mentions 'replicable', or repeatable, which is the crux of why partners want to innovate as a key aspect of alliance strategy.

So, as an OEM or prospective partner, what is in for you to have an innovation agenda with your prospective large IT services company alliance partner?

- Fundamentally, it reminds them why they need you. As discussed in Chapter 2, the technology consultancy, systems integrator or outsourcer needs your product or service to make their offering 'whole' to their client. They provide their core services, but, enterprise solutions being what they are, they also require various components, so they need to partner. Innovating with any alliance partner is rubber stamping that fact. It's an acknowledgement that you are better together and they need you to create solutions and business outcomes.
- It helps you to differentiate yourself in the eyes of the large IT services company, which adds significantly to your value. If you are creating exciting, productive and relevant products and services together then they are probably using IP or facilities that only you have, so it is intrinsically marking you out as essential.
- It helps for you to be seen as a thought leader. Consultancies especially are judged on thought leadership and how they are pushing the agenda; their customers come to them not only to execute, but also to tell them how to do things.

If you can be seen to be helping that process by adding to the knowledge capital within the consultancy, you will become an even more valued partner.
- Repeatability, repeatability, repeatability. Mainly, it comes back to that word. If you create something with a large IT services company, in particular with a technology solutions business like a systems integrator, and you have a reference case (ideally a client implementation) that is working successfully, then you have become part of the fabric of that organisation and how they go to market. You have become the answer to their client's problem. Repeatability will ensure stickiness with your new alliance partner.

So it's obvious what's in it for you, the potential partner, it's about becoming more entwined in the offerings of the large IT services company, which automatically makes you the 'go to' for them. But what is in for them to innovate with you? The reasons are mostly common sense, but my reminding you of them will help you know how to position your proposed innovation or joint solution when the time is right.

- They will obtain new ideas from you. Simple as that. They get to leverage your R&D spend; they get to access your people and their knowledge; and they get to utilise your market insight. In any innovation agenda, the involvement of third parties is essential to bring additional knowledge and perspective. The large IT services companies know this and will welcome your involvement.
- Unique solutions are more profitable. For instance, the more innovative and specialist a systems integrator can make a solution, the less likely it is to be copied or easily replicated. Therefore, it can't become commoditised and the price will remain fair for all parties. Large IT services companies are like all businesses under price pressure, particularly with commoditisation of technology delivery services from off-shore providers, so there is a significant desire to create solutions for clients' problems that are not freely available and easy to commoditise.
- As mentioned above, clients value thought leadership. and it is a motivator for working with consulting firms: they want to access their wealth of knowledge and insight. By providing this, they become more respected and important to the client, so they know that bringing new ideas to the client will help them to remain an important partner. Often, the key value to the consultancy here is that it will help in heading off the competition from an account.
- Working with third parties to create new technology solutions will often bring a large IT services partner into new areas of a client and their business, so the arrangement may help them break into a new department, geography or set of contacts in addition to those they currently work with by providing only their core services. This is a general partnership question and has been covered previously, but it's worth repeating here: the creation of new assets will broaden your partner's offerings and appeal.
- In respect of staff engagement and education, innovation is interesting work. Not all personnel are motivated by money, security, recognition or any other

of the obvious reasons why we choose to work where we do. A major reason can be the desire to do interesting and challenging work. Working on innovation projects helps staff to improve their skills, be creative, be part of something cool, increase their value by being involved in something at the outset. So, a keen innovation agenda will help to motivate and retain good quality personnel.
- Last, but not least, being cool is a good thing. Clients come to the large technology delivery companies very often because they are scalable to the massive challenges that global transformation requires in an enterprise. This is, of course, their core business and essential to them prospering, but the digital revolution and the shift in businesses' desire to differentiate by providing unique digital customer experiences means that it is the cool solutions that can be front of mind for the large enterprises. It's important that their large technology partners align themselves to this new paradigm (more of this later) and innovation in all its forms is certainly part of the answer.

So, for your partner, it's about differentiating themselves in the market and creating new, exciting things for clients to buy. In the process, they need to generate incremental, profitable business while helping their image in front of clients, investors and their own personnel. But what drives the innovation in the first place? After all, it would be easier to continue doing business in the way that we know works and where we have skills already.

Partly, it's down to new product innovation. When there is a new technology development (say 3D printing or autonomous cars) the game changes, so the large IT services company needs to get to work immediately to identify the business value and the business use cases, and work out how an enterprise can take a new product innovation and turn it into extra efficiencies or new revenue streams. This will require a consultative approach to establish the need, and then a plan to transition to the new model – the core competency of a large consultancy or systems integrator. Often, it will be an industry or regulatory change that will fire the innovation agenda. A good example would be the additional regulation brought into the banking sector following the collapse in 2008. Significant process and system changes forced the financial services sector to change the way they were conducting their business, meaning that new ideas and process engineering was necessary to have a competitive edge within the new rules. Finally, and of equal importance, clients need a new angle. The world changes fast as a consequence of consumer adoption brought by technology, globalisation, environmental change and many other macro-economic events, so the large companies that serve them need to be ahead of the game in finding new ways to service the new consumer buying trends. It is the large consulting firms to whom they normally turn to guide that journey.

So, constantly evolving and innovating is essential for the large consultancies, systems integrators and outsourcers to stay relevant, attract customers and drive profit; but how does it happen? Even assuming you have the right relationships and contacts to make it happen, what is the right process to drive an innovation agenda?

> Key learning points: Why does innovation happen?
> 1. If you are planning to build a long-term partnership, it is in your interest to create 'stickiness'. Your solution becomes woven into the fabric of your partner and then you are a key component of their go-to-market message.
> 2. As part of a win–win between you and a large IT services company partner, they rely on you to bring new technology innovation to the table that they can enhance and re-package to increase their credibility.
> 3. Commoditisation is squeezing margins for all. Differentiated innovations help both sides of the alliance partnership equation to offer a product that isn't under extreme price pressure from the competition.

How does it happen?

What are the steps to innovating in an alliance partnership? Who are the key drivers and what are their considerations and motivation? Once created – how do you mutually take your innovation to market and how do you measure success?

We have established that a successfully executed innovation agenda is beneficial to the client and the large IT services company, but this book is about how you work with those organisations and make yourself more valuable to their business. While there is an inherent need and enthusiasm by the end-user client and their services delivery or consultant business partner to innovate, very often it will be up to you to make sure that it's your products and services are the ones forming the solutions. So, let's look at the people within your alliance partner that will help you to integrate into the innovation agenda. In most cases they will be the familiar contacts that you are already working with. It's a question of convincing them of the wisdom of making the investment to create joint assets with your company.

Innovation lead. If you're lucky, your prospective partner will have an innovation lead. Assuming that you can get an audience with this person, then they will be best placed to explain on which criteria their organisation selects partners for joint innovation, and then the process around which they select and execute an innovation project to create a new joint asset. The innovation lead will also then act as, or allocate, a sponsor for the engagement and assist you in connecting with all of the relevant personnel to make the project happen.

Leadership. As part of the ongoing executive governance, it is likely that innovation and mutual asset development will be assessed. As discussed, innovation is important to your partner, so it's likely that the executive sponsorship for the alliance will want to know how you are bringing them new ideas and routes to market. Of course, this senior-level patronage can also help you with the inevitable roadblocks and objections that will occur as you look to push through your innovation strategy.

Alliance lead. This person is always in your corner. They will be goaled on joint innovation and, like the innovation lead, will have the right motivation, contacts and remit to guide you through the legal, political and practical hurdles.

Ambitious technical staff. It is the technical staff that are often most energised and excited by the new creativity and innovation that technical advancements bring. They are normally more knowledgeable and aware of new technology and its benefits. Also, as discussed in the previous section, interesting and exciting work such as innovation projects helps to retain technical personnel – so, the more senior and ambitious technical resources within an organisation will welcome cool and creative projects as they look to develop their skills and job satisfaction.

Vertical industry-focused leadership. As innovation is so frequently addressing specific industry drivers or regulation, the vertical sector executives within the consulting firms are often the most enthusiastically behind any answers to specifically industry-focused business needs. Whether it's measuring oil being dug out of the ground by an energy company or processing parking fines more swiftly by a local authority, the appeal of taking a client a new way of doing business is essential to continue generating fees from that client.

So, innovation looks like most engagements in that it's about establishing who, and then how you get to them. The difference with innovation is that success may be measured slightly differently. While the logical methods of measuring success apply – revenue, new client wins, staff utilisation, profit margins – all of which can be helped by the right approach to innovation, it is also important to measure the success of innovation in other ways; for instance, PR. If an idea or solution is new or revolutionary enough, it will generate column inches or TV coverage, which means that the protagonists will be able to showcase their thought leadership. It will also lead to closer engagement and feedback from clients who respect the consultancy or service provider (and by association their partners, of course) for bringing them the game changing idea and competitive edge. In other examples: attracting awards can be the result from clever or well executed innovation, meaning impressed clients and happier shareholders; and, as discussed already, colleague engagement will always benefit from exciting work and public recognition, resulting in happier and more motivated staff and greater staff retention – a key challenge for the sector.

Key learning points: how does innovation happen?
1. As ever, identify and map out the key stakeholders. Among other questions, ask: Who has most to gain? Who holds the budget?
2. The people with whom you work on a specific industry-focused innovation may be outside of your usual sphere of contacts, which can be a happy by-product of investing in innovation with your partner.
3. There are lots of intangibles to innovation creation, such as the job satisfaction of technical staff, so be clear to map out all of the benefits before making your pitch and think outside of the box from the more obvious new business origination angle.

Who does what and what are the legal considerations of joint innovation?

What are the roles of various alliance partners during the innovation process? What is reasonable to expect in terms of investment and shared risk in asset creation? What are the standard models for managing IP issues and shared risk in project delivery? Also, what is the protocol around exclusivity and what are the legal considerations around competition law when creating assets and going to market together?

The following is a guide and proper legal input is required, but here are the bare minimum considerations from a process and legal standpoint. Every case will be different and will differ greatly based on your resources vs the resources of your potential innovation partner. For instance: Is the client involved? Is it bespoke for a specific client need? What are the dynamics of the deal and the restrictions created by the size of budget? The important thing, as ever, is to strive for a win–win and, while not every agreement around joint innovation has to be so water-tight that it restricts the frontier spirit of innovation, it's a good idea to cover the likely eventualities and to establish expectations up-front.

Probably the most sensible way forward is a teaming agreement. It isn't as heavy as a full contract, but it is usually more detailed than a memorandum of understanding. It gives you the chance to call out who does what as early as possible and allows protection to all parties. As mentioned above, all situations are different and will require different terms, but at a high level, the main components for a teaming agreement to cover joint asset development would be:

Investment to develop. Who does what in the development of the asset? Who will commit the human resources that will be required? What physical resources, such as hardware, software and facilities, are required and who is best placed to provide them? If a war-chest of money is required, who contributes what and how is the money accounted for?

Confidentiality and security. However close and successful the relationship, the issue of confidentiality will be insisted upon by leadership and legal departments before any joint development or go-to-market activity occurs, so a mutual NDA will need to be signed, either separately or embedded into the teaming agreement.

Rights in the IP of the solution. This is something which you should consider and discuss up-front because ownership/licencing rights to the asset will underpin the value proposition. Don't just leave it to the legal team to sort out, have some principles thought through and agreed up-front. The agreement as to ownership and licencing will have consequences for who has the right to exploit the asset (and, for example, to apply for patent protection). What will happen should your relationship dissolve? What will happen if your company, or the partner with whom you're innovating, wanted to recognise it as an asset with value in their accounts? While joint ownership can seem like a fair compromise, in practice it is complex to administer and operate joint ownership; and joint ownership can in fact end up diminishing the intrinsic value of the asset. So, it may make sense for one party to prime and the other to have strong licence rights.

IP of existing assets of the respective companies. This is subtly different from the above point as it is pertains to the IP that you already own which gets embedded into the solution. While happy to see it used in this innovation, presumably both parties wish to retain their pre-existing IP, so this principle should be clear in the teaming agreement and, ideally, the pre-existing IP should be identified to avoid any later argument.

Licencing. This is similar to the IP question. When the 'product or service' is created, how is it licenced to the client and what is the mechanism for ensuring that the client is correctly supported going forward?

Liabilities. Who is accountable for any losses, accidents or client costs in the event that the product malfunctions, or is the subject of an IP infringement claim, or causes financial or actual physical harm to either party or the client's business?

Licencing and pricing. How do you price the invention? Presumably it won't be entirely 'off the shelf', so how is customisation factored into the agreement? What happens in the event of a price negotiation? Who owns revenue streams such as support costs? Most importantly, when the solution is sold, how does each company in the consortium make money?

Go-to-market strategy. There will no doubt be an additional sales and marketing plan to support the asset creation, so this should be referred to in the teaming agreement along with a high-level view of the way in which you will be attracting and supporting new business associated with the invention. It should cover matters such as the target sectors, whether a dedicated sales force will be created, and so on. It is not necessary to go into the minutiae of the sales and marketing strategy in the teaming agreement, just a sense of the high-level approach so that the expectations are not a surprise to either party. It's also important to establish and agree the arrangements for covering the costs of all sales and pre-sales investment.

Disqualified customers. It is likely that each party will have certain clients, countries or vertical sectors that they don't want to cover. This should be called out in the teaming agreement (or probably as an addendum if there is a list) together with what the other parties will do if this occurs in order to service this business. This situation can work both ways. It may be that you or your innovation partner are not permitted to do business in a particular client or highly selective sector, such as defence, so it makes sense to understand how that is addressed when it arises.

Cross-border business. Who will execute sales, marketing, support and so on in the event of a multinational client that has offices in countries not currrently covered by you, your partner or any other essential elements of the solution consortium? Managing this issue is one of the reasons why you want to work with the large IT influencer sector, of course, to leverage their global reach, but it's important to establish the ground rules.

Peripheral business. If the client buys the solution and then chooses to work with you or your innovation partner on work that is not directly related but arose as a consequence of the initial sales (in which you have both invested), is there any obligation on the other party to share that upside?

Resale and ownership. If the project has a 'prime', it is wise to establish under what terms they will acquire the products and services that the other (subordinate) party provides as part of the solution. Once again, this is likely to be a complex matrix and so is best addressed in an addendum or appendix, but it should be referred to at a high level in the document. If delivering a managed service, the same rules apply. It is wise to have the full price list established for, say, a cloud service such as IaaS or SaaS established up-front.

Personnel matters. Are named individuals a condition of the agreement? If so, they should be called out and alternatives given to cover if and when they are not available. It is also smart to agree on what is the protocol around poaching of staff, subject to local applicable employment law.

Exceptions and disputes. While everyone enters an agreement with the best intentions and with a clear idea of how the sales, delivery and support will pan out, clients have a habit of asking difficult questions. A good example of this may be: 'Well, I like your software and I love the idea, but I refuse to buy from [insert name of any partner here].' What happens? Is everyone obliged to walk away, or does your alliance partner accept it and altruistically encourage you as the technology provider (or finance company or services provider or whatever) to go ahead with the project using a different services delivery partner? It happens a lot. A client will not have the same view toward every company in the consortium. These are very difficult decisions and it may be wise to pre-agree what will happen in these circumstances, or, at a minimum, provide for a dispute resolution forum.

Other things you may want to consider. What is the term of the agreement and what happens to the innovation asset after that? What happens in the event that one of the parties is bought or goes out of business? What happens to the asset in the event of a termination from either party?

While I advocate the use of a teaming agreement, I can't stress enough the need to seek correct legal advice as early as possible.

Key learning points: who does what and what are the legal considerations of joint innovation?
1. Agree a strong teaming agreement up-front and consider as many of the eventualities as you can.
2. Take advice as required to ensure that any agreement you make is in compliance with applicable law (e.g. competition law or employment legislation).
3. Pay particular attention to the possibility that the client may not want to deal with one of the partners in the partnership and how you will handle this.

Innovation: a footnote

It was Steve Jobs who said that 'innovation comes from people meeting up in the hallways or calling each other at 10:30 at night with a new idea, or because they realised something that shoots holes in how we've been thinking about a problem'. This isn't a book about innovation or about company culture per se. but there's a footnote about innovation within the technology sector and the new digital sector that deserves to be made. In this chapter, I've concentrated on the importance of doing it right when it comes to innovation and about stakeholder 'buy-in', process, legal rules and the arcane issues of IP, but, in fact, the culture of innovation is meant to be far less constrained. We will look at the impact of Industry 4.0, the dawn of digital and what that means for the IT services sector, but, spoiler alert, the future of innovation will be about speed, taking risks and doing things differently.

In my own dealings with the large IT services companies and their partner companies, the ones that are making an impression have a few cultural common denominators that mean their innovation agenda is working. Her are a few of them:

Be bold. The technology sector and its impact on companies and consumers is moving so fast that it's necessary to take greater risks and grander statements to make an impression.

Eradicate blame and create an environment where it's OK to fail. Success in the digital world will entail new, creative ideas to make the most of the new waves of technology available, such as harnessing the power of social networking, working out what to do with the vast amounts of data that we have and maximising the fact that everyone is now walking around with a mobile phone. Therefore, brave decisions around direction and investments will need to be made. A conservative culture will stifle the out-of-the-box thinking and execution that will be required.

Enthusiasm and belief. New, bold, risky ideas do not sail through organisations unchallenged; they require passion and belief. Lots of hurdles will be put in your way, so you must show significant desire to take the necessary risks and extra effort to really change the game.

It must happen fast. If an idea takes months to get through approval processes, lawyers, budget reviews and support from all levels and stakeholders, the moment will be missed. If you have a good idea, get the support you need to fund it and go ahead, others will be carried along with you. If you procrastinate, you'll lose the first-mover advantage or the wider market will move on and your idea won't make a difference.

There must be a win–win. This is alliances 101; it must look right for all partners before going ahead. That means sharing risk, investment, sales effort, marketing spend, development costs and all of the other facets of inventing and then going to market. And, of course, you need to share the spoils. As always, the alliance must be a case of $1 + 1 = 3$ for the experience to enhance the wider relationship.

> Key learning points: common denominators of successful innovation
> 1. Forget the blame culture and encourage people to take risks.
> 2. What are you waiting for? If it's a good idea, someone else will figure it out and you've missed your chance, so remove the barriers that stop things happening.
> 3. Win–win or no deal. Just because pace and speed are a factor, don't forget to ensure that everyone benefits.

The innovation partner's perspective: Ali's story

Ali (real person, fake name) is an experienced and accomplished alliance lead at a new economy digital vendor. Ali's background is managing large, complex alliances with consultants, outsourcers and systems integrators. Here, Ali talks about his experience of innovating with a large IT services company and what he has learned.

> I first started working with systems integrators in 2000 at the height of the original dot com boom. I've always found innovating and creating joint solutions hugely important. Back then I was working for a fairly niche medium-sized software company, looking after a couple of partnerships: a large consulting firm and a large technology OEM/services company hybrid. They were fairly new associations, so it was mostly about getting out and developing relationships to help them understand the value of the product I was offering. I found that creating joint assets was a really effective way to create traction and it's stuck with me.
>
> The lowest cost of sale for the maximum return is clearly the primary driver for innovating and creating repeatable solutions together. Having something we could mutually drop into a number of clients and demonstrate some IP to a client and something they can spin up very quickly is one reason. However, I think there is also a personal angle here too. My successful innovations and joint solutions usually occurred when someone inside that systems integrator could attach their name to a joint asset, because it could be very powerful for their career. If an asset is successful, and they are associated with that success and the profitability that comes from selling it on multiple occasions on a lower cost of sale each time, then that's certainly goodness for them.
>
> Any company or alliance has the ability to innovate. It's more about who's going to step up and think 'look, I have got a good idea; lets test it out, let's take it to market'. I worked for a boss at a large analytics software company who was good at saying: 'If you think you've got a good idea, put a business case together and just take it forward and make it your own.' He was absolutely right. I have done a lot since; that empowerment and executive support is really helpful.
>
> When it comes to building a successful alliance, the holy grail for an alliance manager can be something that's less tangible, like having a contractor's

badge to get into your partner's building. Because you're in the throes of creating something together, you're suddenly attached to an asset that you can take right across a large systems integrator. It gives you a position to go and broaden your personal relationships, and that makes you more valuable to the company you are working for, and potentially for the company that you could be working for next.

One of the challenges I encountered was funding, which seems strange considering the size of the companies I was looking to partner and build solutions with (i.e. the large global consulting firms, systems integrators and outsourcers). The reason is that everyone inside an organisation like Accenture or Delloitte or IBM Global Services is billable, so the joint solution has to become a passion project. You're relying on what we talked about earlier: does your contact want to get recognised for developing or creating an asset and taking it forward? We had scenarios with people at one large outsourcer, around a retail solution, where we thought we had some great assets to bring our solution together, but we couldn't get the asset off the ground because the executive who was sponsoring it left the firm (because he couldn't get the promotion he wanted) and the solution just withered on the vine.

The large systems integrators like to say they are fast followers and, if there's a market to be made, they can run and dominate it, but in reality they don't do that. In my experience, the biggest thing with creating assets for innovating is having a primed customer. Every time we have done it successfully, there's been a customer that has been ready to buy and who has been driving the development. I look back to one engagement when I was working for the large analytics software company that I mentioned earlier. We created an asset that was an analytics platform, purely based on our technology. The consulting firm that I was partnered with sold it to a large pharmaceutical company. It was the first time in our history as a software OEM that we had stood up what was essentially a cloud environment and changed our software billing mechanism to a subscription model slightly to suit that cloud model. The reason we were successful was that when we sold that initial deal to the large pharmaceutical company, we ended up doing a lot of public social media, a lot of interviews in the trade press and putting together lots of joint collateral, such as ROI [return on investment] models and sending them round internally within the consulting firm. The real success came when the other client managers for the outsourcer could see that there was an existing infrastructure that they could put clients straight on to, so they didn't bear a massive cost of entry. We put a lot of collateral together around both partnership and the asset. The messaging was about risk reduction. The partners of the firm really went for it as it was a proven asset in the field and there was a customer running already. Also, there was a clear proven ROI, so they could see the route to the return. The internal promotion didn't come easily though. There was a lot of shoe leather, as you would call it, We put the social media videos on the consulting firm's internal portal, used enterprise social tools to promote internally and create some noise, and there was a joint intranet for the new platform that we gave a suitably impressive and collaborative name to. I put a lot of work into creating a community of contacts that I would regularly hit with emails containing the links to take them straight to the videos or the ROI tool. That, to me, is what I would consider as business-as-usual when you are looking to create interest inside a SI. Looking back, I think what we did well on that occasion was that we not only had a good idea, we also had a well organised and motivated team that covered delivery, marketing, etc. It wasn't just about asset creation.

While that was a good experience, there are examples of times that I would have done things differently. My main lesson from those experiences was to qualify out sooner. When you realise no-one's biting, walk away, do something different, or else it has a knock effect for future investment.

When I look back on the main motivations for the software companies I have worked for innovating with the large systems integrators and consulting firms, it's actually a lot to do with brand value. They wanted to be associated with that large global firm. And if they got a lot of positive PR from it, perhaps a large consulting firm publicly saying how wonderful their technology is on the back of a joint solution launch, it's great for attracting clients and investors.

There's a lot at stake when you're innovating together. When you think of the wider implications for innovating well or badly, in very extreme examples it could kill the relationship, and in very positive examples it could make you indelibly linked. I think if you do it right there's only positives – as long as there's no channel conflict and the sales team at your company are also going to get paid on that asset. But there is downside if it's going to create channel conflict. You have to think about this carefully as you don't want to compete with your own sales force. Sales force compensation is very important here. If you are trying to create a partnership, and you're not going to pay the sales force of your own company for driving revenues associated with it, then it's not going to work.

Outside of the obvious things, such as a plan and a strong team around you, I think the advice I would give to OEMs looking to innovate with a large system integrator or consulting firm is that you have to be clear on your value, what the value proposition is going to look like, what your value represents to the partner. If you're not clear on that, then it won't work. The other bit of advice I would give would be around cultural alignment. Surround yourself with good people, because a global systems integrator is not going to be interested if you can't enhance their knowledge and proposition. They'll see through people very quickly, as they are very bright people themselves. Last, but not least, find the golden goose for you within the company with whom you are looking to partner: someone that needs a career move, for instance, or someone that's one step away from making the next level, and sell them the idea of how this joint solution can get them there faster.

> Key learning points: Ali's story
> 1. Repeatable solutions are very appealing to the big technology services companies and are an effective way of forging close links and cementing a 'sell with' strategy with them.
> 2. It's preferable to have a customer in mind (or even committed) initially. It increases the urgency and makes the investment case far stronger.
> 3. The creation of the asset is only half of the battle. It's how you market it within the organisation and alliance thereafter that is the difference between a successful product and well-kept secret.

7 Partnering in the new economy

How are the large consulting firms, systems integrators and outsourcers adapting to the digital age, and what does this mean for their partners?

How are the major players restructuring to accommodate the digital opportunity? What skills are they developing? What are the key go-to-market strategies around digital, and how can alliance partners tap into the new commercial landscape to ensure that their products are still relevant?

Let's start by establishing what 'digital' means. The reality is that everyone reading this book will have their own definition, either from their own experience or from the vast amount of media information on the subject. In order to play it safe, let's go with the Gartner definition:

> Digital business is shifting from a future strategic vision by IT leaders and digital leaders to providing a real competitive edge today. Gartner's research indicates that 32% of IT and business leaders at large organisations that have embarked on a digital business transformation say their current business is a digital business.

I choose to read into this that many businesses, though they look like banks or retailers or logistics companies, are now IT companies with processes and systems that are entirely dependent on the data that they possess and how it is processed. This isn't a book about the digital economy or how to master it, so I'll stick to relevant bits that will help you understand how the large IT services companies view digital and how you can then adapt your proposition and approach to complement them.

Q: What are the high-level digital value propositions that the large IT services companies identify?

A: As you would expect, the proposition definitions differ across the many players in the sector, but the IBM high-level digital offerings are logical and highly typical: (i) innovation and business value (i.e. innovating a company's business model to reflect the needs of the digital world); (ii) market and customer management (i.e. helping clients to access and maximise new and existing market sectors and, in the process, improving sales revenues and customer service); (iii) operating and organising model (i.e. technological improvements that make a company and staff more effective, such as value chain optimisation, lifecycle management, and collaboration).

Q: Is digital making a difference to the way that the IT sector and the large consultancies and systems integrators operate?

A: Quite simply, yes. It is a whole new business paradigm and, even though cynics may call the whole digital concept a re-brand for technology business-as-usual, if you want to compete in the market, you need to show that you get it. What is clear is that it is fuelling a whole new boom in IT spend and projects. A report written by TechCity and displayed on the KPMG website states:

> The digital transformation of the UK economy is truly underway. A recent report by TechCity forecasts that the number of digital jobs will grow faster than all other occupations by 2020. It found that 1.46 million people – 7.5% of the entire UK workforce – are currently employed in the digital industries.

Q: Is it large consulting firms or the large IT providers or the clients that are driving the agenda?

A: A bit of all three. The large consultancies are certainly at the forefront when it comes to thought leadership, along with the disruptive start-ups such as Uber, Airbnb and Amazon, in driving the way that digital is transforming markets. But the huge government and media interest in promoting the way that digital is perceived as the most important business driver since the internet means that all corporate clients are keen to be riding the wave. As an example, research by Capgemini Consulting and MIT's Center for Digital Business found that:

> Companies that invest in important new technologies and manage them well are more profitable than their industry peers. Respondents to our survey corroborate this view – they overwhelmingly believe that failure to effectively conduct digital transformation will harm their company's ability to compete.

With this sort of info in the public domain, it is obvious that companies will be looking to their consulting partners to get their digital story straight for their shareholders.

Q: Let's get down to business. How do the large IT services companies make money from digital?

A: The answer is: in the traditional way that they make money from any large, technology-driven projects. Through consultancy, explaining how a business process can be improved and the detailed analysis showing why it makes sense. Through architecting solutions that reflect the new thinking and technological advancements. Through implementation of technology solutions to bring about the change and then through supporting those systems. The dawn of the new digital agenda has brought significant risk to the services sector as smaller, more niche companies often find it easier to understand and champion smaller, more niche technology. So it is the larg,e global (more established) players who have had to fight to stay ahead. But, a full digital transformation for a corporation is a complex, time-consuming project, so it is usually only the large global consultancies and systems integrators that have the breadth to deliver. Additionally, as digital services become more in demand, clients will look to use outsourcers in particular to get up and running quickly.

Q: In terms of structural and cultural change, how are large IT services companies responding?

A: Looking at the organisational change that has occurred to reflect the advent of digital, I would say there are four common denominators across the large consultancies and systems integrators: (i) they are creating and publishing much thought leadership, clearly there is an arms race of knowledge, with all consultancies looking to reassure their clients and prospects that they have the latest and most comprehensive knowledge about what digital means; (ii) they are setting up separate divisions to create space between digital and the rest of their business so that the conservative world of global consulting can be seen as distinct from the funkier culture of digital disruption; (iii) they are addressing the cultural changes required to recruit new staff and transform existing staff into the digital mindset that reflects the new economy. This extract, from the Deloitte Digital website, is very telling:

Life's a little different here. Think inspired pranks, themed conference rooms, gallery-worthy whiteboard art. We're not just a bunch of consultants in jeans. We are creative, visionary minds of many disciplines who put future-forward thinking into projects that push the edges of digital technology. Our clients seek us out for that reason. And what's even better—we have a blast doing it. Who ever said work can't be fun? Around here, that's just what it is. We pride ourselves in our laid-back work environment and distinctive culture. And we also pride ourselves in putting our creative chops to the test and disrupting the status quo each and every day. Sound awesome? It is.

So read into the above what you will. How you refine your offering to reflect the way the global consulting and systems integration sector is addressing the digital world will be important to how you succeed. I would suggest considering the following three aspects of your approach, if you haven't done already.

1. Emphasise disruption

Harvard Business School professor Clayton M. Christensen coined the term 'disruptive technology' in his 1997 best-selling book, *The Innovator's Dilemma*. It is the buzz word of the digital revolution. Christensen talks of there being two types of technology: sustaining and disruptive. Disruption is not always tried, tested and polished, but it is almost always imaginative, simple and revolutionary.

Writing in TechCrunch, Andy Rachleff, co-founder of Benchmark Capital, sums it up well:

> Entrepreneurs in Silicon Valley love to talk about disruption, though few know what it really means. They mistake better products for disruptive ones. Silicon Valley was built on a culture of designing products that are 'better, cheaper, faster,' but that does not mean they are disruptive.

Thought leaders like the large consulting firms love disruption because it is cool and will entail making a difference to the way a client (or even entire market) does business. So, the wise technology OEMs and ISVs will have their story straight as to why their product will help their large IT services partner deliver disruption.

2. Make your product or service relevant to the way that your alliance partner views digital and understand your own digital message

The following extract, from McKinsey's first annual digital business survey, gives good insight to the mindset at play:

> Most C-level executives say the three key trends in digital business—namely, big data and analytics, digital marketing and social media tools, and the use of new delivery platforms such as cloud computing and mobility—are strategic priorities at their companies.

There is an important message in there: make sure your product or service fits into these segments or find a way that it can so that you can resonate with the digital savvy.

3. Align to the cultural shift

It may be about the way that you promote your message within the large IT services company by using a social enterprise tool as opposed to email, or it may be the way that you promote your alliance via Twitter instead of an old-fashioned press release, or it may be the way that you attend meetings at their office in jeans rather than a shirt and tie, or it may be the way that you make your marketing collateral funky and informal, but the important thing is that, if you are dealing with the digital group at your partner, they probably want to do things differently from the traditional way you're used to.

Key learning points: how are the large IT services companies adapting to the digital age?
1. This is a fantastic time to take new and innovative technology ideas to the large IT services companies because they are feeling the pressure of competing in the digital economy against new, sometimes more nimble competitors.
2. Be prepared for a cultural change. The old, conservative image has been shed for jeans and table-tennis tables in the offices of the big consultancies.
3. In terms of the alliance motion, not much has changed. You have a product, they want to deliver services; you just need to figure out how that fits the digital agenda.

What does cloud mean for the large IT services companies and their partnerships?

The generation of acquiring IT hardware and software to install at a client's premises appears to be over. How are the large hardware and software players adapting their business and products to remain relevant to their alliance partnerships and their business models? Do hardware and software companies need partnerships with large IT services companies in the cloud age when delivery is much less arduous and no longer an inhibitor to adoption?

The cloud shift has been a significant source of IT spend in the last five years, with various reputable analysts predicting growth in the region of 30% annually through to 2020. In 2016 we reached the tipping point when the majority of IT was delivered through the cloud.

The answer is that everything has completely changed and yet everything is the same. We need to go back to the very early part of the book to analyse the various ways that engaging with the large IT services companies is impacted by the advent of the cloud as the primary source of compute power. The reality is that the partnering strategy or sales motion in most cases remains unchanged (this is speaking as an alliance professional, *not* a lawyer, who may view things slightly differently; more of that shortly).

Outsourcers or systems integraters as hosters (sell to)

It depends on your perspective. If you are a provider of products or services that could be described as infrastructure (i.e. servers, certain software, networking and the related services), then the chances of 'sell through' and 'sell with' are reduced in projects where the systems integrator is acting as the hoster to the client. The systems integrator will be looking to divert many of the client's workloads to their own hosting environment, meaning that they will not be recommending as much (or any) infrastructure type products and services. This leaves the option of 'sell to', wherein the systems integrator adopts your product while also adopting the same buyer values as one of your end-user clients, such as reliability, resilience, uptime, efficiency, value-for-money, etc. There may be an even greater emphasis in certain elements of the technology stack, such as security, metering and reliability, as these features are the absolute core business of a hoster or outsourcer. If you are a provider of cloud services yourself, or aspire to start selling your product via a cloud model, you need to think carefully about how your offering can complement the cloud services of the outsourcer or systems integrator/hoster as there is a high likelihood of conflict.

Consultants or systems integrators as influencers (sell with)

This is where the specialist cloud hoster, SaaS, IaaS or PaaS vendor can work in a traditional way with the consultancies or systems integrators. Cloud computing transformation is a substantial revenue stream for technical consultancies with services associated with advising and physically helping clients move to the cloud. Services such as business case analysis, operating model refinement, billing, application migration and strategy and enterprise architecture transformation mean that the move to the cloud for most corporations is associated with a significant services investment. Therefore, all of the usual rules apply: consultanices and systems integrators will recommend and integrate cloud products and cloud services to clients as part of the business solution, and you are competing to be the service that they put forward.

Reselling cloud services (sell through)

If your main engagement strategy with the large IT services companies is resale (i.e. they resale your product or service), then your fortunes are effected by the above. Whether you're proving infrastructure, traditional services or cloud services, your engagement strategy with an outsourcer or systems integrator acting as a hoster will be difficult because they will look to provide the infrastructure and cloud services themselves (i.e. retain title and have no need for resale). It's a complex dilemma, though, because, even though the hoster retains title, they are ultimately serving an end-user client (in some cases one specifically, in other cases multiple clients from one server), so at least you are vindicated in selling to the hoster as a channel partner. If that is all your channel strategy allows with a clear conscience, then you aren't undermining your reputation as a channel-focused organisation by selling directly to an end-user.

When it comes to reselling, the commercial model hasn't changed, although the legal framework may prove to be more challenging. The basic principles of reselling remain: you sell the cloud service to the hoster (systems integrator or outsourcer) at one price and they sell it to the client at a higher 'marked up' price. Usually delivered directly from your facility to the client (or their specialist hoster), the legal complications come in the nature of the contractual relationships and associated responsibility, liability, billing and accountability of what is consumed, so a clear contract and good legal support is required.

So, not much is different whether you're selling products, traditional services or cloud services, but it's a brave new world out there, so there must be an angle, a way to steal a march on the competition by being the fastest and most innovative in addressing the new paradigm. Here are a few considerations to help formulate differentiation when partnering in the cloud:

1. One, if not the most important, motivation for adopting cloud services is that it allows clients to save costs through asking a third party (such as a specialist hoster or a systems integrator/hoster hybrid) to manage a task or IT process. Economies of scale are then created by the hosting partner and costs to the client are reduced. IT budgets are unlikely to be reduced, however, so in theory the client has more money to spend on new projects, such as innovation. Where you see a workload migrating to the cloud, don't look upon it as lost revenue, take the opportunity to work with your influencer partner to spend the released budget on new projects. As ever, the saved cost is an opportunity for all.

Partnering in the new economy 141

2. The reselling model is cumbersome when it comes to a cloud transaction and will create delays in realising revenue if you need to invoice the hoster/systems integrator and they need to invoice the client. If you don't have one already, this may be the time to implement a fee programme where you transact directly with the client while compensating the systems integrator on a fee per use (by the end-user client) basis. The systems integrator or consultancy will save the time, expense and risk of getting usage reports and issuing invoices to the client and will, in all probability, realise revenue more swiftly and more efficiently if receiving a fee from you.
3. Like all companies, the large IT services companies love recurring revenues. Cloud-based services are an advantage to them as it creates longer, more lucrative relationships with clients. If you don't have a way of delivering your product to a client or an systems integrator/hoster through a SaaS, IaaS or PaaS model, then it's time to start strongly considering it if you want to appeal to your potential partner, who may have an eye on the stock-price-friendly recurring revenues.
4. If you have sales people goaled on sales into specific end-user clients, ensure that they are confident in your ability to compensate them correctly. When you are billing your product or service via a systems integrator or hoster to an end-user client, particularly where the systems integrator or hoster is providing a shared service, you will find that your sales people are reluctant to work with your large IT services partner if it is difficult to track to which end-user the 'product' is flowing. You may find that your skillfully nurtured relationships are neglected by sales people who prefer to sell directly to end-users when the revenue can be more easily monitored, thereby undoing your hard work in establishing your strategic influencer channel.
5. As outcome-based revenue models become a more common deal shape, then cloud computing models to source the infrastructure for running those services will be become far more appealing. As consultancies and systems integrators look to defer as much of the cost of running the service to when it is used (i.e. when they can take revenue), then a pay-as-you-go cost model of consuming the component parts of the solution from third parties becomes increasingly appealing.

Key learning points: what does cloud mean for the large IT services companies and their partnerships?
1. Make sure that your sales compensation, channel and partner incentive models are up to speed with the cloud era.
2. The cloud model plays perfectly into the outcome-based deal shape and gives you an outcome to differentiate yourself with shared risk.
3. Many of the large IT services companies are making their money through cloud transformation, so don't become fixated with a 'sell to' model; there is still plenty of opportunity to 'sell with'.

Digital marketing: an IT approach vs the traditional agencies

The dawn and growth of digital marketing as an increasingly important means of corporate marketing strategy means that the line between established consultancies and systems integrators and the role played traditionally by advertising agencies and design practices is starting to blur. It's logical that, as advertising strategy and approach becomes more based around clever use of technology and data, the large IT services companies have a more natural role to play, or at least overlap, than traditional marketing and advertising agencies. This is not meant to be a controversial or biased view, just common sense based on the convergence of traditional advertising and technology led marketing using the web, social media and so on. In an article featured on marketing website The Drum, journalist Harriet Kingaby makes the point well:

> The digital revolution has redefined and disrupted not only the products and services offered by advertisers, but the very foundations of the industry itself. Management consultancies and advertising agencies ... have become unlikely foes, locked in a turf war and competing for the attention, budget and bandwidth of the C-suite.

The indicative diagram in Figure 7.1 is based on a diagram in the public domain available from a traditional technology-focused systems integrator.

What is the conclusion?

New relationships will be forged between the technology services sector and the traditional advertising and media agencies as alliances start to form to maximise the opportunities created by analysis of consumer data.

As the consultancies, systems integrators and outsourcers start to encroach upon the domain of the traditional agencies, it is likely that the traditional agencies will encroach upon their core business in return – either by setting up their own groups to perform traditional technology related functions or by creating consortiums of small specialist integrators or consultancies to address the threat. In the future, specialist digital marketing software and service providers will need to ensure that they are covering the technology influencer sector as enthusiastically as they have been the traditional agencies. If you're a technology vendor selling those digital marketing products or services, your partner base is expanding and you need a strategy to cover the entire spectrum of new partners you may encounter.

As the skills within marketing increasingly become technology based, so the likelihood of commoditisation and therefore off-shoring increases, meaning that traditional agencies will potentially need to forge relationships with global outsourcers. Like all business disciplines, digital marketing is a highly specialist and technical area and that isn't the remit here, but it's important to remember that the large consumer businesses spend more money on advertising than they do on IT, so, as more of a crossover between technology and advertising and marketing becomes common, it is inevitable that the scale, skills, efficiencies and transformation experience of the large IT services companies will become more relevant

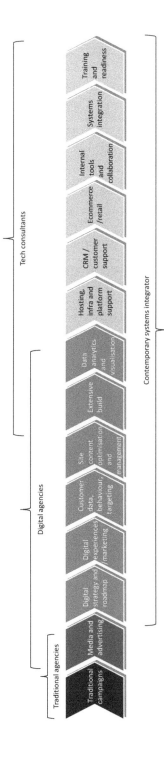

Figure 7.1 The emerging overlap between the digital agencies and the tech consultancies.

and they will start to refine their message to address the opportunity. So, have a clear idea where your proposition fits.

> Key learning points: digital marketing vs the traditional agencies
> 1. The lines are getting blurred between IT and the digital/creative agencies.
> 2. There is likely to be further consolidation between the IT sector and the advertising and media agencies, which will open up a whole new set of partnering opportunities.
> 3. The established off-shore resources of the large systems integrators and outsourcers will become appealing to the new media agencies as they start to compete in a more competitive commoditised market.

The Internet of things and Industry 4.0

A lot of what can be said about the Internet of things (IoT) overlays with the other sections in this chapter, so I'll endeavour to make the points as distinct as possible.

Like digital, if you asked people what the IoT is, you would get a whole host of different answers (insert into a search engine and you'll see what I mean). According to the *Oxford English Dictionary* (as good a place to start as any) it is: 'The interconnection via the Internet of computing devices embedded in everyday objects, enabling them to send and receive data.' According to Gartner, there will be nearly 26 billion devices on the IoT by 2020, so, in short, it's potentially the biggest technology wave that we have seen for a while and is the sort of market development that could actually move the dial on a country's gross domestic product (GDP). If you are in data analytics, security or cloud services, or you develop user interfaces to display data, then this is great news, but, then, you know that already.

To put the IoT into its wider Industry 4.0 context, the following is from the ever reliable Wikipedia:

> Industry 4.0 is a collective term embracing a number of contemporary automation, data exchange and manufacturing technologies. It had been defined as 'a collective term for technologies and concepts of value chain organisation' which draws together Cyber-Physical Systems, the Internet of Things and the Internet of Services.

So, it's a pretty important subject and, unsurprisingly, the large IT services companies are leading the way in advising companies how they can access the huge benefits to be derived from the new revenue streams now available from this aggregation of data.

From the perspective of the large IT services companies, the journey, and the host of services provided, will look similar to other large IT delivery projects: strategy, architecture, design, security, integration, data analysis, project management, support. In terms of what this means for the established technology sector, I like this piece written by Barb Livesay in *Redmond Channel Partner*, a publication for Microsoft channel partners:

When you boil down the Microsoft IoT value proposition, it's pretty straight forward:

- There are a huge number of devices, machines, sensors and other 'things' collecting data.
- The data needs to be gathered and stored somewhere.
- The data needs to be put into a context where it can be integrated, combined, analysed and reported.
- In order for that data to be understood and applied to present and future decisions, it needs to be winnowed, organised and presented in a user-applicable form.

I like this explanation because it goes a long way to stripping down an IoT project into easy chunks that providers of IT services and products can understand. It's mainly about data: how to gather it, how to process it, how to analyse it and how to use that newly gathered analysis for business benefit. But there is a more interesting story buried in here in the sentence that reads 'devices, machines, sensors and other "things" collecting data', which says to me that our previous perception of client server computing is very much under review. For the last 20 years, we have mostly associated client server computing with traditional computer networks of servers and PCs. This has evolved over the years into routers, hubs and other network nodes, but the IoT is opening up the client server world to a whole new set of network constituents. Instead of PCs and routers, the 'clients' will now be cars or fridges or windmills or plant machinery.

As a company looking to forge partnerships to access this new sector, you may need to review your current partner ecosystem and decide whether your traditional partnerships are still relevant or whether the IoT will mean forging relationships with companies that you have not previously encountered, such as sensor manufacturers.

In terms of building your story to work with the large influencers, the usual rules apply: make sure that you are clear where your proposition fits in relation to Industry 4.0; identify the key personnel within the organisations that are running the IoT or Industry 4.0 strategy; and do what you can to become an embedded part of the proposition. The sector may be revolutionary, but embedding in your alliance partner to maximise the new revenues is not.

Key learning points: what does cloud mean for the large IT services companies and their partnerships?
1. IoT will create technology networks of devices and components, such as sensor technologies or other industrial items, that will open up a new sphere of alliance partnership opportunities.
2. Much of the revenue for the large IT services companies is in the collection, processing and presentation of data, which leaves a substantial amount of the project from which you can benefit.
3. In many ways, nothing has changed – this still resembles a client server computing model, so don't over-think it. All of the principles covered in this book apply.

What does the future hold for the IT services sector and how does that affect you, the partner?

In a world realigning with digital, the cloud and the benefits and challenges of globalisation, it is obvious that the IT services sector is well placed to continue to deliver the, often revolutionary, transformation that large enterprise clients require. As a partnering strategy, a continued close alignment with the business opportunity for partners still endures. The influence that the large consultancies, systems integrators and outsourcers have, the huge revenues that are being driven by the major technology trends such as cloud, IoT, mobility and digital transformation, and the increased revenue opportunity from globalisation and additional IT spend from developing nations, means that the technology services market has never been in a stronger position.

This position should mean they can wield further power in their prospective partnerships, but is this correct? It's certainly correct to say that major investment in technology to compete in the digital economy together with the extra spend opportunity streams for emerging markets will bring new revenue streams, but with globalisation also comes competition and the new digital technologies are more about agility, innovation and speed to market than about scale, so the need for innovative partners to stay current, relevant and able to diversify into new uncommoditised markets has never been stronger. Play to your strengths and consider how you can help your potential alliance partner overcome some of the challenges in the new, globalised digital world.

Don't rely on your relationship with IT

According to Gartner:

> … budgets from IT departments will stay flat to very slightly up through 2019. Most of the increase in C&I spending will come from line-of-business budgets. Business units will spend increasing amounts of money on newer front-office digital technologies. As a result, by 2019, spending by business units will make up 50% of the C&I market.

So, while you may feel that you can have the IT team covered and leave it to your consulting partner to cover 'the business', it may be time for a re-think. Spend more time on your business case and make friends with the business as they will be driving your projects more and more. Make sure that you have those bases covered when engaging with the influencers. Of course, this shift to 'the business' validates your decision to partner with the consulting sector who traditionally control that stakeholder group.

Have your cloud partner strategy and commercial model straight

The trend to cloud will continue and it will affect the revenues of the large IT services companies. The analysts say that cloud revenues will continue to grow as corporations move more workloads to the cloud. This will mean strategy and transformation revenues for the consultancies and systems integrators and more core cloud revenues for outsourcers and off-shore service providers. As previously discussed, it will also create efficiencies that will translate into additional services revenue for new projects. However, there is a risk to consultancies and systems integrators here. The rise of the SaaS model will mean that many IT vendors' delivery models will reduce the need for integrator involvement; also, the delivery of PaaS and IaaS will reduce system integrator delivery revenues that were previously earned from on-premise solutions. You may be one of the companies that is by-passing this spend and benefitting by making your offering more attractive to end-user clients – good for you. However, it won't ingratiate you to your partners, so think carefully about how you build them into the solution, either by delivering services revenues or through other commercial models such as influencer fees.

Provide a generous services blend and an opportunity for a working margin to negate commoditisation and off-shoring

The ability to off-shore work and also to access extra sources of labour is putting the IT services market under significant price pressure. The answer for the large IT services companies is to improve their blend of specialist uncommoditised services. This is where the partnerships come in. New technologies, new business sectors, new methods of doing business do not generally lead to commoditiser price sensitive services, so helping your partner to discover and master new technology areas using your projects and innovation will be welcomed.

Industry transformation encourages incremental IT spend

Be industry relevant. Bring your consulting firm, system integrator and outsourcer alliance partners technologies that are disrupting industries or addressing regulatory change in sectors. This point mirrors the point above; commoditisation is a challenge, so we are all looking for industry change that is driving new business innovation. Specific industry-focused technologies tend to do this more than pan-industry solutions, where a race to the bottom becomes common.

Be agile and cool

The digital economy feeds on innovation, imagination and speed to market. Large organisations find it a challenge to live up to this. They are political, slow to react, busy satisfying legacy clients with old contracts and addicted to the revenues that keep their share price high and their investors feeling safe. So they need to partner with smaller, more agile companies that understand and can take them into new market areas. This is where you come in. Niche, expert and agile is viewed as a positive business model in the digital economy and large IT services companies will increasingly look to partner with companies that can help them appear this way to their clients and prospects.

In short, the large IT influencers are at constant pressure from price and from new market entrants attacking their clients and sectors with new disruptive ideas. Addressing commoditisation and the threat from contemporary technologies and business models can be achieved by identifying the companies that can work with them to use their niche industry and technology insight and help the big, established players discover the new business models and opportunities available in the new economy.

Key learning points: what does the future hold?
1. Increased commoditisation from off-shoring and new market entrants means that this is a good time to bring your partners new and innovative technologies and solutions so that they can be differentiated.
2. The large IT services companies are precisely that – large. So be the one in the relationship that helps them to force the agenda by being the cool, agile party which makes them view the market opportunity in a different way.
3. Cloud is not going away, it is the new normal. So have your partnering-in-the-cloud story straight.

The digital disrupter's perspective: Phil's story

Phil is an alliance lead at one of the new digital giants* (aka new economy companies or digital disruptors). His role is to partner with a portfolio of the large consultants, systems integrators and outsourcers. His story is interesting because he recently joined this company from one of the more established technology corporations** and his approach to partnering has altered to address that change. As with all interviews, Phil is a real person but his story has been deliberately anonymised (*think: Facebook, Apple, Amazon, Twitter, Uber, etc.; **think: CISCO, IBM, HP, Fujitsu. etc.).

> I've been working with large global IT services firms for 15 years. I like it because it's challenging. I like the thought process and the work that goes into building a plan, because it's different with every systems integrator. I like that you have to fully understand and address the objectives of your partner and it involves people, it involves management, it involves governance, it involves soft powers as well as hard powers. Complex alliances work is like developing a business if you do it properly, and that's what's interesting.
>
> Probably the toughest thing to handle when it comes to alliances work, as opposed to face-to-face sales, is that you don't have ultimate control on the second or third party involved in the alliance. When things aren't going right, you can influence your own side of the house, but on the other side of the house you can only control by impact and influence and sometimes that is problematic.
>
> When you've primarily worked in the business of marrying together large technology companies and large systems integrators, you are actually quite

susceptible to macro-economic issues and mergers and acquisitions. Particularly when the large technology companies diversify to address a changing technology sector, alliance partners can be friends today and competitors tomorrow. They could disappear through acquisition or be subsumed, and that brings about some uncertainty in the planning phase. It means that you have to be on your game all the time and to be ready for that and deal with it. It happened to me recently, and it upset an alliance plan that had been progressing steadily for two years.

The current OEM I am with now are constantly assessing conflicts of interest with the systems integrators and outsourcers because there is constant overlap as the business models of the large digital giants and the services companies, with whom their predecessors partnered, start to converge. I see it a lot in the sector. You have a client manager in your own company who can be downright hostile if they know you are working with certain alliance partners because you are feeding the enemy. As there's now so much overlap, that's a big cultural problem. Of course, it does depend on the nature of your own company and how they manage that potential conflict through incentives and objectives.

My new company is more of a west coast culture, far more dynamic. It's a huge step up in terms of pace of working and development of product and go-to-market from where I have worked previously. The company doesn't plan for years, we plan for months. The rate of change, the agility in market and the organisation structure is very fluid. I've noticed as well that the digital giants are more collaborative, with a flatter management structure – and the management are more approachable. The new economy companies are on a learning path. They don't have the heritage of the big IT behemoths of yesteryear, you know, the companies that have been around a long time, so they are still learning their trade. They are growing at a huge pace in terms of market presence, and they don't have the reputation in the market place that the traditional guys do, so they are always having to fight and make their name in the enterprise sector; whereas, the traditional guys have it slightly easier in some ways in that they are already ensconced.

Another thing I have noticed since moving to my new company is that, culture wise, there is far more of an employee agenda and employee consideration because they appreciate that the personnel, as opposed to the products, are the life blood of the company. In traditional, publicly quoted technology firms, with all of the attendant margin pressure, I don't think that is the case.

There's always a bit of tension around recruitment too. The new economy companies are a real draw for people who are currently working for, or traditionally attracted t,o the big SIs. The technologies they represent are typically cloud and there's only going to be a very few people that are going to be able to provide the cloud at that scale at that price point in the future, so I think traditional systems integrator work is under pressure. A lot of experienced people can see where the future is, so those new economy companies with the sexy images and high quality brands are quite attractive as employers.

The million dollar question that you want me to answer is: 'What are the implications for partnering?' Well, it's not necessarily straight forward. Let's talk about culture for a minute. I mentioned that the pace of change at the new economy companies is significant, and that their agility is significant, and that doesn't lend itself to easy partnering at all. The big consulting firms are more risk averse and process driven, for instance, and, as you can imagine, when you have two organisations working at different speeds, you have to bridge that gap.

The other thing is that the new economy companies are typically representing cloud services, so when they look for alliance partners, often partner profitability is a question. How can that alliance partner make money out of representing your service? Put another way: 'What's in it for me?', because that isn't always obvious. When we used to sell hardware or pre-packaged software, that question was more straight forward. However, in the new economy, when representing someone else's cloud business it isn't always clear how that alliance partner is going to make money, because the ownership of the service to the client is less clear-cut. I think that, in terms of working with partners, there needs to be a good understanding of how it needs to be approached, the skills that they need, how each company makes money out of it, how the solution's going to be supported and also, last but not least, how an alliance partner can drive value using somebody else's cloud *and* protecting their own IP.

Despite all of this, the new economy companies still attract alliance partners of all sizes because the growth rate in those companies and the market is so significant that the partners want to be part of it. But they are also attracted by brand value as well. That being said, there are downsides in this cultural incompatibility. For instance, agility and development cycles are challenging sometimes. What I mean by that is the new economy companies are growing and morphing so fast that it's hard sometimes for them to be coherent to a partner who is used to some level of stability and tradition. So, from a cultural perspective, there is a misalignment there once again.

I think the saving grace for the big IT services companies is in thought leadership. You can't underestimate the quality and depth of the global consulting firms' and system integrators' industry knowledge. They really understand the business drivers of a solution and the challenges of a given industry or sub-industry. The new economy companies have amazing technologists, but they don't have that deep industry knowledge. So, if you look at building solutions to address a business problem, the new economy company may provide the platform to build on, but the IP and the business solution is still dominated by the global consulting firm.

On a personal level, I am nearly twice the average age at my new company, but I would make a bet that the average age at new economy companies will increase over the next few years. Why? Because they want to grow significantly in the enterprise space and, even in the new technology environment, they need experienced, credible people liaising with the the enterprise and alliance world, so experience counts. Flashy new technology isn't everything if it isn't delivered the in the right way, and it needs to be delivered by credible and experienced people for it to be effective. Enterprise clients still want to see some war wounds and battle scars, and for people to know their business. The new economy OEMs are growing really quickly, they are all lean businesses and they need experience to know what works, so having worked in the alliance world with other major accounts really works when you are building partnerships. I wouldn't underestimate for one minute how that experience is needed, even by the latest big technology companies. Leadership never goes out of fashion.

If I ran a start-up right now, I would only involve a large global services firm if they were going to help me grow my business and get to the big markets. So, it's about access to markets. Although, I would say that the very nature of tech start-ups means that they would only go to the large global alliance partners if they absolutely had to, in order to accelerate or to keep their investors happy. The big corporations, now, are happy to work with start-ups that aren't household names in a way they haven't been willing to do previously.

Nowadays, when I am working with the large systems integrators, I have to explain to them that if they want to engage effectively with my company, the stakeholder map is different from what they are used to. The chief digital officer, chief transformation officer and chief marketing officer are three roles that are important for an alliance lead looking to partner with arguably the most powerful people in the building. The other stakeholder that is important is the head of product engineering, because the new economy companies are totally reliant on product and differentiation. It's a technology company at the end of the day, so having the best thing available is really key. Engineering heads often lead global armies of developers and are under a lot of pressure to reduce development cycles to get the next 'thing', function or feature out and stay just ahead of the pack. They are usually operating at a VP, if not SVP, level and are generally very long standing employees and extremely powerful.

When I look at the really excellent graduates now, I think they are more aware of the new economy companies first. They know the companies and brands, so they are more familiar than they would be with a consulting firm or system integrator. Even so, there is an appreciation that the big IT services firms are very high quality, provide fantastic training and are a really great opportunity for advancement; plus, they have a global reach and so are still very attractive, even with the lure of the digital giants out there.

At the end of the day, I may now work for the latest hot company, but the lessons are the same as they have always been. Be a good listener, try and understand the heritage incumbency and focus of your partner, focus on the win–win–win and good things will happen. What I mean by that is: the win for the client, the win for the alliance partner and the win for your company. If you find an activity or opportunity that ticks those boxes, then you are probably on the right track. To do more of that, make sure you have a very good alliance person, because they do make a difference – and, of course, make sure you have got good sponsorship.

Key learning points: Phil's story
1. The pace of change at the big digital disruptors is different from the old technology companies, and it's essential that their partners match that.
2. Be prepared to become familiar with a new stakeholder map in the new digital companies. They are technically led and much of the power sits in the senior technical or product management roles.
3. The business models, and even the technologies, might have changed, but the most important lesson of sales hasn't – listen!

8 The 10 steps to success

That's about it really. Plenty to do, but with organisation, support and the right attitude, success is within your grasp. Everyone will take something different from this book, based on their particular circumstances and partnering aspirations. However, if you don't have the time or inclination to read and digest every aspect of this book, keep in mind the following 10 steps. They will put you in good stead.

Rule 1: have congruent goals

This really is lesson number one on day one of all sales and business relationships: make sure you establish and maintain a win–win. It's essential to all successful alliances and never more true than when partnering with a large IT services company.

We have looked at the importance of identifying, setting, targeting and then tracking the achievements of our mutual goals and needs from any relationship. Put concisely, I would describe this as 'have congruent goals'. Ensure that you fully understand the motivations of your partner, the limitations of their scope and what success really means for them. Ensure that you set realistic, measurable, mutually agreeable goals for each engagement and conscientiously report on them.

This is true at a strategic level, but also at every level of the engagement. Before you start any meeting, put yourself in the shoes of the person on the other side of the desk who is representing the large IT services company and ask yourself: 'What are they trying to gain here?', 'How will it help them get to their wider goals?' and, cliché alert, 'What does success look like?' If it's not obvious, then ask. No-one will object. They will see it as refreshingly honest and sensible, because it doesn't happen as much as you would think. Just because it is a direct and slightly obtrusive question, it doesn't need to be impolite or discourteous:

> Before we start, can we have a quick re-cap of our roles, objectives and what we all want from this meeting and how that enables our wider, mutually successful relationship together?

or

> I think it's important for us both to explain what we are looking to achieve in this meeting so that we can ensure we are all working toward the right outcome.

or even

> I want to be entirely transparent and explain what success looks like for me and my organisation and why we regard this meeting as so important to our strategy. I think it is equally important for you to describe how this relationship/deal/opportunity/pursuit will help you move toward your wider corporate/departmental/personal goal.

Then, at the end of the meeting, make sure that you re-cap and decide if you achieved what you set out achieve and that you are still on track for a win–win. If not, establish what needs to change in order to get there and how you can do things differently.

The above approach is very tactical and meeting specific, but it is true of the wider relationship also. You need to be true to yourself and your company by ensuring that you execute profitable, sustainable business, but you also need to ensure that your relationship is good business for your partner and be aware that the same is true at each level of the organisation with whom you are working.

When times get tough and inevitable bumps in the road occur, it is going to be important to take a step back and remind your partner why you are both working together and why it's important to stick with it for the long term. It's also good to use those congruent goals to inspire personnel at the lower levels of the organisation that you will encounter along the way. They will usually respond favourably to a wider strategy relating to why the large IT services company is investing to make the relationship a success. A gentle, yet convincing, lever to make sure that everyone remains on message, and pulls out the stops to attend your meeting, is to invest their resources in your idea and to keep deliverables on schedule.

Chapter 2 highlights some of the tangible, measurable benefits of an alliance for a large IT services company, such as additional services revenue, resale revenue or cost avoidance, and explains the strategic imperative to partner at the basic level in order to complete their solution, but the 'win' for the services provider should never be assumed or taken for granted. Sometimes their need to partner with an OEM or different services company is obscure, such as a specific defensive play within a client or a foothold in a new innovative growth market. The important thing is that you understand what it is and how your offering enables it and makes it happen. Solid alliance management and governance on the part of the large IT services company will usually ensure that they are pursuing the right relationships and aims, but make sure that it's a question that you frequently ask yourself and your stakeholders also: Is this delivering what you need and do you understand what we need as well?

The ultimate endorsement is the ability to create a reference and a credential at the end of the engagement. This will only be possible if both companies have achieved a mutually successful win–win.

Rule 2: identify and really manage the right stakeholders

As explained in Chapter 2, while it is tempting to go straight to the top, the right stakeholders in a large IT services company alliance partner are not always the most senior management. The people who help you to get established and can tangibly benefit your business are often in middle management, the finance department or concealed in the technical architecture department. The successful alliances understand the roles and personnel that are relevant to each individual project or sales pursuit and how they can most efficiently map on to them.

Of course, it's important to have senior-level support within any alliance to ensure that your plan is well funded and your proposition has the support of the people in the organisation who set and implement the strategic direction; but, it is also possible to go too senior. While the leadership can endorse you and believe in your alliance, it is the technical architects or the client teams that will decide if your product or service is right for their engagement.

Any area of the organisation can be a sweet spot for your offering. For instance, if you are selling innovative technology that transforms a business process, then the management/business consultants will be your main cheerleaders. If your product saves delivery time and cost, then it is the financial arm of the systems integrator or outsourcer, or the delivery lead of the engagement who will get behind you. If your proposition is uncommoditised and offers a significant margin opportunity when sold, it is the sales people that will get behind you. If what you are offering is stable, mature and reliable, the technical team will be your advocates. The point is this: know your stakeholders, hone your message and make sure they are bought in. Ultimately, it will always come down to risk and reward. Different roles within the large IT services company will support you based on what your product offering brings them. Can they make money, and will they avoid the substantial cost of a poorly delivered outcome?

In an ideal world, the best approach is to use your own company to create peer relationships within your new alliance partner whenever you can. Making connections and fostering relationships between your organisation and the personnel of the corresponding alliance partner is the most efficient and comprehensive way to be embedded; your leadership to their leadership, your finance director with their finance leads, your sales manager with their senior salesperson, your technical architect marking their technical architects.

Due to the typical size of the alliance partners we talk about in this book, it probably isn't going to be possible to make peer relationships at the very top of the organisational structure, so be sensible. Perhaps the leadership of an industry group or large client engagement is the correct aspiration. Instil a sense of responsibility and ownership within your organisation for the relationships to work and explain their role to everyone. This means that the first sale you make is to your own company. Get them to accept the fledgling alliance and have them feel accountable. If you're reading this as an account manager, the clue is in the name: it's time to start managing.

The other thing to consider when you're mapping a peer-to-peer relationship approach is that it's not all about job titles. There is an even more effective tool to keep your organisation close to your alliance partner, and that is the power of personal connection. The logical thing to do is to ask the finance leads or the technical people to connect. That is undoubtedly important from a practical perspective, but sometimes the chemistry of other relationships just work. Often it's as simple as supporting the same sports team, having children the same age, living in the same neighbourhood or having mutual friends. Just look for the connective tissue between your extended team and the stakeholders within the large IT services company that you want to nurture. It needn't be sleazy or insincere, people like to deal with others with whom they have affinity, so it makes common sense in a people business where personal relationships still prevail despite the weighty nature of the business and the sometimes conservative personalities.

Once the connections are made and the congruent goals are established, make sure that you create a rhythm to the relationship. Regular meetings, touchpoints and calls will keep people engaged and vested in the alliance, and provide the necessary heads-up to identify problems before they de-rail the relationship. The smart move is to make the meetings as far in advance as you are able because you will find that making meetings every month or week will not happen. The diaries of busy people are normally booked for the short term. Meetings in advance are worked around and have a greater chance of remaining in place. This is obvious, but worth reminding ourselves. Stick to the rhythm of the business, have an agenda, have a clear outcome for the meeting and, most of all, ensure that everyone present is getting value from it (put thought into this), then the meeting schedule will be maintained and the alliance will prosper.

Last, but not least, be pragmatic, not obsessive. You may not have the right contact, you may not have the right cast-list for the governance meeting, you may not have a senior enough sponsor, but do it anyway. If you wait for the perfect alignment, the months will pass you by. Get the ball rolling and use the momentum to get to the perfect set of relationships over time.

Rule 3: get someone's mortgage dependent upon you

As soon as you can, strive for your alliance partner to get skin in the game by recruiting or training dedicated alliance or delivery personnel whose existence is reliant on your success.

On a basic, practical level, you need someone inside the tent. This will save you a huge amount of work and will expedite your business plan and progress within the alliance significantly. They will understand and can guide you around the structure of the organisation: the culture, the business drivers, the clients and, probably most important, the key personnel that are relevant to you progressing your agenda. When plotting your business plan, these are all essential.

It stands to reason that you want that person exclusively (i.e. managing only your relationship as opposed to multiple alliance partnerships). Having their destiny intrinsically wrapped up with yours means that you will have a high quality relationship owner as your guide and fighting for you. If the large IT services company does not see your potential relationship important enough to fund a dedicated owner for it, but you are convinced of the value to them and to you, then consider partly or entirely funding one yourself. They are geared up to take investment from outside sources to pay for short-term project-based work (it is, after all, their core business), so the model will be familiar and straight forward to implement. As a fallback scenario, get a relationship owner to at least have your alliance as part of a portfolio of alliances they manage. The important thing is that you have an advocate and someone to be your eyes and ears. When arranging a meeting to discuss a certain project, account or engagement opportunity, an internal email from a colleague to your target contact within the business will have a greater chance of being read and acted upon than an external email, especially from an unfamiliar company.

There is also the intelligence aspect of being inside the company firewall that your counterpart will enjoy. From their insight, you will learn about the company direction of the large IT services company, competitor activity, company restructuring information and any personnel changes that affect you. This can allow you to change direction swiftly and effectively.

Consider also that you will need to plan a communications campaign into your alliance partner. In Chapter 4 I talked about the importance of having an awareness strategy into the large IT services company. Gaining access to the sort of newsletters, enterprise social tools and intranets required to do this can only be achieved from within the organisation, so you need someone not only to advise you about the most effective methods but also the practical ability to post the content.

The power of personal connection should also be acknowledged here. Your advocate will spend time in the offices of their employer, sitting next to colleagues in the office, dining with them in the restaurant, drinking with them in the pub and mingling at community meetings. In every interaction he or she will be talking about their role and promoting the alliance. Potentially, this could be hundreds of touch points each month creating awareness of your product or service. In terms of awareness building, there is no substitute for this.

Once you have your dedicated contact, transparency is key. Create an environment of trust and openness immediately and you will find that your approach is replicated. This will give you access to the kind of important facts about the business motivations of your alliance partner that you need. It goes without saying that trust should be absolutely sacrosanct and the quicker you earn it, the swifter your integration into these sometimes huge organisations will be.

There's another important factor to consider as well. That is the emotional impact of making this investment. When the large IT services company has made an investment to fund a relationship owner, immediately there is a compelling commercial imperative to make the relationship work. An investment of £200,000+ (in terms of deploying someone from chargeable work to be dedicated to relationship management) is material and will mean that the relationship will have senior support to thrive. Also, when your partner has put that level of skin in the game, your own leadership will sit up and listen. It will mean that you will be afforded more patience and support when you are promoting your prospective relationship internally. This is an important dynamic (see Rule 4).

So, if you can convince your newly formed partner, or indeed your own company, to make the investment in a dedicated relationship owner, what sort of person do you want? He or she needs to be well connected. A network, particularly a network that is relevant to your offering, is important. This leans toward someone with longevity of employment within your alliance partner or with a background of delivery or business development within the area to which your offering is relevant. As shown in Chapter 3, the large IT services companies can be hierarchical, so having someone fighting your corner with an impressive job title will usually have greater impact.

Ideally you want someone who knows your business. The staff of the organisations with whom you aspire to work will expect their colleague to be able to qualify and pitch the benefits correctly in order for them to feel comfortable to bring your company into their engagement.

He or she must be well organised with good interpersonal skills. There is a lot to do and consistent rhythm is important. If forced to choose, I would go for this personality type over someone who was an out and out salesperson. You can perform the relationship building role yourself, but you need someone to create the framework. Notwithstanding the above, ideally your candidate should like people and be comfortable standing up and being your advocate in all sized groups. Finally, they should be ambitious and keen to make a name. What you are looking to achieve together is hard work, sometimes risky and will require passion and conviction, so you need someone who will have the courage for the journey and be prepared to raise their head above the parapet for you.

Rule 4: ensure that you have understanding leadership

The process of identifying and meeting the correct personnel within a large IT services company, establishing teaming and commercial terms, identifying an appropriate client or project on which to engage and then supporting a bid process through to a successful sale and delivery will take months and often years. A well-funded alliance programme and an understanding, long-term-focused management is essential.

Scenario 1: you already have the end-user client support

Let's look at the best case scenario. You have a client that has expressed an interest in working with you. They like your product and you have the right support within the client. Then they come back to you and say that they intend to integrate your product as part of a tender process or larger project implementation on which they are working with one of the large IT services companies. Even in this best case scenario, you will need to reach out to the correct personnel within the client's chosen services partner (assuming that you have been given a contact name by the client), make contact, be put in touch with the personnel with whom you can work to include your offering (architects basically), then agree the commercial terms under which you will be included (see Figure 8.1). The tender process may well begin at this point, which will add much more time and bring in the risk of your new friends not being successful in the tender process.

Sometimes it's a blessing to come to the process post tender, but you will still have to take the time to embark on the journey of technical and commercial approvals before your product is accepted. This scenario is largely out of your hands. If it is your client's wish that they engage with you in this way, you have little choice in the matter and, in this scenario, the relationship with the systems integrator is immaterial to the timeline of the deal. Some time (and extra risk) may be added by agreeing terms with the large IT services company, but ostensibly, this is a fairly typical sales cycle and similar to what you would expect even if there was no large IT influencer involved.

Scenario 2: realising revenue from a standing start

This is where it starts to get very risky and costly. You decide in a meeting that you need a strategy to work with a consultancy firm, systems integrator or outsourcer. This may have come about because the leadership of your company have read one of the many reports suggesting that this is the way to penetrate the large clients or projects, it may be that that you are encountering these organisations in all of your large engagements or prospects, or it may be that you have been recruited specifically for the task of setting up a channel for working with this sector. Whatever the reason, you have decided on the strategy, so you will need patience and investment. See the diagram in Figure 8.2 to highlight the stages. From conceiving the idea to getting paid for your first deal, this could be an 18-month journey and even then doesn't guarantee success if the projects you back don't turn into live projects, or indeed your partner is not successful in winning the projects at bid stage.

As we can see in Figure 8.3, time investment also means financial investment. This is an estimated example of how much a company could invest in staff costs (not including management time or additional infrastructure costs such as demo equipment, software customisation, etc.) and is predicated on the salary numbers assumed in the diagram. This scenario ends in a sale, so there is a happy ending and a high likelihood that this cost outlay will be recouped. Of course, this diagram only demonstrates one sales cycle. It is likely that, once the alliance manager has created his plan and started to gain traction within his large IT services company, he or she could work various opportunities simultaneously, which would mean significant payback on this invesment if those opportunities turn into sales. So it's highly hypothetical, but should provide an indication of the investment required to execute a channel strategy into the sector.

As mentioned previously, the first sale that needs to be made is to your leadership and your investors. They need to be re-assured that this is a viable approach.

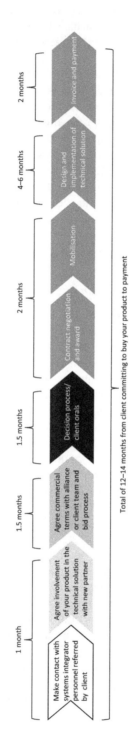

Figure 8.1 Timeline of an engagement for implementation of a medium sized IT project where a client has asked a large IT services company to involve you. Overall project value circa £20m.

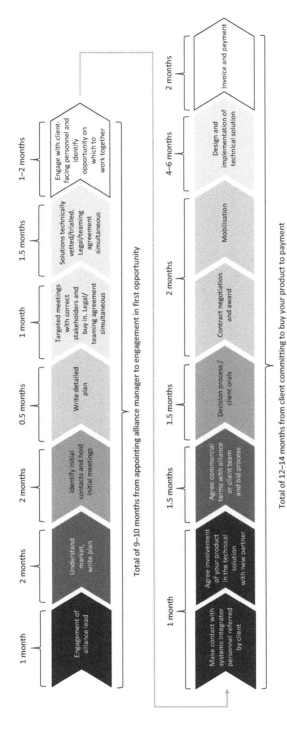

Figure 8.2 Timeline of an engagement where you are starting on alliance strategy from scratch from appointment of the alliance manager.

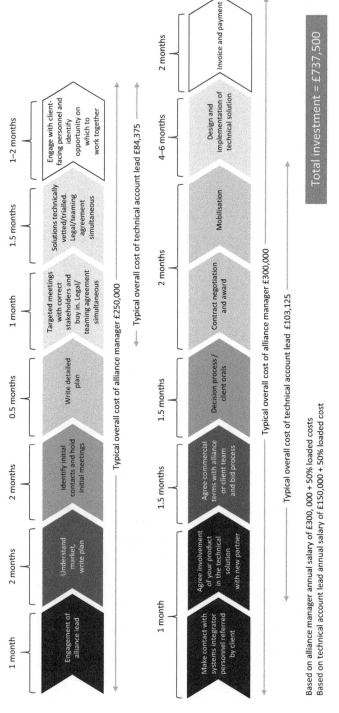

Figure 8.3 Time and expenses overlay of an engagement where you are starting an alliance strategy from scratch from appointment of the alliance manager.

DEAL SIZE: By working with the large IT services companies, you will become involved in larger deals and projects	CORRECT LEVEL OF ENGAGEMENT: Better (more senior) relationships within the client will mean swifter deal closure and revenue realisation	A VIRTUAL SALESFORCE: Investment in channel strategy creates economies of scale and provides a capable and well connected sales force taking your offering to market	INNOVATION = REPEATABLE: Innovating and creating shared assets will create a stickiness that will endure, guaranteeing a route to market for years to come	CREDIBILITY: The global IT services players have a reputation for quality, security and impartiality, which can benefit your brand	REDUCED ADMIN and CREDIT RISK: Managing multiple client relationships is costly; consolidating customers to a few large organisations with whom you transact saves costs and credit risk
	Increased revenue				
	Swifter revenue realisation and higher percentage of deal closure				
			Efficiency savings		

Figure 8.4 Bottom and top line financial benefits of a well executed alliance strategy with the large consulting, systems integrator and outsourcing sectors.

It's therefore worth remembering why we have embarked on this journey so that you can overcome the inevitable concern and objections (see Figure 8.4). At a high level, we touched on the most common objections in Chapter 4, but, in order to give you a 'cheat sheet' of the key benefits, be armed with the following before you go and ask the CFO for the funding to grow your alliance strategy:

Deal size. By working with the large IT services companies you will become involved in larger deals and projects. Partly this is because they are usually only hired to substantial projects and partly because they work mainly with large clients. So, the pay-off takes longer, although when it comes in it will be more substantial in size.

Correct level of engagement. Time spent in getting 'buy-in' from the senior client-facing personnel in the large IT services company will almost always translate into better (i.e. more senior) relationships within the client because they tend to operate at a business level in the C-Suite. So, while the cost investment is substantial, it will ordinarily result in saved time in getting to the real client decision makers.

A virtual salesforce. Like all channel strategies, investment in channel strategy will create economies of scale by providing a capable and well connected sales force taking your product/offering to market. So, while the timeline of a possible return on your activities is unappealing, the multiple deal cycles within which you can be involved will negate the long-term risk.

Innovation = repeatable. When you innovate and create shared assets with any alliance partner, particularly if you enjoy success in winning mutual business this way, you will create a stickiness that will likely endure and guarantee a route to market for years to come.

Credibility. The global IT services players (particularly the ones listed in Chapter 1) have a reputation for quality and security in terms of financial stability and delivery capability. In short, a partnership will bring you the reflective credibility and inclusion onto supplier lists that it may be difficult for you to access without this partnership. They are also known for impartiality, and their word is respected more highly than that of a provider of a particular technology, who obviously has a personal agenda, so endorsement, for instance from a technical consultancy, is valuable to your standing.

Reduced admin and credit risk. Managing multiple client relationships isn't a nice problem to have because it is costly, particularly if you are selling your product via a service model that involved constant metering, monitoring and piecemeal invoicing. If you can consolidate your list of customers to a few organisations with whom you transact, it can significantly reduce your credit risk as well as your back-office admin costs.

Rule 5: appetite for risk

Large IT projects are complex, and clients expect as much of the risk as possible to be taken by the delivery partner. In turn, the large IT services companies will expect their partners to share in that risk. It is often the supplier that has the most tolerance to this shared commitment that can differentiate and qualify to partner in the most lucrative projects.

When your product is involved, it goes without saying that the cost of pre-sales and sales processes, such as bid submission, will be provided free of charge by you, the partner, but there is also an opportunity to take this to the next level. As explained in Chapter 3, the large systems integrators and outsourcers are increasingly moving to a gain-share or outcome-based model, where they will be expected to absorb much or all of the up-front costs of the solution/service being delivered to the client (or directly to their customers).

This model means that the upside for them will be the unlimited savings or revenue wins of the client. These might include being paid a fee for costs saved when owning the cheque clearing process for a retail bank (an example of gain-share) or receiving a fee from a car dealership for every car sold via a sales lead generated from a digital marketing solution (an example of an outcome-based model). In either instance, the solution creation and management will be of substantial cost to the systems integrator or outsourcer because they own the asset (albeit shared, with complimentary services being delivered to other clients in order to create economies of scale).

The large IT services companies, like all businesses, do their best to minimise risk. Therefore it makes sense for them to find partners that will share the up-front cost and risk of the solution/service to the client. As a partner, this business model may result in delayed revenues, or indeed lower revenue than predicted, while the desired cost savings or increased revenue for the client take a while to be realised. But you do have the security of knowing that your partner probably has a great deal more to lose that you do in a failed outcome-based investment model. Considering their industry knowledge, your partner is probably confident of the viability of the investment. So, while the gain-share or outcome-based business model has inherent risk, it is a way of differentiating your company and taking a major step toward to becoming more embedded in the go-to-market strategy of your alliance partner.

In many cases, it doesn't have to be as absolute as giving away your product or service in return for forecasted or projected revenues. Sometimes it is as simple as sharing the liability on delivery. Many projects have penalty clauses for late or failed delivery, so, where you can help the delivery partner to offset those costs, you will be regarded favourably.

Shared risk is often a model that suits a new company looking to make an impact in the market with a specific large IT services company because many large or more established players find it difficult to show this degree of flexibility due to shareholder or director-level squeamishness. When you start the discussions about how your product or service will be used and implemented, delve into the shared risk expectations between the client and the systems integrator or outsourcer and see if you can make your offering while sharing in the potential upside of recurring revenues from a successful project. As ever, your internal revenues (software already developed or resources already recruited) will have low cost to you, but high perceived value to your alliance partner or their client, thereby creating a lucrative win–win.

Rule 6: be prepared to show preference

If you are determined to establish a strategic alliance with a specific consultant, systems integrator or outsourcer, it may be expedient to elevate that partner to preferred bidder status in certain situations in order to create a lasting impression. Large software and hardware companies are often reluctant to do this as it can compromise their wider channel integrity; however, it is always noted and remembered by them if they win business through a unique level of endorsement.

This topic was covered in Chapter 4 under the section 'Show Preference', so probably requires only a basic re-cap here. It's a difficult subject and, once again, is a concept that is often easier to adopt for new entrants to the market or smaller technology OEMs with less-established channels. Policy (and maybe even the law) is an enemy of this tactic, so the bigger you are, the tougher it is; but getting off the fence to show commitment will be remembered by the personnel involved in the bid. Having your endorsement on the bid document or in the customer presentations stating that your partner (the specific large IT services company) is your favoured partner owing to their superior skills at configuring, architecting or implementing your product (or integrating your service) will differentiate you as a trusted and favoured long-term partner.

To navigate the political mine field, many OEMs get around this concept with tiered support or discounts based on deal registration models. This is a very effective way of granting a preference to the services partner and also allows you to defend your decision to your other channel partners. A typical example of this would be an extra discount granted to the partner that first alerts you to a specific opportunity. If the partner is doing their job correctly, that will always be them (as opposed to, for instance, a VAR, who is normally brought into the sales cycle far later and often at the behest of procurement department). If the additional support of a discount provided to the large IT services company for alerting you to the deal is substantial enough, then it will effectively commercially differentiate them in a way that makes them unbeatable in the contest. This model of tiering different fee levels for an involvement in different aspects of the sales and delivery journey can, of course, also be applied to resale margins, with perhaps a higher margin given to partners who originate a sale or who had previously nominated a client for joint pursuit.

When you are forced to bid with various partners, there are ways of supporting specific partners that you think have a stronger ethical right to the business, such as granting them the superior pre-sales resource or providing them with additional product data or demo equipment. Of course, this needs to be executed within strict ethical and legal boundaries and be defensible, but may be justifiable when rewarding the partner that has actually created the opportunity in the first place. It's always advisable take advice in this area.

Preference is a valuable tool to creating a close long-term relationship, but it's value shouldn't be entirely invested in this way. It can also be a handy negotiating tool and a bargaining chip to be used to secure that meeting you have been trying to make with a certain department at the large IT services company or that client introduction that you have been asking for.

Rule 7: get credentials

The projects in which the large IT services companies are involved are usually substantial and lucrative, so they cannot afford for them to go wrong as it impacts their profitability and, more importantly, their client relationships and reputation. Therefore, when selecting a supplier or partner for a project they will always ask: 'Do we have a successful record with [XYZ]?'

I cannot emphasise this enough, credentials are the way forward. First, it's great advertising. If you can get a good-quality client credential or reference project professionally created and written up, it is the ultimate way of showing your customers (both within the alliance partner and your external clients) that you have a successful relationship. The more public you can make it, the better. First base is a private credential that can be used in restricted circumstances such as bid submissions or presentations with other prospects under NDA. The next level is a reference that can be used in internal literature and freely within client discussions. But the ultimate is a full public credential backed up with press and PR; nothing gives the relationship a more assured seal of approval.

As we have covered in almost every section so far, the large IT services companies are the embodiment of businesses that are about maximising return (selling more and at higher profit) while minimising risk (avoiding costs or reputational impact), so the security of knowing that their own organisation has previously worked successfully with you is important when the project lead, system architect or client lead is considering your product to be involved in their bid. It also shows a degree of implementation skills within the business and so gives the sales or bid leads the confidence to put forward the product knowing that their organisation has the ability to deliver.

Finally, and in many ways most importantly, it gives your alliance partner the feeling that, if they put forward your product, they are playing on home turf. If your partnership has the strongest client story, then risk-averse and time-constrained personnel will opt to put your product forward if they think that they have the killer differentiating story to win the business. After all, why would they put forward a different product if they knew that their competitor had the greater skills or superior delivery experience and therefore a more attractive selling story?

It's obvious, but the credential should have two versions. One for the 'outside world' (i.e. external clients or prospects) that emphasises the client issue, the way that the partnership addressed the issue and the saving or financial return that was achieved. The other version will be aimed at your internal personnel and will include the above information, but also focus on the delivery ease, cost saving and where each department of the alliance partner achieved profit.

Rule 8: be prepared to be flexible

In the bid or contracting process for a large IT project, the bidders will be asked to agree to an extensive amount of complicated criteria. This will entail a set of partners taking a pragmatic approach toward commercial, delivery and legal terms in order to conform to the client's needs.

It's not just about showing preference. Client demands, particularly on the more complex and technical projects, are many and varied, and an ability to share the pain of a particular term, condition or commercial need is essential. There is a recurring theme across many of these golden rules: shared pain is the way to make a long lasting relationship with the large IT delivery players.

Sometimes this means addressing legal terms, especially in outcome-based deals. It may mean taking a higher level of accountability. It may mean changing IP to accommodate clients who are investing significant amounts of knowledge of their process into a solution. Or it may be as simple as amending credit terms to see payment for the cost of your product or service in line with when the increased revenue or cost savings are made by the client or when the delivery partner gets paid.

Sometimes, the flexibility needs to be around commercial terms. It's often necessary to help an alliance partner win a bid or a piece of business by hitting a specific price point at time of tender. While this feels like you are taking all of the pain, remember: all projects executed by consultancies, systems integrators or outsourcers are based on either cost savings or increased return for a client. So, consider taking a hit up-front in return for a share of the benefit later in the project. Apart from anything else, it will allow you to understand better the work that the large IT services company is doing and give you the opportunity to get closer to their business.

The notion of lowering your quote to hit a price point could be to beat the competition, could be to maintain the margin for your alliance partner or could be just to hit the client budget price to allow the deal to happen. For whatever reason, it's in everyone's interest for you to be entrepreneurial and imaginative in the way that you price in order to make the deal happen.

The margin point is relevant. Large IT services companies have shareholders (public or private). This means that their gross margin expectation is a KPI for their share price. As mentioned previously, the upshot of this is that a certain margin needs to be realised by the large IT services company in order not to dilute their market-declared profit margin and impact their share price. So, while the margin expectation looks excessive, it is often imperative to make it 'good' business. If you can't make it happen, it may affect your desirability to that particular partner in the future.

Once past the bid stage, and assuming a successful outcome, there are also ways to differentiate your company during the delivery and support phases by showing flexibility. First, it may make sense to tailor your support model to reflect the deal economics (as mentioned above). That might be to phase the support costs to later in the 'run' period of the project when the profit is being realised by the client and the delivery partner. It is also a smart idea to take a close look at how you can ensure you aren't encroaching on your partner's core business of providing services wrapped around the delivery of a project. Are you used to providing certain services that your alliance partner is expecting? This is more likely to occur than you think, so be conscientious in discussing this as early as possible and be prepared to compromise on who takes which roles for the long-term health of the relationship.

The other stage of the project and delivery lifecycle you may want to consider is the product support services. The prime contractor (your partner) will ordinarily provide support (service desk) services to the client as part of the project implementation or 'run'. This will allow first line call logging, so consider a reduced cost for your support services based on the fact that initial call logging and basic support will be provided by the large IT services company (who will only contact your support services after initial diagnosis).

The moral of the story here is that clients hire the large IT services companies to do complex and intricate projects by definition. The ability to reconcile the risk of the project with its return is essential when assessing all bids, so any help that partners can provide in sharing the risk (and maybe later the reward) is valued and remembered.

Rule 9: work very hard

If you haven't got the hint already, let me reiterate: the personnel in consulting firms, systems integrators and outsourcers work very hard and are very smart. A full commitment mentality to please the customer is the norm, not the exception – and they expect the same from their partners.

Sales, alliance formation and relationship management is naturally a demanding occupation. In this respect, you don't now need to be reminded that excelling takes long hours, especially when you factor in travel, meetings, admin and preparation together with hospitality and entertainment, which tend to be evening and weekend pursuits. To make an impression in the large IT services company takes a large amount of application. As has been highlighted repeatedly in this book, the breadth of roles and complexity of the organisation structures within these large, often global organisations, not just over the entire organisation, but often just related to a specific client or project, requires a great deal of time and patience. It takes time to make the contacts you need (including lots of blind alleys) to get to the right decision makers for a project or client engagement. It involves managing many stakeholders (see Chapter 4 on using all of the resources of your organisation to make life easier for yourself here). You may get lucky early and make the right sort of connection immediately, but understanding the complex structure will probably take time and mean many meetings before you fully understand. It's an unfashionable view, but it's a numbers game: lots of phone calls = lots of meetings = the right contacts = the right outcomes. Eventually.

And then, just when you fully understand the movers and shakers and the people making the decisions around the project that can positively affect you and can lay the foundations for a successful relationship going forward, they get headhunted or leave, or move roles, or change to a different project, or go to work for the client. Like all new economy businesses, IT services organisations exist in a very fluid job market, so your work is never complete.

So, hard work is a given, but there are certain factors of the way that a large IT services company conducts their business that makes them uniquely challenging. First, the main constant is the culture of hard work and long hours. If you are working with them on a pre-sales or delivery basis, you will be expected to keep up and maintain the same level of effort and intensity – the success-at-all-costs and client satisfaction culture that drives all of the successful global players. In Chapter 3, within the Career Levels and Performance Management section, we covered the competitive nature of performance management systems which encourage long hours and quality work at all times. That culture pervades all of the touch points of their business, including their relationship with their partners. Everyone wants to think we are in it together, so ensure that you are as committed as your alliance partner contacts when a deadline or deliverable needs to be hit. Either way, they will remember it.

Second, as previously discussed, the sort of business and sales pursuits that you will be working on with your new alliance partner will be very deadline oriented. All projects are strictly governed by a project plan that is sacrosanct, so when deadlines need to be achieved you will find some long, unsociable hours being worked by the delivery or bid team. They will want you to be standing shoulder-to-shoulder with them and be available as they work into the night for their go-live or their architecture diagram submission.

Third, and this should not be under-estimated, is the practice of additional or 'side of desk' roles within a large IT services company. Very often, especially in sales and business development scenarios, the personnel working on a sales cycle, new client pursuit process or bid submission are also committed to a simultaneous client delivery project, meaning that much of the work required to complete the tender response is done outside of usual office hours. As a bid deadline nears and the workload and pressure increases, additional personnel are brought in to add expertise or an extra pair of hands to the submission, and these are also hours that are found outside of someone's day job, The upshot of all this is that much pre-sales work with which you will be involved will be out of office hours. You are supporting a 24×7 operation, so be prepared for this. If you are not available, they will move to another supplier or partner if a deadline is in jeopardy. This is not done out of spite or punishment, but out of necessity, and you are back to square one.

Finally, the global nature of these businesses means that personnel from many countries or time zones are likely to be involved in your projects. This will increase because outsourcing and utilising off-shore resources for delivery is becoming more commonplace, so, even if your team 'in-country' are on course and working normal hours, you will likely be pulled into supporting activities and working along with contacts in other geographies at the most inhospitable of times.

Like it or not, your new alliance partners work long hours, so whether by design or necessity you may end up working many of those hours. For you to be fully accepted and valued as a partner, an equal commitment is appreciated and even expected. As with all sales and partner development roles, if you aren't servicing that client, someone else will.

Rule 10: be resilient

According to dictionary.com, resilience is: 'The ability to recover readily from illness, depression, adversity, or the like; buoyancy.' In business, I would put it another way: there will be more bad days than good days and the ability to bounce back is the thing that differentiates the successful people from the also-rans. To quote Colonel George A Custer: 'It's not how many times you get knocked down, it's how many times you get back up.'

It's the one thing that we all need, but is very difficult to teach. We can all read books on time management, closing techniques, making cold calls, creating strategy and all of the other skills that a successful alliance professional needs, but it is the power of resilience that will have the greatest effect on your destiny.

I have good news, though. Even if there are more bad days than good, if you get it right, the good days will make it all worthwhile. The companies that we have talked about in this book by their nature have long established and deep relationships already, which they are reluctant to compromise, so there will be lots of doors slammed in your face before you find the right person and the right project.

There are a lot of variables when you are in the business of large IT delivery projects. You may not get to the right person. If you do, you may not have the right product (on this occasion). If you do, and the systems integrator likes the product, and the price and terms are agreeable to all concerned, you are still probably competing with others to be included as part of the solution. If that goes well, and you get selected as the partner of choice, there is also the little matter of the large IT services company that you backed going on to win the business. You could have done everything right and have a great product, but it's likely that your product and its cost is only a small part of the overall project, so you probably have very little influence on the overall outcome. So, even though you have done everything right, victory is often snatched from you.

Let's look at it optimistically. Even the scenario where your alliance partner is not selected for the work will be good for you in the long term. You will have made friends and supporters along the way that will be invaluable in the future. Also, it is possible that the client will have liked what they learned of your product or service during the unsuccessful bid process and may ask the successful delivery partner to build your product into their project. In most cases, the original large IT services company will give their blessing to this so that they can see you succeed in the spirit of partnership (it's also possible that your fee registration process may pay them even if they don't win the implement work).

Technology is moving fast. No-one has a right to be an incumbent provider or partner, so there are always openings. This can, of course, work against you, but also in your favour, so if at first you don't succeed, don't worry. It is all time well spent, if you have made the right connections, for the next bid or project.

The intangible in the professional lives of all sales, alliance and relationship management people is that not everyone is going to like you. This is even more likely when working with the large IT services companies, where there are so many different roles and personality types in every project or engagement team. It's especially important to be pragmatic and not take any bad experiences personally. The drawback of the technology sector is that it does attract technical and analytical people, who are by nature suspicious of people trying to forge partnerships, so be prepared to deal with odd tricky character along the way.

A positive mental attitude and fortitude is a quality greatly valued by all at your alliance partner. The work is demanding, tiring and often frustrating, so they recruit people with a large amount of resilience because that is what is required to have the staying power to make a successful career. The same needs to apply to you.

9 How to put what you have learned into practice

Do you really want to do this? If you have the right level of belief in your product and company, the drive, the work ethic and an understanding boss with deep pockets, then it's time to start planning for success. But the important word there is *if*.

To qualify out at this stage is a sound decision if you don't have the right proposition or support or deep enough pockets to make it work. Qualifying out will save significant money and may even save your job. The cost of getting it wrong is months or even years spent establishing relationships, vying for acceptance against superior products or inferior products from better funded companies and, even when you are accepted, pouring tens of thousands of business development pounds into bids that may well fail through no fault of your own.

But you can't play at it either. If you want to compete seriously, put your plan together, sell it to your leadership or investors and start to work on whatever relationships you have to get a foothold. Better still, ask your most loyal customer to do it for you – if they have a partner from their favoured consulting firm, systems integrator or outsourcer on speed-dial maybe that is the answer.

If you have a good plan, work hard, follow the rules and get it right by establishing a mutually appealing go-to-market alliance strategy with the large influencers, you will gain access to the most powerful business decision makers leading the most lucrative projects at the world's largest companies.

Good luck.

Glossary and definitions

Word or term	Literal or standard definition	Context of this book
Alliance partner	Individual, company, country or other group that join forces (ally) together for mutual benefit; in modern business this usually means to work together to create a stronger proposition to customers	In most cases this describes the organisations represented by the reader of this book, i.e. the aspirant alliance partner that wants to ally with the large IT services company, or the term could be used to describe the large IT service company or a third party that also wants to combine with either of these companies.
Black box	A self-contained unit in an electronic or computer system where the component parts are hidden and invisible to the function of the solution	Like turnkey, used to denote a complete solution of the type that can be created when an alliance partner (at whom the book is aimed) works with a large IT services company. By definition, these solutions will often entail product and services. *See also* Turnkey.
BPO	Business process outsourcing	A sub-set of outsourcing that involves contracting the operations and responsibilities of a specific business process to a third-party service provider.
C-Suite	Term used to describe the most senior personnel (usually board level) within corporations. So-named from the use of the letter C to denote chief, i.e. CEO, CIO, CFO	Usually used within this book to describe the seniority of the personnel within target end-user client organisations to whom the large IT services companies can provide access if successfully engaged.

(*Continued*)

Word or term	Literal or standard definition	Context of this book
Client	Individual or company that is a customer	Describes the 'end-user' client in the chain, i.e. the company or corporation who will be the eventual owner or user of the service. In instances where the large IT services company is the end-user, such as when they are asking a host and hold their own infrastructure, this has been clearly noted.
Client engagement	When working with a client	Used to describe a project or similar activity where the large IT services company is contracted to provide a deliverable for a client ranging from a small piece of management consultancy to a large complex computer system.
Close to the box services	Services that are closely linked to the implementation of a specific technology, usually hardware	Used in this book to denote services that are ordinarily delivered by the technology OEM (usually hardware related, but not always) and are closely linked to the implementation and installation of a technology; therefore, delivered by the technology OEM as opposed to the large IT services company.
Cloud	Remote IT systems accessed via the internet where services such as storage or processing can be delivered in an on-demand model	Cloud in this book refers to cloud computing and the providers. Unless stated specifically, this may include private, public or hybrid cloud.
Colleague engagement	Personnel satisfaction	Not to be confused with client engagement, colleague engagement is a measure of the satisfaction of a member of a company's personnel. Usually used in the context of this book in relation to activities that an alliance partner can undertake with a large IT services company to improve the job satisfaction of their staff.

Glossary and definitions 175

Word or term	Literal or standard definition	Context of this book
Deck	PowerPoint presentation	Often the deliverable for a consulting or strategy project.
Deliverable	The piece of work (product or service) to be delivered as the end result of a discrete project	The end product or service that is delivered to the client by one of the large IT services companies who this book is about.
Delivery partner	Supplier for whom a company has contracted a piece of work for completion	As Deliverable, this term is used as a catch-all for the systems integrators, consulting firms and outsourcers about whom this book is written, but specifically in the context of one of these companies that has been formally contracted by a client for a specific project.
Digital	Originally used to describe data in the form of binary digits. The term has many modern day meanings, but is most commonly used to describe most electronic or computerised technology, e.g. digital watch, digital camera	Used in this book to describe 'new economy' businesses and technology providers that use modern IT methods such as capture, manipulation and presentation of data to create a differentiated business benefit.
Experienced hire	An experienced new recruit to any organisation	A term used frequently within consulting firms to describe any member of staff that has joined the company not straight from education, having worked in a full-time paid position for any business prior to joining the consulting firm.
HR	Human resources	Refers to the people who comprise the workforce, or assets, of a company as well as the department who manages the employment and performance of those people.
IaaS	Infrastructure as a service	Describes the delivery of virtualised hardware services such as storage or processing power on a subscription model.

(*Continued*)

Glossary and definitions

Word or term	Literal or standard definition	Context of this book
Incremental	Additive or accretive	Used to describe business or business benefits that otherwise would not have been created without the partnership.
IP	Intellectual property	Intangible property that is the result of creativity, such as patents, copyrights, etc.
ISV	Independent software vendor	A software company usually distinguished by not being a large multinational household name.
IT influencer	An organisation that either contracted or informally influences clients to procure specific IT products or services	Used a catch-all term for the systems integrators, consulting firms and outsourcers about whom this book is written. Influencer is more likely to pertain to companies at the early stage of the cycle, i.e. consulting firms, but not always. See Figure 2.1 Venn diagram in Chapter 2 for a representative list.
KPI	Key performance indicator	Measures of business success; used to describe the metrics that measure the success of alliance engagements.
Large IT services company	Any large organisation that is involved in the consulting or delivery process of IT projects	This is a catch-all term for the systems integrators, consulting firms and outsourcers about whom this book is written. See Figure 2.1 Venn diagram in Chapter 2 for a representative list.
Management consultancy	An organisation that helps other organisations to improve performance either through increased revenue or improved efficiency by providing advice or recommending business solutions	One of the four key target constituent groups of the book. Wider definitions and example companies are given in Chapter 2.
NDA	Non-disclosure agreement	A contractual, usually legally binding, confidentiality clause entered into by alliance partners and/or clients as standard practice when embarking on any project or discussion in which non-public company information and data will be shared.

Glossary and definitions 177

Word or term	Literal or standard definition	Context of this book
OEM	Original equipment manufacturer	The source creator of a product. Usually used in this book to describe a typical company for whom this book is intended, i.e. a hardware or software company that creates or assembles their own products.
Offering	Something offered or provided as a contribution	A solution to satisfy a client need that, in some cases within this book, may be the offering of the aspirant alliance partner or may be the offering of the large IT services company or may be a joint offering created or delivered mutually.
On-premise	IT solution located on the user's premises as opposed to a cloud model	As per the standard definition, where a solution (hardware and software) is sold and implemented on a client's premises as opposed to remotely in an off-site datacentre or a cloud model.
Outsourcer	A company that specialises in delivering business services to other companies who have 'outsourced' that process or activity to the outsourcer	One of the three key target constituent groups of the book. Outsourcing is a wide group, this book concentrates more on the activities of the large IT outsourcers and business process outsourcers defined and listed in Chapter 2.
PaaS	Platform as a service	This term here denotes application infrastructure services such as middleware, application platform integration, business process management and database services.
Proposition	A suggested solution, scheme or outcome	Usually used in this book as a description of a solution to satisfy a client need. In some cases, it may be the proposition of the aspirant alliance partner, or may be the proposition of the large IT services company, or may be a joint proposition created or delivered mutually.

(Continued)

178 Glossary and definitions

Word or term	Literal or standard definition	Context of this book
Retail title	To be the eventual owner of an item	Used to denote when a company ends up as the eventual owner of an item, i.e. they 'retain title' and it is not resold or passed on to another company. Usually used to describe when a large IT services company 'retains title' of hardware or software in order to provide a managed service.
RFP	Request for proposal (or pricing)	A formal process wherein a company requests bidders to provide a final (often legally binding) proposal for goods or services. Often preceded by an request for information (RFI) – a process at an earlier stage which is non-binding and designed to down-select partners for RFP consideration.
SaaS	Software as a service	Delivery of software via the cloud, as opposed to on the client's premises. Usually accessed via a subscription model as opposed to a licence model.
SLA	Service level agreement	An official commitment between the service provider and the client where the service quality, availability, responsibilities and so on are set out and agreed.
SOA	Service-oriented architecture	A collection of services that communicate with each other.
Systems integrator (SI)	A company or individual who ordinarily combines hardware and software products from disparate providers to deliver a complete integrated solution	One of the four key target constituent groups of the book. Wider definition and examples companies are discussed in Chapter 2.
Technical consultancy	aka IT consulting. As a management consultancy, but specifically advises clients how the use of IT products can improve business performance	One of the four key target constituent groups of the book. Wider definition is discussed in Chapter 2.

Glossary and definitions 179

Word or term	Literal or standard definition	Context of this book
Third party	A person or company involved in a situation who is not one of the primary participants	Usually pertains to you, the aspirant alliance partner, or in some cases the large IT services company (where they are intending to be involved in a transaction or cycle which is already occurring between a supplier or customer).
Turnkey	A comprehensive offering that is delivered as a complete solution	To describe a solution of the type that can be created when an alliance partner (at whom the book is aimed) works with a large IT services company. By definition, these turnkey solutions will often entail products and services.
Vendor	Any seller or provider of a product or service	Used in this book interchangeably with OEM to describe an originator of a product or service such as a hardware manufacturer or a software company; a typical company to whom this book is aimed.

Additional reading

You may wish to consider the following books for more background context. The book descriptions are lifted directly from Amazon.com or from the publishers' websites. I have given the dates of the latest printed version I could find. In some cases these books are somewhat older and, given the fast moving nature of the sector, some of the content may be outdated, but the industry insight and history will still be interesting and relevant.

Consulting, outsourcing and systems integrator sector

The Vault Guide to the Top 25 Consulting Firms (2009)
Naomi Newman

Offers an inside look at management consulting careers and the firms that shape the industry in Europe. Based on surveys of consultants, this title provides the inside scoop on firm news, firm culture, pay, diversity initiatives, hiring process and more, as well as rankings of the top 25 consulting firms. Latest version I could was 2009, but will still be relevant as most of the players will still be active and important.

Outsourcing: All You Need to Know (2014)
Dr Sara Kathleen Cullen, Dr Mary Lacity and Dr Leslie P Willcocks

This book is the definitive guide to leveraging the external services market for business advantage. Based on 30 years of research into over 2,100 organisations and advisory engagements throughout Europe, the Americas, Asia Pacific and Africa, three world authorities detail the frameworks, lessons and practices that inexorably produce high performance.

The Business of Systems Integration (2005)
Edited by Andrea Prencipe, Professor Andrew Davies, Michael Hobday

This book is the first to systematically explore systems integration from a business and innovation perspective. Contributors delve deeply into the nature, dimensions and dynamics of the new systems integration, deploying research and analytical techniques from a wide variety of disciplines, including the theory of the firm, the history of technology, industrial organisation, regional studies, strategic management and innovation studies.

The Outsourcer: The Story of India's IT Revolution (2015)
Dinesh C. Sharma

The rise of the Indian IT industry is a remarkable economic success story. Software and services exports from India amounted to less than $100 million in 1990, and today come close to $100 *billion*. The 'miracle' of Indian IT is actually a story about the long work of converting skills and knowledge into capital and wealth. With *The Outsourcer*, Sharma offers the first comprehensive history of the forces that drove India's IT success.

Inside a consulting firm, outsourcer or systems integrator

How to Survive a Career in Consulting (2015)
John Kumar

If you are one of those people enamoured with a career in consulting, this is just the book for you. It is a no holds barred look at the industry, with a focus on getting a job at a consulting firm, surviving while there and ultimately making a move out. Whether you have worked in consulting before or are totally unaware of the industry, you will be sure to learn something new in this tongue-in-cheek look at working in a big-name consulting firm.

How to Become a Big Four Management Consultant (And Whether You Should Even Want To) (2013)
Benjamin Monk

The author goes through all the advantages and disadvantages of a career in consulting, based on his own experience globally and backed up with examples from across the sector. There are sections that examine what skills and knowledge recruiters look for when hiring both graduates and experienced hires. The book also looks in more detail at two of the activities that are key to consulting: sales and thought leadership. It's designed to help people understand the real pros and cons of consulting and, if that doesn't put you off, to show you exactly what skills and behaviours you will need to demonstrate or acquire if you are to succeed as a management consultant.

The Firm: The Inside Story of McKinsey, The World's Most Controversial Management Consultancy (2015)
Duff Macdonald

They helped invent the bar code. They revolutionised business schools and created the corporate practices that now rule our world. McKinsey employees are trusted and distrusted, loved and despised. They are doing behind-the-scenes work for the most powerful people in the world, and their ranks of alumni include the chairman of HSBC and William Hague. Renowned financial journalist Duff McDonald uncovers how these high-priced business savants have ushered in

182 *Additional reading*

waves of structural, financial and technological shifts, but also become mired in controversy across the years.

The Trusted Firm: How Consulting Firms Build Successful Client Relationships (2006)
Fiona Czerrniawska
   This unique journey through the new consulting terrain looks at how leading consulting firms worldwide create a platform for success: what values they need, who they recruit and what recruitment processes work best, how they keep their finger on the pulse of the market and how they match the right people to particular jobs.

Accenture 34 Success Secrets: 34 Most Asked Questions on Accenture – What You Need to Know (2014)
Tina Serrano
   Accenture PLC is a transnational administration advising technics facilities and subcontracting corporations. It is the world's greatest advising firm, calculated by earnings, and is a constituent of the Fortune Global 500 catalogue. The book contains 34 answers, much more than you can imagine, comprehensive answers and extensive details and references, with insights that have never before been offered in print. This all-embracing guide offers a thorough view of key knowledge and detailed insight and introduces what you want to know about Accenture.

Alliance management

The Strategic Alliance Handbook: A Practitioners Guide to Business-to-Business Collaborations (2014)
Mike Nevin
   This book enables readers to understand the commercial, technical, strategic, cultural and operational logic behind any alliance and to establish an approach that is appropriate for the type of alliance they are seeking and the partner organisation(s) with whom they are working. Whether you are an alliance executive responsible for the systems, strategy and performance of your organisation's alliancing programme, or an alliance manager needing to ensure the success of a given partnership, *The Strategic Alliance Handbook* is an essential guide.

Strategic Alliance Management (2012)
Brian Tjemkes, Pepijn Vos and Koen Burgers
   Mastering the art of managing strategic alliances allows firms to radically improve their performance and this book provides a detailed, evidence-based approach outlining the design, management, and evaluation of these alliances. Elaborating on the decision-making structures apparent during each stage in the alliance lifecycle, and elucidating cases from across the world, *Strategic Alliance Management* offers a systematic framework that provides insights into the development and deployment of alliances.

Alliances: An Executive Guide to Designing Successful Strategic Partnerships (2014)
Ard-Pieter de Man

Strategic alliances are increasingly common among modern corporations and a hot topic in today's business schools. Most managers don't have the experience or sufficient knowledge to create a functional alliance governance structure. This is a sophisticated guide to crafting successful partnerships, offering a combination of carefully designed checklists, up-to-date examples and scenarios from around the world, and the tools needed to ensure that all elements of an alliance are taken into account and fully assessed.

Cooperative Strategy: Managing Alliances, Networks, and Joint Ventures (2005)
John Child, David Faulkner, Stephen Tallman

Strategic alliances are increasingly common, as many organisations look toward various partnering arrangements. This second edition extends the first edition's clear and comprehensive survey of strategic alliances, presenting different disciplinary perspectives (economics, strategy, organisation theory) and numerous examples from the corporate world.

Index

Page numbers in *italics* refer to figures; those in **bold** refer to glossary terms.

account-based stakeholders 107
account mapping 109–10, *111*
accreditations 60–1, 105, 117
administration 164
age of employees 150–1
agility 97, 120–1, 147, 150
alliance best practice: establishing goals 103–6; going to market 109–14; governance and tracking 116–18; objections to 101–3; perspectives on 22–4, 65–9, 96–100, 118–21, 131–2, 148–52; stakeholder management 106–8
alliance leads/managers 55, 125
alliance partners **173**
analysts 78
anatomy of IT projects 41–4, *45*
arbitrage *see* labour arbitrage
architecture of IT projects 42–3, 47–9
associates/associate consultants 78
audience of book 4–9
awareness 113

behaviour 75–6
belief 130
'Big Four' 36–7
billing revenue 81–2
black box **173**
blame 76, 130
boldness 130
BPO (business process outsourcing) 34, 84–5, **173**
business analysts 78
business case for IT projects 41–2, 45–7
business development 117
business leverage 64
business models: alliance in the new economy 96–100; billing revenue 81–2; career models 77–81; co-opetition and ethical walls 94–5; culture 70–7; deal shapes and shared risk 82–9; fee programmes 91–3; going client-side 89–90
business process outsourcing (BPO) 34, 84–5, **173**

careers 72, 76–81, *80*
case studies: alliance excellence in the new economy (Georg's story) 96–100; alliance partner's perspective (Gavin's story) 118–21; client-side perspective (Paula's story) 22–4; digital disrupter's perspective (Phil's story) 148–52; innovation partner's perspective (Ali's story) 131–4; navigating routes to market (Stephanie's story) 14–16; why partnering is win-win (Peter's story) 65–9
case team leaders 78–9
channel networking as benefit of partnership 63–4
chargeable hours 81–2
Christensen, Clayton M. 137
client engagement **174**
client sales lead 56–7
clients: definition **174**; perspectives of 22–4
client-side consultancy 89–91
close to the box services **174**
cloud: definition **174**; impact of 139–41; strategy and models 146–7
collateral 113, 115
colleague engagement 124–5, **174**
colleague respect 75–6
commercial considerations: alliances and 99–100; preference and 168
commoditisation 123, 142, 147–8

communications strategies 114–16, *115*, 157
compensation models 38, 109, 133
competitiveness 60–1, 72
confidentiality 74–5, 127
conflicts of interest 128, 149
congruent goals 153–5
consultants (career level) 78
consulting firms: cloud services and 139–40; culture 70–7; overview 31–4; reasons for use 17–19
co-opetition 94–5
core business: focus on 19–20; preference and 168
corporate social responsibility 75
cost avoidance 105
cost saving 61–2, 141
credentials 106, 167
credibility 164
credit risk 164
cross-border business 128
C-Suite **173**
culture: alignment 133; colleague respect 75–6; corporate social responsibility 75; decks 76–7; digital age 138; of disrupters 149; diversity 73; hard work 71–2, 169–70; of innovation 130–1; integrity and reputation 74–5; of IT influencers 70–1; knowledge capital 73–4

data 145
deadlines 72, 170
deal bringing 112–14
deal registration 166
deal shapes: business process outsourcing (BPO) 84–5; fixed price contracts 84; gain-share 85–7; outcome-based 87–9; overview 82–3, *89*; smaller companies 98; time and materials 83
deal size 164
decks 76–7, **175**
deliverable **175**
delivery 117
delivery partner **175**
Deloitte 36, 37, 137
design of IT projects 42–3, 47–9
detached view 18–19
differentiation 60–1, 124–5
digital 135, **175**
digital age: adapting to 135–8; cloud 139–41; digital marketing 142–4; a disrupter's perspective 148–52; the future 146–8; Internet of things (IoT) and Industry 4.0 144–5
digital agencies *143*

digital marketing 136, 142–4
discounts 109, 166
discrimination 75–6
disputes 129
disqualified customers 128
disruption 137–8, 148–52
diversity 73

Electronic Data Systems (EDS) 38
emotion 18–19, 157–8
engagement levels 164
engagement managers 78–9
engagement strategies 27–8
enthusiasm 130
entrepreneurial mindset 97
Ernst & Young 36, 37
ethical walls 94–5
exceptions 129
executive stakeholders 107
experience 18, 150–1
experienced hire **175**

failure 130
fee programmes 91–3, 141
financial benefits 20, *163*
fixed price contracts 84
flexibility 21, 98, 167–9
focus 18, 19–20
forecasts 117
functional stakeholders 107
funding of joint solutions 132

gain-share *86*
goals 153–5
go-to-market strategy 109–14, 128
governance 107–8, 116–18
government bodies 38–9

hard work 71–2, 169–70
hosting 139
hours of work 170
HP 38
human resources (HR) **175**

IaaS (infrastructure as a service) **175**
IBM: co-opetition and ethical walls 94; as services and vendor hybrid 37–8; value propositions 135–6
implementation of IT projects 43, 49–51
incremental **176**
independent bodies 38–9
independent software vendors (ISV) **176**
Indian pure plays 35
Industry 4.0 144–5

Index

influence as engagement strategy 27, 28, 33
infrastructure as a service (IaaS) **175**
innovation: culture of 130–1; definition 122; how it happens 125–6, 131–2; partner's perspective (Ali's story) 131–4; repeatable 164; roles and legal considerations 127–9; why it happens 122–5, 131
innovation leads 125
integrity 74–5
intellectual property (IP) 18, 127–8, **176**
intelligence 157
internal IT systems, selling to 10
Internet of things (IoT) 144–5
investment 59–60, 127
IP (intellectual property) 18, 127–8, **176**
ISV (independent software vendor) **176**
IT consulting *see* technical consultancy
IT departments, future of 146
IT influencers **176**
IT projects: anatomy of 41–4, *45*; architecture 42–3, 47–9; business case 41–2, 45–7; implementation 43, 49–51; key personnel 53–7, *58*; support 43–4, 51–2; timelines *160–2*; typical scenario 45–52, *53*

job titles 78–9

key performance indicator (KPI) **176**
key personnel 53–7, *58*
knowledge capital: culture 73–4; personnel and 102; technical knowledge 19, 62; traditional and disrupters 150
KPMG 36, 37

labour arbitrage 20
large IT services companies: benefits of partnerships for 58–65; definition **176**; history as influencers 1–3; risks of working with 3
leadership: innovation and 125–6; stakeholders 107; success and 158–64
legal considerations: alliances and 99–100; co-opetition and ethical walls 95; of joint innovation 127–9; preference and 168
legal team 57
leveraging 64
liabilities 128
licencing 128
Livesay, Barb 144–5

macro-economic issues 149
managed procurement 12–14

management consultancy **176**
management consultant (career level) 54
managers 78–9
margins 102–3, 147, 168
marketing: funds 105; IT and traditional 142–4
materials 83
McKinsey 138
meetings: establishing goals 153–4; relationship-building 156; review meeting content *108*
mergers and acquisitions 149
metrics 117
milestones 117

networking 63–4
non-disclosure agreement (NDA) **176**

OEM (original equipment manufacturer) **177**; *see also* vendor
offering **177**
off-shoring 20, 147
on-premise **177**
operational benefits 62–3, 99
organisational change 137
original equipment manufacturer (OEM) **177**; *see also* vendor
outcome-based models 28–9, 87–9, 141
outsourcer: definition **177**; as hosters 139; overview 28–31; reasons for use 19–22
ownership and innovation 129

PaaS (platform as a service) **177**
partners (career level) 79
partnerships: benefits for large IT companies 58–65; disrupter's perspective 150–2; objections to 101–3; as win-win 65–9, 130; *see also* alliance best practice
pay-as-you-go models 141
peer relationships 155–6
performance management 78–81
peripheral business 129
personal connections 99, 156
personnel: alliance manager 55; client sales lead 56–7; control and 102; of IT projects 53–4, *58*; legal considerations 129; legal team 57; management consultant 54; procurement/supplier management/product management 55–6; project manager 56–7; solution architect and technical architect 54–5; success and 155–8
personnel satisfaction 124–5
platform as a service (PaaS) **177**

political barriers 18–19
PowerPoint 76–7
preference, showing 113–14, 166, 168
pre-sales support 166
PricewaterhouseCoopers (PwC) 36–8
pricing 128
principles 79
problems, deep focus on 18
procurement 55–6
product management 55–6
product support 168–9
profit 59–60
project leaders/managers 56–7, 78–9
project-based stakeholders 107
promotion: awareness/training 113; internal and external 113–15
proposition **177**
pyramid staffing 78–9

qualified leads 105
qualifying out 133, 172
quality capabilities 21
quotes 168

Rachleff, Andy 138
recruitment in disrupters 149–50
regulation and innovation 124–5
regulatory bodies 38–9
relationship owners 156–8
relationship-building 155–8
relevance 138, 147
repeatability 123, 164
reputation 74–5
request for proposal/pricing (RFP) **178**
reselling: cloud services 140–1; as engagement strategy 27, 28, 33; fees or margins 105; innovation and 129
resilience 170–1
resources: access to 18; cost saving through 61–2
respect 75–6
retail title **178**
retaining title 27–8
revenue: of product 105; for services 104
revenue streams: navigating *13*, 14–16; recurring 141; selling through 11–12; selling to (for client use) 12, 14–15; selling to (managed procurement) 12; selling with 10–11, 15
RFP (request for proposal/pricing) **178**
risks: of alliances/partnerships 3, 101–3; appetite for 164–5; reduced credit 164; reducing 132–3; shared 85–9, *86*, 164–5; success and 164–5

roadblocks 117
round-the-clock service 21, 170

SaaS (software as a service) **178**
sales cycles and alliances 102–3
sales force: incentives 109–10; virtual 164
sales revenue 104
security 127
selling: to (for client use) 12, 14–15, 139; to (for internal use) 10; to (managed procurement) 12–14; through 11–12, 140; together with partners 64–5; with 10–11, 139–40
senior analysts 78
senior associates/associate consultants 78
senior executives 79
senior managers 79
service level agreement (SLA) **178**
service-oriented architecture (SOA) **178**
services and vendor hybrids 37–8
shared risk-reward pricing model 87–9
shared services 20
showing preference 113–14, 166, 168
SLA (service level agreement) **178**
SOA (service-oriented architecture) **178**
social media 132–3
'soft dollar' 105
software as a service (SaaS) **178**
solution architects 54–5
solutions: as benefit of partnership 59; uniqueness of 124–5
speed 130
staff augmentation 17–18
staff engagement 124–5, **174**
stakeholders: categories *107*; disrupters and 151; identifying and managing 155–6
success, steps to: congruent goals 153–5; credentials 167; flexibility 167–9; hard work 169–70; key personnel 156–8; leadership 158–64; resilience 170–1; risks 164–5; showing preference 166; stakeholder management 155–6
supplier management 55–6
support: IT projects 43–4, 51–2; product support 168–9
systems integrators (SI): cloud services and 139–40; definition **178**; overview 25–8; reasons for use 17–19

teaming agreements 95, 127–9
technical architects 54–5

technical consultancy *143*, **178**
technical knowledge 19, 62
technical staff and innovation 126
tendering process 158–9
third party **178**
thought leadership 122–3, 136–8, 150
tiered fees 166
time and materials 83
tracking 116–18
trade bodies 38–9
training 113
transparency 157

trust 98–9
turnkey **178**

value propositions 97–8
vendor **179**; *see also* OEM (original equipment manufacturer)
vertical industry-focused leadership 126
vertical sector alignment 107
vertically aligned niche consultancies 35–6
vice presidents 79
virtual salesforce 164